Cultural Landscapes

BALANCING NATURE AND HERITAGE
IN PRESERVATION PRACTICE

Richard Longstreth, Editor

University of Minnesota Press | Minneapolis | London

A different version of the Fall Caribou Crossing National Historic Site case study in chapter 9 previously appeared as part of Guy Swinnerton and Susan Buggey, "Protected Landscapes in Canada: Current Practice and Future Significance," *The George Wright Forum* 21, no. 2 (2004): 78–92; used with permission. Two of the case studies and part of the conclusion in chapter 9 were originally published in *Cultural Landscapes: The Challenges of Conservation,* World Heritage Papers 7, UNESCO World Heritage Centre (2003): 94–98; reprinted with permission.

Published by the University of Minnesota Press
111 Third Avenue South, Suite 290
Minneapolis, MN 55401-2520
http://www.upress.umn.edu

Library of Congress Cataloging-in-Publication Data

Cultural landscapes : balancing nature and heritage in preservation practice / Richard Longstreth, editor.
p. cm.
Includes index.
ISBN-13: 978-0-8166-5098-9 (hc : alk. paper)
ISBN-10: 0-8166-5098-5 (hc : alk. paper)
ISBN-13: 978-0-8166-5099-6 (pb : alk. paper)
ISBN-10: 0-8166-5099-3 (pb : alk. paper)
1. Landscape assessment. 2. Cultural property—Protection. 3. Landscape protection. I. Longstreth, Richard W.
GF90.C85 2008
712—dc22 2007049870

Printed in the United States of America on acid-free paper

The University of Minnesota is an equal-opportunity educator and employer.

15 14 13 12 11 10 09 08 10 9 8 7 6 5 4 3 2 1

Cultural Landscapes

Contents

Preface

THIS book is the outgrowth of the Fourth National Forum on Historic Preservation Practice, held at Goucher College in Towson, Maryland, on 18–20 March 2004. The objective of these conferences is to provide an all-too-rare opportunity for people working in the preservation field to hear and discuss current issues that are complex and often the source of disagreement or misunderstanding.[1] This exchange is conducted on "neutral ground," as it were, in the halls of the academy rather than under the aegis of a preservation organization so that all participants may feel unencumbered in expressing their views. From its inception in 1997 through 2004, the forum was in large part possible through generous funding from the National Park Service. De Teel Patterson Tiller, former Deputy Associate Director for Cultural Resources, deserves much of the credit for supporting the initiative conceptually as well as monetarily. Park Service personnel from the Historic Landscape Initiative and Hampton National Historic Site made special contributions to this conference. Goucher College provided an ideal setting and admirable support through the offices of Megan Cornett, Noreen Mack, and Craig Henderson.

A number of academic institutions offering instruction in the historic preservation field served as cosponsors, including Boston University, Columbia University, George Washington University, Goucher College, the University of Cincinnati, the University of Delaware, the University of Kentucky, the University of Minnesota, the University of Oregon, and the University of Southern California. Equally important was the cosponsorship by the Historic Preservation Professional Interest Group, American Society of Landscape Architects; the Alliance for Historic Landscape Preservation; and the Historic Resources Committee, American Institute of Architects.

The papers presented at the conference were chosen from a large number of abstracts sent in response to a widely distributed call. The review committee consisted of David Ames, Kenneth Breisch, Shaun Eyring, Lucy Lawliss, Robert Mack, Hugh Miller, Richard Wagner, and myself. The selection process was based solely on the merits of the proposals received rather than being shaped in part by a concern for comprehensiveness or for attaining a balanced program in terms of subject matter, viewpoint, speaker background, or geographic areas covered.

The committee also reviewed an initial draft of the papers. The proceedings were printed as David Ames and Richard Wagner, eds., *A Critical Look at Cultural Landscape and Historic Preservation* (2004). Of the fifteen papers presented, ten were developed further for this anthology; the invited paper prepared by Robert Melnick for the opening address was likewise adapted for publication. I wrote an introductory essay to emphasize some of the difficulties and challenges in using a cultural landscape approach in preservation to complement the numerous successful examples analyzed in the chapters that follow.

I am grateful to David Ames and Richard Wagner for their overall coordination of this project, which has made my job easier in innumerable ways. Shaun Eyring assisted in reviewing and making valuable suggestions for several of the chapters whose content extended beyond my areas of expertise. Paul Groth kindly gave a careful read of a chapter. Appreciation goes to the authors for producing such insightful work and for responding to my editorial queries and comments. Each chapter has been prepared so that it may stand on its own, but I have minimized redundancies and otherwise structured the material so that it contributes to a larger, coherent whole.

Special thanks go to Pieter Martin and others at the University of Minnesota Press, including Mary Keirstead, Rachel Moeller, and Andrea Patch, for making the production of this book a pleasure. No less appreciation is due the reviewers of the manuscript for offering numerous suggestions that improved its structure and content.

This book makes no attempt to be comprehensive in scope. Quite to the contrary, its contents are but one of what need to be many more contributions to a vast, rich, and diverse subject. The authors' range of professional expertise, concerns, outlooks, and opinions indicates that preservation from a cultural landscape perspective is indeed more multifaceted than has traditionally been the case. These varied conceptual frameworks will enrich but also change policy and practice in the field. Whatever the outcome, preservation may well be a substantially different phenomenon a generation hence as the concept of cultural landscapes becomes more widely embraced.

In its organization, the book is divided into two basic spheres, interpretation and management, although most chapters consider at least some aspects of both. The chapters address new approaches to considering the significance of landscape features that have generally been overlooked or deemed unimportant. They discuss an array of optimal new practices for stewardship, examining ways in which ongoing change can be effectively managed so that it is compatible with and perhaps can even enhance the historic resources in question. In crafting their arguments, the authors draw on the now substantial array of literature on cultural landscapes and build on the still meager body of work that focuses on cultural landscapes and preservation. What distinguishes these essays is their detailed examination of case studies within a larger conceptual framework. As a result, the material should afford valuable guidance for people of numerous specialties working in the preservation field and should also encourage expanding the perspective of all of us who care about the enormously rich legacies of our environment.

Note

1. Issues examined in the three previous meetings were historical significance, integrity, and design. A refined version of the first conference was published as Michael Tomlan, ed., *Preservation of What, for Whom? A Critical Look at Historical Significance* (Ithaca, N.Y.: National Council for Preservation Education, 1999). A book of selected, revised papers from the third conference will be issued as *Design and Historic Preservation: The Challenge of Compatibility,* ed. David Ames (Cranberry, N.J.: Associated University Presses, forthcoming).

Introduction: The Challenges of Cultural Landscape for Preservation

RICHARD LONGSTRETH

THE concept of cultural landscape has evolved over several generations. Yet that concept is still relatively new to the field of historic preservation, and while it has made a substantial contribution, it remains misunderstood or marginalized in many quarters.[1] Indeed, the number of preservationists who have not heard of the term or have only a vague notion of what it represents is substantial. Cultural landscape—or simply "landscape," as it is known in some circles—is frequently misconstrued as being synonymous with designed landscape—a garden, park, campus, boulevard system, and the like—or with landscaping—the act of manipulating topography, ground surfaces, and plant material. For some, cultural landscape applies primarily to rural settings or to those created by an ethnic or racial "other"—Pennsylvania Germans, Cajuns, Hopi. Similarly, some construe the concept's pertinence to "different" places such as New Mexico, but not to their own backyards. Irrespective of such misunderstandings, many preservationists tend to view cultural landscape simply as comprising physical entities—comparable to historic districts, for instance—instead of also as a *method* of considering, analyzing, and evaluating places.

The idea of a cultural landscape is at once simple and complex. Studying cultural landscapes entails natural and man-made components of the environment and the ways in which they have changed over time, issues explored by Heidi Hohmann and Bonnie Stepenoff in the chapters that follow. How these components relate to one another is a central point of the inquiry as well. Those relationships may be harmonious, or they may be disparate, even conflicting, as Hillary Jenks underscores. Both components and their relationships are analyzed not just in the physical dimension but also in the functional and associative ones. The significance of the landscape may be rooted in a single event or in a slow, gradual process, as Courtney P. Fint and Nancy D. Rottle discuss. Likewise that significance may stem from a single phenomenon—the creation and use of transportation corridors analyzed by Susan Calafate Boyle and Michael Caratzas—or multiple ones, as noted by Randall Mason. Finally, cultural landscapes may also entail natural settings, unaltered by, but imbued with special meaning for, humans—a point Susan Buggey and Nora Mitchell emphasize. Julie Riesenweber discusses cultural geography's key historic contribution to the study of cultural landscapes and suggests that more recent tacks taken in that discipline may likewise be instructive. But a number of the other essays underscore the fact that the *application* of the cultural landscape concept to preservation endeavors now necessitates the involvement of many professional spheres, drawing from a variety of hard and social sciences, humanistic fields, and design professions. Such work challenges all those involved not simply with thinking broadly and inclusively, but doing so with others who have different skills and, perhaps, different concerns and priorities. To compound the situation, cultural landscape analysis also presumes varied readings of the place in question, some of which can be quite personal, as Robert Z. Melnick's concluding chapter elegantly delineates.

In contrast to entities that are commonly the focus of preservationists' attention, a cultural landscape is given no inherent qualitative status. By its very designation, a historic district carries a recognition not shared by many other places. A certain degree of age and integrity is also an important preservation yardstick that likewise denotes specialness. Yet any part of the land can be seen as a cultural landscape—from a dump site to a thoroughbred horse farm, from the corridor along a multilane freeway to a network of nature paths, from a utilitarian domestic yard to a national park, from a squatter settlement to an elite suburban enclave. Changes that have eroded the historical value of a place may nonetheless be important contributors to a cultural landscape. Is this concept, then, really an aid to preservation, or are its parameters sufficiently different that the two are best kept at a safe distance from one another?

At the most basic level, a familiarity with cultural landscape studies can be of immense benefit in broadening preservation's horizons. The routine practice of survey and registration continues to be conducted in most quarters as an object- and design-oriented one. A farmstead is discussed and evaluated primarily for the residence and perhaps for some of its outbuildings but seldom for its setting—its paths of circulation, fence and field patterns, water sources, landforms, or character and arrangement of plant material, both natural and cultivated, and how and why all of these facets may have changed over time. Key components of the landscape, ones that do much to define physical character as well as provide insights on its evolution, are commonly ignored or accorded marginal status in preservation studies of almost every kind of area, including institutional campuses, residential neighborhoods, commercial centers, and even public open spaces.[2] If nothing else, greater understanding of landscape can improve our knowledge of such places and also our treatment of them. With notable exceptions, preservation practice has been notoriously lax in how spaces around buildings and other objects of veneration are developed. The Main Street sidewalks and streets that have been embellished with new pavements, plantings, light standards, and other ornamental fixtures or the railroad station, handsomely restored, with grounds turned into a quasi park are simply latter-day versions of the elaborate, imagined gardens bestowed upon many eighteenth- and early-nineteenth-century houses several generations ago.

A cultural landscape perspective can also aid in the treatment of the architectural components of settings. Should the temporal or functional relationships between a building and its landscape be severed? That disconnection occurs frequently due to the exigencies of economics. The farmhouse whose farm has become redundant can still be retained as a dwelling, and even if the once cultivated land is now a residential tract, the transformation may be considered a preservation victory if the building itself is sensitively treated and given an adequate buffer zone from its neighbors.[3] Studied as a cultural landscape, the results can be seen as a logical response to forces beyond an individual's capacity to change and a telling manifestation of their time. Among the hundreds of thousands of properties that have been preserved in recent decades, a sizable portion have seen extensive change to their environs since the period from which their historical significance emanates.

But what about *restoration* when the landscape has changed? The process may be justifiable when change is multifaceted and ongoing, as is the case when restoring a building, open space, or other entity in an urban setting. A "restored" Central Park in New York is not inappropriate, even though it is surrounded by an urban landscape radically different from when the park was originally developed, because that perimeter setting of houses, apartment buildings, hotels, and institutional quarters of many kinds has always been in the process of change. Restoration may also be warranted when the process can be applied to especially significant parts of a landscape even though insufficient information exists to restore others. A well-restored mid-nineteenth-century hacienda in the upper Rio Grande valley may be worth the effort for the insights it gives on a long-vanished domestic environment and way of life even if the acreage of which it was once the hub cannot be brought back to a comparable state. Yet when the landscape has enjoyed stability over an extended period of time, altered primarily by small-scale, incremental changes, returning some components to an earlier condition may be questionable.

Montpelier, a large plantation that became one of the most ambitious country places in Virginia Piedmont during the early twentieth century, for example, is currently (2007) being restored to the time it was occupied by James Madison (Jr.) and his family (Figure I.1).[4] A thorough investigation of building fabric yielded sufficient information to justify restoration on documentary grounds, and there is no question that the significance of the property's intimate association with Madison far exceeds that of other occupants. As restored, the fabric can tell us much about the fourth president and the influence his predecessor in the White

Figure I.1. Montpelier, Orange County, Virginia, ca. 1755 (for James Madison Sr.); extensive additions, ca. 1797–1800, portico 1809–12 (for James Madison Jr.); extensive additions and alterations begun 1902 (for William du Pont); du Pont changes demolished 2004. General view of main house and its immediate grounds. Photograph by author, 2003.

House, Thomas Jefferson, had on shaping this domicile. Yet in its reconfigured form the house sits in a landscape that is largely a product of the twentieth century by its du Pont owners—a grander, more varied, and more genteel landscape than it was in Madison's time. Moreover, as substantial sums are poured into the house, some of the barns and other major outbuildings of the du Pont era languish (Figure I.2). The life of Montpelier as a celebrated breeding farm for race horses and an elite social center is being subordinated for an earlier, more elusive, but also ostensibly more visitor-appealing one with a founding father. At the same time, the du Pont landscape will serve as a convenient foil; its understated elegance is a far cry from what would have been its character as a large, working plantation operated by slave labor.[5]

If cultural landscape analysis can offer warnings against unadvisable decisions in preservation, it can also guide practice in a positive way. The yield of information and insights should be an incentive in itself, for such probing can put even well-known places into a wholly new perspective. Fort Ticonderoga, near the foot of Lake Champlain in northern New York State, is a telling illustration. With both French and English fortifications constructed during the eighteenth century, the site played a significant military role in the French and Indian and the Revolutionary wars. William Ferris Pell, a rich New Yorker, purchased the

Figure I.2. Montpelier, general view of decaying early-twentieth-century barns northeast of main house. Photograph by author, 2003.

site in 1820 as a country estate but also to preserve the now ruined bastion as a shrine to the nation's early history—a highly unusual step at that time. Six years later, he constructed The Pavilion near the lake shore below the bluffs on which the ruins stood (Figure I.3). The new building appears to have served the unorthodox dual function of gentleman's retreat and inn for well-heeled visitors. By 1840, The Pavilion was converted to full-time commercial use, still placing it in the first generation of hotels serving a predominantly recreational function in a scenic rural area.[6]

The most extensive changes made to Fort Ticonderoga, however, began in 1909 when, after buying out other family members, Stephen H. P. Pell initiated the fort's reconstruction as a public destination. What is probably the first major, historically motivated undertaking of its kind in the United States continued in phases until 1940. Concurrently, Pell began collecting artifacts associated with the site and with eighteenth-century military engagements more broadly. Visitor facilities included a ticket and souvenir pavilion (the Log House), expanded several times between 1909 and the mid-1920s, and a log stand for the Fort Ticonderoga Pottery Works, another Pell enterprise. Pell also adapted The Pavilion into a summer house for his family, rendering the place more sumptuous than it had

Figure I.3. The Pavilion, Fort Ticonderoga, New York, 1826 (for William Ferris Pell); alterations and additions 1908–9 (for Stephen H. P. Pell). Alfred Bossom, architect. Photograph by author, 2004.

previously been and erecting a new service wing, but otherwise making only minor modifications to the building's fabric.

Pell's architect, the aristocratic British transplant Alfred Bossom, imbued much of the tract with the feeling of a great, early-twentieth-century country place—a type with which he was well familiar.[7] At the main entrance lies a gatehouse, playing in variation motifs Bossom employed for the fort's barracks. A long drive winds through what was originally a deer park and is now mostly maturing woods on the site of the siege of the French fort. Amid the deer park landscape that is still maintained rise French earthworks, the only known example of their kind in the nation. The drive thence descends to the ridgeline of the peninsula on which the fort sits, lined by Norway maples planted in the mid-twentieth century, framing open fields where a panorama of the setting begins to unfold (Figure I.4). Instead of terminating at a great residence, however, the drive ends unceremoniously in an ungraded parking lot, much like those employed at hotels of the period in western national parks. Entry to the fort itself remains through the Log House, now a rare surviving example of the first generation of rustic commercial establishments catering to tourists. The fort has changed little since 1940, although the exhibition fixtures inside are being modernized to protect artifacts more effectively. A reconstruction of the mid-eighteenth-century east building, erected by the French to house supplies and gunpowder, began in 2005 based upon newly discovered documentation.[8] While such a project would be untenable in many circumstances, as part of a complex that is entirely remade, the realized new building will be only the latest chapter in a century-old sequence.

Figure I.4. Fort Ticonderoga, main drive. Photograph by author, 2004.

A long "rear" drive extends from the car lot down the bluffs on which the fort rises to fields, now cultivated for hay. Both this drive and its spur leading to The Pavilion are lined with mature green ash trees, planted around the time of the house's conversion (Figure I.5). Bossom designed a large automobile garage and a two-story log playhouse as adjuncts to the renovated dwelling. Set amid a broad lawn, apple orchard, and early-nineteenth-century locust trees as well as younger ashes, The Pavilion also boasts expansive formal grounds, named "The King's Garden" by Stephen Pell because of its location near utilitarian gardens serving both French and English garrisons there more than a century before. Bossom designed the matrix for this feature, enframing it with walls that suggest a fort in miniature, turned inside out. The prominent landscape architect Marian Cruger Coffin created a vibrant, yet understated garden within those confines after World War I. While the house experienced almost no alterations during the Pells' residency, which lasted until 1987, thereafter the untended garden completely deteriorated. As an initial step in bringing this area into the public realm, the garden was meticulously restored to its original state, the research beginning in 1993 and work on-site completed eight years later (Figure I.6).

Most of this remarkable array of components in the Fort Ticonderoga landscape remained excluded from the story until recent years. The reconstructed fort was long presented, appreciated, indeed, venerated, as an authentic site of Colonial American history. Its other historical values—as one of the first protected ruins in the United States; as one of the first endeavors in what is now termed heritage tourism; as the site of an early resort hotel (one of a very few from that era to survive in recognizable form); as a historical reconstruction then completely unprecedented in its size, scope, and importance; as both a historical

Figure I.5. Fort Ticonderoga, rear drive, entrance to Pavilion drive at left. Photograph by author, 2004.

Figure I.6. The Pavilion, "Kings Garden," 1910. Alfred Bossom, architect. Planting beds redesigned, ca. 1920–21, Marian Cruger Coffin, landscape architect; Coffin garden restored, 1997–2001, Lucinda Brockway, landscape architect. Photograph by author, 2004.

site and a country retreat, tended for more than 150 years by a prominent family that still maintains its stewardship; as among the earliest historical properties fashioned specifically for automobile tourists; as an elegant early-twentieth-century country place that includes farmland and, now, one of the best restored gardens of its genre readily accessible to the public—are all aspects of the fort's legacy that have become recognized within the past two decades. What has sometimes been dismissed in preservation circles as "merely" a reconstruction should be valued for that very attribute, as well as for other closely related features that comprise the extraordinarily rich Pell legacy.

The challenge facing Fort Ticonderoga and many places like it is how to maintain and interpret so multifaceted a legacy. The Pavilion stands vacant, in need of extensive repairs, its unusual configuration resisting new functions. It can, and probably should, be restored to its state in the 1960s, when Stephen's son, John, and his wife, Pyrma, commissioned Sister Parish, among the foremost interior decorators of the mid-twentieth century, and her partner Albert Hadley to recast the furnishing scheme using family pieces from the eighteenth and early nineteenth centuries.[9] So presented, The Pavilion could tell multiple stories—of the house, of family history, of the Pells' own presence on the site in the early nineteenth and a major portion of the twentieth centuries, and of the significant changes to the dwelling that continued to occur until near the end of Pell occupancy.

The great majority of tourists today visit the fort because it is—or appears to have been—a fort: to see its features, exhibits, performances (drills, reenactments), and other events. Many who come probably do not care about, and some would probably not understand, some of the other significant aspects of this landscape. But The Pavilion grounds have now attracted a following in their own right, and additional work is likely to broaden the audience further. That objective is also likely to be enhanced as plans to interpret the tract's long and rich American Indian heritage are developed. At the heart of the challenge that the concept of cultural landscape brings to the fore is preservation that addresses the concerns and values of multiple groups, not just one or the dominant one, and does so in a way that each of those constituencies can learn from components beyond its own sphere.

Since the early 1980s, the National Park Service has taken a leading role in the advancement of a landscape approach to preservation. This initiative at first focused on agrarian settings under its tutelage but was soon applied to the parks more broadly with growing importance given to cultural resources developed to serve the parks themselves.[10] Just as Fort Ticonderoga is more than a Colonial site, so such venerated preserves as Grand Canyon, Crater Lake, Mount Rainer,

Yosemite, and Great Smoky Mountain national parks are more than natural wonders. The value of the hotels, museums, ranger cabins, roadways, overlooks, and many other components of park infrastructure are now seen—and protected—as enhancing the landscape rather than compromising its extraordinary natural features. The great park hotels and increasingly other parts of this infrastructure are proving ever more popular in themselves, reinforcing the role of preservation as an agent in expanding public interests.[11] As monumental as this shift in official policy and public attitude alike has been, the greatest difficulty remains reconciling the coexistence of natural and man-made components of landscapes deemed "wild."

In the strict sense of the term, *wilderness* as lands that have never experienced human intervention is almost impossible to find, a point Robert Z. Melnick emphasizes in his essay. Yet in recent decades, as a matter of policy and practice, wilderness has come to mean something very different: land that will no longer be subject to much human presence. People may traverse such territory but not in machines, and they cannot alter it or even allow earlier forms of human occupancy to remain. Wilderness in this sense is a human, as well as a natural, creation. This tactic is eminently sensible for areas that have long since ceased to harbor human settlement if they ever did so and whose natural features deserve such protection from an increasingly intrusive society, but they can be counterproductive in places where the human record is recent and meaningful. Environmental historian William Cronon has argued persuasively that in such cases the impact of human settlement is an important part of the equation even in designated wilderness areas. Using the Apostle Islands National Lakeshore in Wisconsin—"a much altered but rewilding landscape"—as a case in point, he cautions:

> If visitors come here and believe they are experiencing pristine nature, they will completely misunderstand not just the complex human history that has created the Apostle Islands of today; they will also fail to understand how much the natural ecosystems they encounter here have been shaped by that human history.

He concludes:

> In a very deep sense, what they will experience is not the natural and human reality of these islands, but a cultural myth that obscures much of what they most need to understand about a wilderness that has long been a place of human dwelling.[12]

A landmark initiative to achieve a balance between wild and historic landscapes has been achieved during the past decade in the Adirondack Mountains of New York, spearheaded by a regional preservation group, Adirondack Architectural Heritage (AARCH). The focus of this effort has been Camp Santanoni (begun

Figure I.7. Camp Santanoni, near Newcomb, New York. Main residence, 1892–93 (for Robert Pruyn). Robert H. Robertson, architect. Photograph by author, 1982.

1892), one of the earliest and most ambitious of the huge rustic domiciles developed as a self-sufficient compound in a remote, largely natural, private preserve (Figure I.7).[13] When the state purchased the 12,663-acre tract in 1972 for incorporation as part of the Adirondack State Park Forest Preserve, farsighted officials recognized the camp's historical value, and acreage around the building complexes and the five-mile drive that leads to them were not designated "wilderness." Yet no steps were taken to protect the camp. Strong pressure came from some environmental groups to have the camp destroyed, which their leadership believed was mandated by the state constitution.[14] Still, preserving the camp was a priority of AARCH from its founding in 1990. Working closely with the Town of Newcomb, in whose jurisdiction the complex lies, AARCH built private-sector and political support, securing an agreement in less than two years with the state Department of Environmental Conservation, steward of the Forest Preserve. Further negotiations led state officials to approve in 1995 the designation of a "historic area" within its lands as being constitutionally acceptable. Three years earlier, AARCH began work to stabilize and repair the now rapidly deteriorating components of the camp, rescuing fabric that was near failure and raising public consciousness at the same time.

Finally, in 2000, the governor signed the measure that set aside tracts totaling over thirty-two acres as the historic area—a major precedent for preservation that has received far less attention nationally than it deserves. A full commitment now exists from the state to protect the critical mass of the camp that still stands. The main residential compound and several other buildings have been restored, saved from what would have otherwise been swift ruin. Additional buildings remain in a perilous state, however. In 2004 the barn burned, and the prospects for its reconstruction are uncertain. Furthermore, as significant as the Santanoni accord is, its current stipulations prevent retrieval of the open, working landscape that until the 1970s was an integral part of the farm (Figure I.8). Creating a living history farm, where the story of the operation that sustained the camp for some eighty years could be told, would respect the land and be a further draw for the rising number of visitors to the premises. Pressure to keep the land "wild" makes such a venture problematic at present. Concern over preserving other cultural resources in the Forest Preserve—early-twentieth-century fire towers, an early-nineteenth-century blast furnace, a late-nineteenth-century fishing camp, and now another large private camp, built in 1939–40—underscores the need for more sweeping provisions, even as they may trigger counter initiatives from some environmentalists. The debate is far from over.

Just as the concept of cultural landscape can mitigate polarized views of nature versus artifice, so it can bridge divisive opinions on the relative importance of "architecture" versus "history." The segregation of these terms into categories was codified by National Register criteria and other documents emanating from the National Historic Preservation Act of 1966 and reflects long-term attitudes among preservationists in the United States. This bifurcation can wreak great mischief, for it reduces "history" to intangibles—associations with persons, events, and the like—robbing it of any physical dimension. Thus, Mabel Dodge Luhan's extraordinary adobe house (1918–21) in Taos, New Mexico, was initially proposed as a national historic landmark on the grounds of her involvement with that community's celebrated art colony, while the dwelling and its landscape were presumed to be inconsequential, even though they are poignant embodiments of the owner's personality as well as a singular example of twentieth-century design.

Figure I.8. Camp Santanoni, barn *(left)*, begun 1902, Edward Burnett, architect; later additions; burned 2004. Creamery *(right)*, ca. 1904, probably Delano & Aldrich, architects. General view, showing encroachment of vegetation over former fields and pastures of farm complex. Photograph by author, 1982.

Similarly, by employing "architecture," or an allied design category to describe the physical dimension, the significance of all things, including landscapes, may be assessed using a yardstick that is only one of many factors involved in shaping the built environment and oftentimes has no relevance to the resources at hand. Thus, a community garden created during World War II at the rear of a 1920s apartment building was judged noncontributing, even though it formed an important part of many residents' lives for most of that building's existence, because the garden was not designed and bore no formal relation to the "architecture." Reliance on "architecture" can also foster the taste prerogative—the unthinking, snobbish notion, still cherished in many preservation circles, that physical things are assessed by some immutable, yet never articulated, canon of formal attributes.[15] Looking at the built environment as a landscape can expose the pernicious effects of such predilections, but old habits die hard.

An especially unfortunate case of the "history" versus "architecture" dialectic—one that is likely to become infamous if current plans are realized—is the impending destruction of the former visitor center (now called the Cyclorama Building) at Gettysburg National Military Park. Designed by Richard Neutra in 1959 and dedicated three years later, the building was the flagship of the National

Figure I.9. Visitor Center (now Cyclorama Building), Gettysburg National Military Park, Gettysburg, Pennsylvania, 1959–62. Neutra & Alexander, architects. Photograph by Thaddeus Longstreth, 1963.

Park Service's Mission 66 program, which provided not only long overdue infrastructural improvements but also played a pioneering role in the advancement of historic site interpretation as part of public history (Figure I.9). Vienna-born Neutra, conscious of lingering North-South animosities and having experienced the effects of monarchal rule firsthand, dedicated his efforts to one of his foremost heroes, Abraham Lincoln, and to the causes of freedom and peace. Conceptually the scheme was developed not just to facilitate visitation but as an instrument to advance global harmony at the height of the Cold War. The lessons to be learned from the battle were not just ones of military engagement and of strife in America's past; they were essential ones for the present if holocaust was to be averted and lasting peace attained.[16] These and many other facets that make the building one of national significance were never investigated by park managers, who continue to downplay its importance and insist that it violates hallowed ground. Early on in the process, the then state historic preservation officer and the president of the National Trust for Historic Preservation concurred that the building should be removed on the basis that it was an intrusive feature on the battlefield, standing near the heart of General George Pickett's tragic and decisive charge.

Once a campaign was launched to save the Neutra building and the case made for its significance, decision makers still maintained an "either-or" perspective. In sanctioning demolition, the Advisory Council on Historic Preservation issued an opinion that irrespective of how important the building might be, it was nonetheless incompatible with the park; the Battle of Gettysburg's significance far transcended that of the building. The leadership of the National Trust has also staunchly adhered to this view. In recent communication with Neutra's son, president Richard Moe observed: "the prevailing view [at the National Trust] is that the battlefield is the historic resource that the park is intended to preserve and, regrettably, it's difficult to do that properly when the building is on part of the battlefield."[17] The leadership of the World Monuments Fund disagreed and placed the building on its one hundred most endangered properties list in 2005.

What remains the prevailing official perspective toward the Neutra building not only ignores the intent of the design, it takes an unduly narrow view toward the continuum of commemoration that is central to the park as a landscape and to its meaning for many visitors (Figure I.10). The new general management plan gives the terminal date for the park's period of significance as 1933—the year the National Park Service assumed custody!—even though numerous commemorative markers have been added since then. In place of the building will be a landscape "restored" to its 1863 appearance. Yet restoration is impossible, for the site is one of the richest places of combat memorialization in the United States—a landscape in which the building can be seen as an integral part. Furthermore, a flanking highway and mid-twentieth-century commercial establishments along it stand as conspicuous indications of the passage of time. If realized, the quasi–re-created patch of 1863 landscape that is planned will always be surrounded by an environment of substantially later vintage.[18]

Interpretation of the battle will continue whatever the outcome, as Julie Riesenweber remarks in her essay. Her observation also intimates the slippery slope that the concept of cultural landscape can create for preservation if it is used in certain ways: demolition of the building and the creation of a new, open setting are just part of the ongoing changes to foster interpretation. In this way cultural landscape bears analogy with the concept of anti-restoration—or anti-scrape as it is frequently called—which has become a determinant of preservation policy in many parts of the world. Taken to its extreme, anti-scrape would prevent any change in the name of preservation or for any other reason as it would sanction all changes made up to the time of designation. But the practice of preservation, like the crafting of history, is of necessity a selective act that is impossible to conduct in a purely neutral fashion. Rather, practice must be guided by reason, principle, knowledge, and fact. Much the same applies to cultural landscape, which is a construct no less than the idea of anti-restoration or of historical significance.

Misapplied, cultural landscape becomes an excuse for passivity in the preservation field, with the implicit assumption that historic resources—and natural ones as well—do not suffer serious depletion in a laissez-faire climate. Used with purpose and imagination, on the other hand, cultural landscape can, and should, be an essential underpinning of preservation, opening a whole new chapter on our understanding of, and respect for, the world around us. The essays in this book

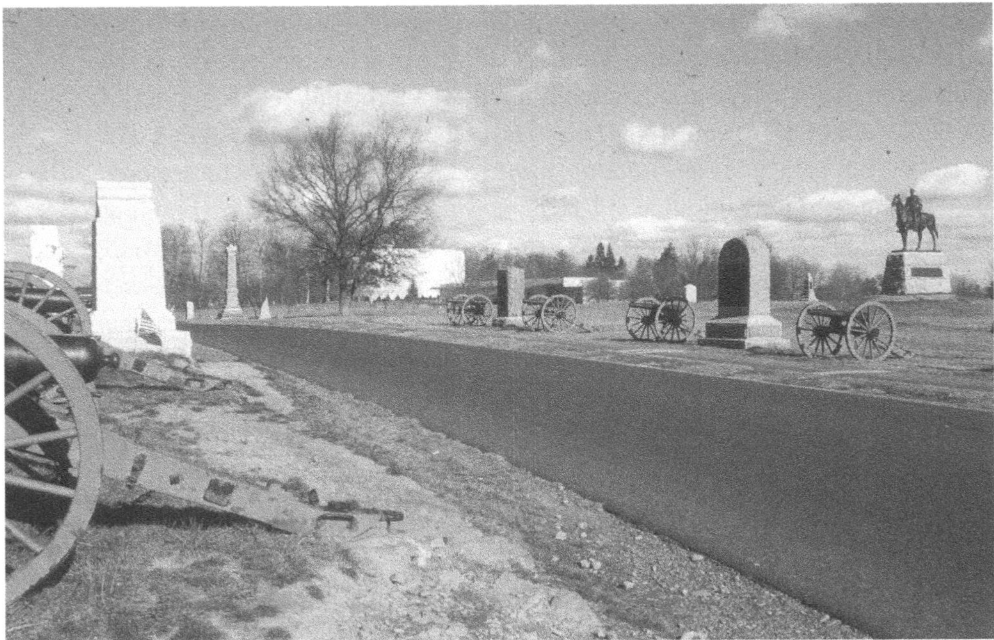

Figure I.10. Gettysburg National Military Park, general view of commemorative monuments along Hancock Avenue, Visitor Center in background. Photograph by author, 1999.

analyze some of the many beneficial aspects of the process, not just for preservation but for the natural and cultural worlds as well. Most of them are case studies, analyzing the intricate process of applying the cultural landscape concept to a wide variety of situations. The places addressed range from a caribou crossing in the new Nunavut territory of far northern Canada to state parks in Oklahoma and Missouri, from Little Tokyo in Los Angeles to a 4-H summer camp in West Virginia, from the Cross-Bronx Expressway in New York to a still largely rural island in Puget Sound, and from transportation routes in the American West to a notorious prison site in far southeastern Australia. The scope of issues the chapters that follow analyze substantially enhances our understanding of the great promise this realm of endeavor holds. The challenges are indeed opportunities.

Notes

1. For further discussion, see "Introduction: Why Cultural Landscape Preservation?" in *Preserving Cultural Landscapes in America,* ed. Arnold R. Alanen and Robert Z. Melnick (Baltimore: Johns Hopkins University Press, 2000), 1–21; Paul Groth and Chris Wilson, "The Polyphony of Cultural Landscape Study: An Introduction," in *Everyday America: Cultural Landscape Studies after J. B. Jackson,* ed. Chris Wilson and Paul Groth (Berkeley: University of California Press, 2003), 1–22; Genevieve P. Keller and J. Timothy Keller, "Preserving

Important Landscapes," in *A Rich Heritage: Historic Preservation in the Twenty-First Century,* ed. Robert E. Stipe (Chapel Hill: University of North Carolina Press, 2003), 187–222, 514–16; and Julie Riesenweber, "Landscape Preservation and Cultural Geography," chapter 1, this volume.

2. I base this observation not only on longstanding experience and discussions with colleagues but also on my position as chair of the Maryland state review board for the National Register of Historic Places. Maryland's program is widely considered to be a strong one, yet the problem persists in getting the authors of nominations to examine the places in question from a landscape perspective.

3. This statement should in no way be construed as condoning the loss of farmland or open space generally; it merely recognizes that in some cases such preservation cannot be achieved.

4. For discussion of the restoration and its rationale, see Mark R. Wenger and Myron O. Stachiw, "Recent Investigations at Montpelier," *Forum Journal* 18 (fall 2003): 18–27; Richard Moe, "The Essential Montpelier," *Preservation* 55 (November-December 2003): 6; Kirstin Downey, "Authentic Madison," *Washington Post,* 29 October 2005, F1, F8, F9; Scott Harper, "Restoration May Polish Montpelier's Profile," *Washington Post,* 4 May 2006, T18; Philip Kennicott, "Madison's Makeover; Project Is Restoring the Dignified and Sturdy Character of His Oft-Altered Home, Montpelier," *Washington Post,* 13 August 2006, N1, N5, N6; Cybèle Trione Gontar, "Rediscovering James Madison's Montepelier," *Antiques* 117 (April 2007): 120–29; and Jonathan Mummolo, "Madison Trash Heap Yields Stuff of History," *Washington Post,* 17 October 2007, B1, B10. The house has never figured prominently in histories of Virginia architecture. See, for example, Mills Lane, *Architecture in the Old South, Virginia* (Savannah, Ga.: Beehive Press, 1987), 103. Charles E. Brownell, Calder Loth, William M. S. Rasmussen, and Richard Guy Wilson, *Buildings of Virginia: Tidewater and Piedmont* (New York: Oxford University Press, 2002), 129–30, outlines the importance of the property as a twentieth-century country place.

5. Concerning the plantation landscape, see John Michael Vlach, *Back of the Big House: The Architecture of Plantation Slavery* (Chapel Hill: University of North Carolina Press, 1993); and Vlach, *The Planter's Prospect: Privilege and Slavery in Plantation Paintings* (Chapel Hill: University of North Carolina Press, 2002).

6. Concerning the military history of the fort, see Edward Pierce Hamilton, *Fort Ticonderoga: Key to a Continent,* reprint ed. (1964; Ticonderoga, N.Y.: Fort Ticonderoga, 1995). Concerning later developments, see Alfred Bossom, "The Restoration of Fort Ticonderoga," *Eighth Annual Report of the American Scenic and Historic Preservation Society* (Albany, N.Y.: J. B. Lyon, 1913), 610–18; Bossom, *The Restoration of Fort Ticonderoga or Fort Carillon, New York State, U.S.A.,* privately printed, ca. 1925, copy at Fort Ticonderoga archives, Ticonderoga, N.Y.; Lucinda A. Brockway, "Of Garrison Grounds and Pleasure Grounds: Plants and People at Fort Ticonderoga, New York," *Plants and People: The Annual Proceedings of the Dublin Seminar of New England Folklife* 20 (1999): 116–30; Brockway, *A Favorite Place of Resort for Strangers: The King's Garden at Fort Ticonderoga* (Ticonderoga, N.Y.: Fort Ticonderoga, 2001); Nicholas Westbrook, "Ticonderoga in Print: Prints from the Fort Ticonderoga Museum Collection," *Imprint: Journal of the American Historical Print Collectors Society* 26 (spring 2001): 2–18; and Carl R. Crego, *Fort Ticonderoga* (Charleston, S.C.: Arcadia, 2004). I am grateful to Nicholas Westbrook, director of Fort Ticonderoga, for additional information.

An 1826 guidebook, issued when The Pavilion was under construction, noted that "Ticonderoga shall become one of the stopping places [for steamboats] . . . and a fine inn is also erecting there" (Brockway, *A Favorite Place,* 31). The earliest known newspaper account of The Pavilion was recently discovered by Fort Ticonderoga Association trustee Karla von Fumetti Standt in the *Pittsfield* [Mass.] *Sun* of 29 May 1829. It notes: "The taste and elegance of [Pell's] mansion and gardens, and the high state of improvement of his farm, are by no means the least attractive objects, to the numerous visiters *[sic]* who have, of late, frequented the place." These descriptions, correlated with the building's highly unusual plan in which the main block is flanked by ranges of small rooms, originally accessed by a covered breezeway, with somewhat larger spaces at each end, suggest that Pell had the house built to accommodate more than the usual number of guests, who may or may not have been of his choosing.

7. For background, see Dennis Sharp, ed., *Alfred C. Bossom's American Architecture* (London: Book Art, 1984).

8. The Magasin du Roi, as it was known, was blown up by the French in 1759 when retreating from British forces during the Siege of Carillon. The exterior of the new building is based on a plan recently discovered in the New-York Historical Society archives. The interior will be totally new, housing a public education center.

9. All furnishings from this period were inventoried and placed in storage when the house was closed, enabling a thoroughly accurate restoration. Excellent illustration of the house from this period is found in Mark A. Hewitt, "Living with Antiques: The Pavilion, Ticonderoga, New York," *Antiques* 125 (July 1988): 130–41. See also Desmond Gunniness and Julius Trousdale Sadler Jr., *Palladio: A Western Progress* (New York: Viking Press, 1976), 164, 168–69, and plates. Concerning Sister Parish, see James A. Abbott and Elaine M. Rice, *Designing Camelot: The Kennedy White House Restoration* (New York: John Wiley & Sons, 1988); Mark Hampton, *Legendary Decorators of the Twentieth Century* (New York: Doubleday, 1992), 196–213; *Parish-Hadley: Sixty Years of American Design* (Boston: Little Brown, 1995); and Apple Parish Bartlett and Susan Bartlett Crater, *Sister: The Life of Legendary American Decorator, Mrs. Henry Parish II* (New York: St. Martin's Press, 2000).

10. The pioneering study was Robert Z. Melnick, with Daniel Sponn and Emma Jane Saxe, *Cultural Landscapes: Rural Historic Districts in the National Park System* (Washington, D.C.: National Park Service, 1984). Hugh Miller, then the Park Service's chief historical architect, assumed a central role in spearheading the effort.

11. Linda Flint McClelland, *Building National Parks: Historic Landscape Design and Construction* (Baltimore: Johns Hopkins University Press, 1993); Harvey H. Kaiser, *Landmarks in the Landscape: Historic Architecture in the National Parks of the West* (San Francisco: Chronicle Books, 1997); Ethan Carr, *Wilderness by Design: Landscape Architecture and the National Park Service* (Lincoln: University of Nebraska Press, 1998); and Arnold Berke, *Mary Coulter, Architect of the Southwest* (New York: Princeton Architectural Press, 2002) document this legacy. Christine Barnes, *Great Lodges of the National Parks* (Bend, Ore.: W. W. West, 2002) was written as a companion to a PBS Television series, both clearly oriented to a larger segment of the general public.

12. William Cronon, "The Riddle of the Apostle Islands: How Do You Manage a Wilderness Full of Human Stories?" *Orion* 22 (May-June 2003): 36–42, quote on p. 38.

13. The main residence was designed by R. H. Robertson in 1892 and completed the following year. A sizable farm complex was designed ca. 1902 by Edward Burnett, and

an equally impressive gate lodge in 1905 by Delano & Aldrich. A detailed history of the camp is given in Robert Engel, Howard Kirschenbaum, and Paul Malo, *Santanoni: From Japanese Temple to Life in an Adirondack Great Camp* (Keeseville, N.Y.: Adirondack Architectural Heritage, 2000). Chapter 10 therein documents the protracted effort to preserve the camp. See also "A Milestone Year at Camp Santanoni," Adirondack Architectural Heritage *Newsletter* 10 (winter 2000–01): 1, 3.

14. Passed in 1894, Article XIV of the state constitution stipulates the removal (either through destruction or neglect) of all buildings and structures on Forest Preserve land—a measure intended to protect the park from the then abundant pressures for development. Unlike virtually all other state, as well as national, parks, the Adirondack State Park's boundaries encompass private land in addition to that held by the state, which is designated the Forest Preserve. Still comprising less than half the acreage within the boundaries, actual Forest Preserve land is a galaxy of tracts, varying greatly in size and acquired over some twelve decades. For background, see Frank Graham Jr., *The Adirondack Park: A Political History* (Syracuse, N.Y.: Syracuse University Press, 1978); and Phillip G. Terrie, *Contested Terrain: A New History of Nature and People in the Adirondacks* (Syracuse, N.Y.: Syracuse University Press; and Blue Mountain Lake, N.Y: Adirondack Museum, 1997).

15. For further discussion, see Richard Longstreth, "Taste versus History," *Historic Preservation Forum* 8 (May-June 1994): 40–45; and Longstreth, "Architectural History and the Practice of Historic Preservation in the United States," *Journal of the Society of Architectural Historians* 58 (September 1999): 326–33. Concerning the community garden, see Longstreth, *History on the Line: Testimony in the Cause of Preservation* (Washington, D.C.: National Park Service; Ithaca, N.Y.: National Council for Preservation Education, 1998), chapter 5. An excellent analysis of the pitfalls of such an approach for cultural landscapes is provided in Catherine M. Howett, "Where the One-Eyed Man Is King: The Tyranny of Visual and Formalist Values in Evaluating Landscapes," in *Understanding Ordinary Landscapes*, ed. Paul Groth and Todd W. Bressi (New Haven, Conn.: Yale University Press, 1997), 85–98, 224–26.

16. Concerning the building, see W. Boesinger, ed., *Richard Neutra, Buildings and Projects* 1961–66 (Zurich: Verlag für Architektur, 1966), 156–65; Thomas S. Hines, *Richard Neutra and the Search for Modern Architecture: A Biography and History* (New York: Oxford University Press, 1982), 243–45; Sarah Allaback, *Mission* 66 *Visitor Centers: The History of a Building Type* (Washington, D.C.: National Park Service, 2000), chapter 3; and Ethan Carr, *Mission* 66*: Modernism and the National Park Dilemma* (Amherst: University of Massachusetts Press, 2007), 162–63. A detailed analysis of the building is contained in the national historic landmark nomination, prepared by Christine Madrid French and myself on behalf of the Society of Architectural Historians and posted on http://www.mission66.com/cyclorama. Among the more useful pieces covering the controversy are the following: Thomas Hine, "Which of All the Pasts to Preserve?" *New York Times*, 21 February 1999, AR 48; John Beardsley, "Another Battle at Gettysburg," *Landscape Architecture* 91 (September 2000): 128, 125; Mark Rozzo, "Who Chooses History?" *Los Angeles Times Magazine*, 27 June 2004, 14–17, 31; and Herbert Muschamp, "Martial Plans: The Enduring Relevance of a Modern Masterpiece at Gettysburg," *New York Times*, travel section, 20 May 2007, 60–61.

17. "A Problem of Common Ground," Advisory Council on Historic Preservation report prepared in compliance with the provisions of the Section 106 review process by Herbert M. Franklin, Bruce D. Judd, and Parker Westbrook, 10 May 1999; e-mail from Richard Moe to Dion Neutra, 25 August 2004, copy provided by Dion Neutra.

18. "Final General Management Plan and Environmental Impact Statement, Gettysburg National Military Park, Gettysburg, Pennsylvania," 2 vols., National Park Service, June 1999. Concerning memorialization, see Reuben M. Rainey, "Hallowed Grounds and Rituals of Remembrance: Union Regimental Monuments at Gettysburg," in *Understanding Ordinary Landscapes,* ed. Groth and Bressi, 67–80, 223–24; and Thomas A. Desjardin, *The Honored Dead: How the Story of Gettysburg Shaped American Memory* (Cambridge, Mass.: Da Capo Press, 2003).

A fortunate by-product of the controversy has been the Park Service's initiative to assess its extensive legacy of the Mission 66 program. Four visitor centers of the period have been designated national historic landmarks as a result, and many other such resources are likely to be protected in the future.

PART I

Interpreting Landscape

1. Landscape Preservation and Cultural Geography

JULIE RIESENWEBER

When preservationists think of cultural landscapes, they usually regard them as something resulting from the impact of human activity on a natural environment. In the secretary of the interior's guidelines, for example, a cultural landscape is "a geographic area (including both cultural and natural resources and the wildlife or domestic animals therein), associated with a historic event, activity, or person or exhibiting other cultural or aesthetic values." The geographer Arnold Alanen and landscape architect Robert Melnick emphasize that these places may be found "virtually everywhere that human activities have affected the land."[1] Such definitions treat landscape as a material thing and stress the impact of culture on nature, though National Park Service guidelines do so indirectly by alluding to culture through the idea of cultural resources and linking cultural landscape as geographic area with preservation's concept of significance through historical association. Preservation thus presents landscape in a way that cultural geographers associate with Carl Ortwin Sauer, who coined the term *cultural landscape* for his discipline during the 1920s. Sauer's approach to landscapes still reverberates today, yet few geographers have been involved in discussions about cultural landscape preservation, which has instead been dominated by persons trained as architects, landscape architects, or historians of the built environment. So while cultural geographers have given much attention to the concept of landscape over the past forty years, especially, and many no longer define cultural landscape as Sauer did, the more recent geographic thought has not penetrated discussions about landscape preservation. Here I outline the evolving idea of landscape among geographers and suggest the implications these shifts may have for the preservation of cultural landscapes.

The term *cultural landscape* was introduced in Sauer's seminal work, "The Morphology of Landscape" (1925).[2] This work was in part motivated by its author's dissatisfaction with the environmental determinism then popular among colleagues. While Sauer agreed with many of them that geography's central questions revolved around the relationships between human beings and their environments, he thought people had as great an effect on the physical environment as it had upon them. In "Morphology" Sauer argued that the study of landscape should be geography's primary concern, since the concept mobilized a "peculiarly geographic association of facts." He defined landscape as "an area made up of a distinct association of forms, both physical and cultural," while the cultural landscape was something "fashioned from a natural landscape by a culture group. Culture is the agent, the natural area is the medium, the cultural landscape the result."[3]

In Sauer's formulation, landscapes, whether physical or cultural, were material things. They were real and knowable through the visual sense. "Geography is a science of observation," he wrote in 1956. "The geographic bent rests on seeing and thinking about what is in the landscape. . . . In some manner, the field of geography is always a reading of the face of the earth."[4] "Morphology" outlined a method for that reading, which adapted techniques for tracing geomorphologic and topographic change to the investigation of cultural landscapes. Whether employed by physical or cultural geographers, the morphological method relied on the observation of landscape forms. For cultural landscapes, observable landscape forms included features such as population, housing, and transportation networks. Sauer's goal in observing, mapping, and analyzing such cultural landscape features was tracing landscape change and deciphering the successive layers of residue left on the land by human occupation.

This historical approach dominated cultural geography in America through the first half of the twentieth century.[5] Not only did Sauer's students continue his approach, but some also focused it to emphasize the very stuff with which historic preservation has traditionally been concerned. Fred Kniffen, for example, spent the majority of his career researching buildings and adapted Sauer's method of observing landscape forms to classifying building types and mapping their distribution. Yet while Sauer had been concerned with both natural and cultural landscape forms, explicit mention of the former all but disappeared from Kniffen's work. For Kniffen, all landscapes were cultural landscapes in that all contained traces of the "cultural strains" that occupied them.[6] While Sauer sought to define regions by mapping a combination of natural and cultural forms, Kniffen hoped to delimit culture regions and reveal culture relationships through cultural forms alone.

Other members of the "Berkeley School" of cultural geography, so named for the institution at which Sauer was based for most of his career, provided similar conceptual, methodological, and substantive orientation to landscape scholars and preservationists from many universities and backgrounds. One of the more influential of these is Peirce Lewis, who argued that "all human landscape has cultural meaning," and that this meaning might be understood by reading the landscape as if it were a book. "The human landscape is our unwitting autobiography," Lewis wrote, "reflecting our tastes, our values, our aspirations, and even our fears in tangible, visible form."[7]

A disciple of Kniffen's, folklorist Henry Glassie, made an important contribution to the conceptual and methodological interactions of cultural geographers, architectural historians, and historic preservationists, as well as some of his own colleagues. Like Kniffen, he mapped regions based on the distribution of material culture forms.[8] Glassie's dissertation, subsequently published as *Patterns in the Material Folk Culture of the Eastern United States,* employed a version of Sauer's morphological method. He insisted that geographical methods, rather than the historical ones traditionally employed by architectural historians and folklorists, were best for documenting and analyzing material folk culture, because they exhibit "major variation over space and minor variation through time. . . ." "When ordering his data," Glassie maintained, "the student of folk culture should listen more closely to the cultural geographer than to the historian, for he must labor in the geographer's dimension and shares a major goal with the geographer—the establishment of regions."[9]

While Glassie's treatment of material folk culture legitimized the architectural study of common buildings, attention to landscape as a whole rather than its component parts fell by the wayside in his translation of Sauer's morphological method to architectural investigation. Nonetheless, many of the historic resource surveys initiated in the 1970s by state historic preservation offices utilized a methodology with its basis in the morphological method devised by Sauer, adapted to buildings by Kniffen, and applied to material folk culture by Glassie.[10] While Glassie's work indirectly exposed folklorists and architectural historians to Sauerian cultural geography and its morphological method, it was J. B. Jackson who made the concept of cultural landscape a familiar one within the design professions. Although he never undertook advanced training in, nor identified himself as a member of, any academic discipline, Jackson became interested in French regional geographers and their treatment of landscape while in Europe during World War II. To further his interest, he founded, edited, and published the journal *Landscape* between 1951 and 1968. Sauer invited him to teach several occasional seminars at Berkeley in 1957. Within ten years, Jackson was involved with the departments of architecture and landscape architecture at both Berkeley and Harvard. In a recent tribute, geographer Paul Groth and architectural historian Chris Wilson noted the unique alliance between the design fields and historic preservation, emphasizing the importance of Jackson and his journal to preservationists as they began to consider historic districts, entire communities, and rural landscapes.[11]

But not long after preservationists started their massive survey efforts nationwide in the 1970s, cultural geographers began to challenge their own assumptions. In 1980, James Duncan published a critique of geography's "superorganic" notion of culture, arguing that it gave culture an existence above and beyond the people who transmitted it. This concept portrayed culture as internally homogeneous, downplayed individual agency and choice, and thus overlooked means by which culture operates.[12] Duncan's critique had important implications for landscape geography because if *culture* was a problematic term, then so was *cultural landscape.*

Initially, cultural geography's reformulations of the landscape concept involved questioning its status as a material thing. Drawing from both art historical investigations of landscape painting and Marxist theory, the historical geographer Denis Cosgrove proposed that landscape is as much an idea as a tract of land, and connected its emergence as an idea to capitalistic economic and social formations. Landscape, he maintained, is "a way of seeing—a way in which some Europeans have represented to themselves and to others the world about them and their relationships with it, and through which they have commented on social relations." In other words, landscape is an epistemology, "an historically specific way of experiencing the world developed by and meaningful to certain social groups." Whereas Sauer conceived landscape as an array of visible, material forms—especially socially constructed forms—Cosgrove considered landscape "not merely the world we see . . . [but] a construction, a composition of that world" that represents the world in much the same way as a landscape painting.[13] While Cosgrove's analysis does recognize social aspects of landscapes, his analysis further differed from Sauer's in emphasizing individual action(s) over social ones in the making and remaking of landscapes, something Sauer and his followers had largely ignored.

Cosgrove's definition of landscape led him to find limitations in the morphological method. Observation alone is insufficient for accessing the deeper meaning of landscapes, he argued, because "formal morphology remains unconvincing as an account of landscape to the extent that it ignores . . . symbolic dimensions." Cosgrove urged geographers' attention away from landscape's material forms and toward "the symbolic and cultural meaning invested in these forms by those who have produced and sustained them, and that is communicated to those who come into contact with them." Accepting "the ambiguity and severally layered meanings of landscape does not excuse us from careful examination of them and of their origins," he insisted. "Rather, it obliges us to pay rather greater attention to them than we have done in the past, for it is in the origins of landscape as a way of seeing the world that we discover its links to broader historical structures and processes and are able to locate landscape study within a progressive debate about society and culture."[14]

While conceiving landscape as representation downplayed its material aspects, in later work Cosgrove argued with coeditor Stephen Daniels for a reconciliation of landscape's dual material and immaterial character: "This is not to say that landscapes are immaterial.... They may be represented in a variety of materials and on many surfaces—in paint on canvas, in writing on paper, in earth, stone, water and vegetation. A landscape park is more palpable but no more real, nor less imaginary, than a landscape painting or poem." Since "every culture weaves its world out of image and symbol," and landscapes are symbols or representations invested with meaning, they reasoned, landscape scholarship itself contributes to the process of constructing meaning as "every study of a landscape further transforms its meaning, depositing yet another layer of cultural representation."[15]

Other geographers have regarded landscapes and their representations together as related texts, and in applying literary theory to landscapes solidly link them with social processes involving ideology and power. Rather than following Lewis in assuming an unmediated or direct relationship between the landscape and the observer, James and Nancy Duncan considered landscape meaning to be fluid, shaped by the observer's ideas and social position as well as by the circumstances of the reading. "Texts are not 'innocent,'" they wrote. "They are not transparent windows through which reality may be unproblematically viewed."[16] While different individuals may take different meanings from the same text, as geographer Donald Meinig has pointed out, the Duncans stressed that there simultaneously exist commonly held understandings and interpretations of them, shared within social groups called textual communities.[17] Such a community tends to prefer certain readings or understandings over others and eventually takes these privileged interpretations for granted. Following this line of thought, the Duncans defined landscapes as "texts which are transformations of ideologies into a concrete form."[18]

As texts of concretized ideologies, landscapes are indeed not "innocent." What Stephen Daniels called landscape's "duplicity" results from the way in which it is always present and often overlooked, yet it is constantly communicating and reinforcing power relations, and thus is connected to ongoing "socio-political processes of cultural reproduction and change." Conceiving landscape as discourse, or "the social framework of intelligibility within which all practices are communicated, negotiated, or challenged," geographers taking a critical approach have pointed out that as they translate social and cultural beliefs and values into visible form, landscapes convey these as appropriate, true, or "natural."[19] Landscapes are instruments of cultural power as they mediate such processes of concretization and naturalization, and they are all the more powerful because they are the taken-for-granted settings of daily life. Landscape can thus be considered "discourse materialized," or the "tangible, visible articulation[s] of numerous discourses." While terms such as *materialize* connote a lack of fluidity, landscapes as materialized discourses are, like social life, never static. As Richard Schein wrote, "landscapes are always in the process of becoming—no longer reified or concretized—inert and there—but continually under scrutiny, at once manipulable and manipulated, always subject to change, and everywhere implicated in the ongoing formulation of social life."[20]

During the past twenty years, then, cultural geographers have employed social theoretical insights along with economic, political, and aesthetic considerations to mount a critique of studies that treat cultural landscapes exclusively as things and depend on unmediated observation as method. Rather, they now suggest, landscape is as much image, symbol, signifier, and materialization of ideology or discourse as a material thing. Most importantly, this work has changed landscape "from a noun to a verb," to borrow a phrase from art historian W. J. T. Mitchell, by pointing out the ways in which landscape participates in the construction of both its own meanings and forms of society.[21] Historic preservation, on the other hand, often utilizes a concept of cultural landscape that originated in the 1920s, made its way into the design professions in the 1960s, and was employed by landscape architects who began to consider landscape preservation in the 1980s. But historic preservation, too, has changed greatly over the past three decades. The emphasis on evaluation within context begun in the 1980s, for instance, signals awareness of some of the theoretical issues with which cultural geographers have grappled.

Recent geographic scholarship has important insights to offer preservationists as they increasingly grapple with the concept of cultural landscape. Preservation is, on the one hand, a social and political movement and, on the other, a set of institutionalized practices that expressly seek to retain, stabilize, and breathe new life into material remnants of the past. The secretary of the interior's *Standards* defines preservation, that most general of interventions that lends the movement its name, as

> the act or process of applying measures necessary to sustain the existing *form, integrity* and *materials* of an historic property. Work, including preliminary measures to protect and stabilize the *property*, generally focuses upon the ongoing maintenance and repair of historic *materials and features* rather than extensive replacement and new construction.[22]

Grounded in notions of fixed real property, preservation is concerned with visible, material things that survive from the past and with maintaining in the present their appearance in the past.[23]

While material—or historic fabric—is pivotal in certifying the historicity of particular places and supporting their preservation, integrity is the quality through which preservation assesses how closely that material maintains a semblance with that of the period of historical significance. According to the National Register of Historic Places guidelines, integrity demands "the authenticity of a property's historic identity, evidenced by the *survival of physical characteristics*" that existed during a particular time in the past.[24] As an idea centered on the physical characteristics of historic places, the very notion of integrity is connected to theories of landscape that regard it as a material thing. Since such survival is the result of stasis, occurring only when there has been little change to a building or landscape over time, it is no wonder that preservation has difficulty grasping the fluidity and a sense of process many geographers now emphasize in examining landscapes.

Those preservationists most closely involved with cultural landscapes recognize the difficulties in applying to them evaluative criteria originally developed primarily for buildings. Others have likewise questioned the possibility and advisability of capturing landscapes and halting their change through preservation.[25] J. B. Jackson maintained that part of our appreciation of historic landscapes stems from their very endurance and ongoing change: from the fact that they are a living and integral part of the world.[26] The preservation-sensitive folklorist Bernard Herman has drawn an analogy between preservation and taxidermy, implying that stopping change takes landscapes and buildings out of the organic world, an act that often means stopping life.[27] Alanen and Melnick echo the voices of critical landscape geographers in characterizing cultural landscapes as both "product and process," and consider them significant not only as relics representing a particular point or period in time but also for their fluidity, endurance, and subtle presence in the face of ongoing physical and ideological change.[28] Perhaps preservationists would find useful a distinction between historic landscapes, which through their high degree of material integrity particularly evoke some period or event in the past, and cultural landscapes, significant places in which some traces of the past endure yet undergo constant change.

While integrity is a concept explicitly tied to the material characteristics of historic resources, the connections between significance and materiality are subtler. National Register guidelines imply that the fabric of those resources embody significance *if* integrity is present.[29] Thus, significance is bound up with materiality. This relationship has led some preservationists to observe that integrity is the "fifth criteria for eligibility." Catherine Howett, for example, observed that, in practice, integrity is even more important than significance because "no matter how historically important a site or structure may have been, if its present condition fails to meet standards of integrity... it cannot qualify for listing in the National Register of Historic Places."[30]

By placing concepts such as significance and integrity firmly within the realm of socially constructed meaning, recent geographical thought challenges historic preservation's assertion that materiality carries historical authenticity. This position also suggests that the preservation movement itself is socially constructed, thus questioning whether preservation's goals and values are universal and "true." As architectural historian Catherine Bishir, who spent most of her career in North Carolina's state historic preservation office, argued, preservationists are a distinct social group with distinct beliefs acquired through specific training and practice.[31] Preservation professionals thus constitute a community, which takes as commonplace the sense of significance framed by federal historic preservation policy. Most Americans, however, are not part of this community and do not necessarily share the distinct connotations of concepts such as significance and integrity.[32] For most people, a significant place or event is one that has had great impact on their or other people's lives. All of us who have worked with historic buildings and landscapes have talked with people who value material remnants of the past because of their associations with personal, family, or community history. Most value places because of the memories associated with them, because these memories and the attached places are part of who they are. The insights of critical landscape geography might, then, lead us to a sense of significance closer to this popular meaning. From both the popular and discursive points of view, what is important is not that which is unique and monumental, celebrates success, fits into some canon, or has remained unchanged but that which most decisively shapes how we view and interact with the world.

Preservationists thus might follow cultural geographers' lead in asking not simply what landscapes reflect but also what they shape. One seemingly diverse array of landscapes decisive in shaping social interaction are those Schein characterizes as "racialized." Such landscapes are "particularly implicated in racist practice and the perpetuation of (or challenge to) racist social relations."[33] Examples include neighborhoods redlined through zoning, deed covenants, and financial practices; those developed expressly for sale or resale to African Americans and other ethnic and racial groups; suburbs that separated whites in quasi-rural settings; gated communities; and rural black communities such as Nicodemus, Kansas. Less obvious are racialized landscapes such as the courthouse square in Lexington, Kentucky. Site of the Fayette County Courthouse since Lexington's founding in the 1780s, the square has long borne statues of Confederate General John Hunt Morgan and John Breckinridge, who was a U.S. senator and vice president. Both men were slave holders, and although the "cheap side" of the square was the site of a slave market before the Civil War, this fact was not commemorated until October 2003, when a group of African Americans was finally successful in having a historical marker placed there. Prior to the recent dedication of the historical marker commemorating the Cheapside slave market, the landscape both reflected the racist practice of omitting African Americans when interpreting the past and shaped social relations by implying this was the "normal" or appropriate way of doing things.

As Schein has noted, understanding landscape's place "in the social relations and spatial arrangements of daily life" involves questions about how one "particular and identifiable cultural landscape in this place is related and connected to landscapes and social processes in other places."[34] While this sense of networks and flows of meaning and power recalls preservation's notion of context, it also challenges its scalar categories of local, state, and national levels of significance. It further provides opportunity for considering new ways in which landscapes might be significant, for making connections between places separated in time and space, and for finding significance in landscapes that might otherwise have been thought unimportant. Landscapes are indeed texts that tell stories. Part of the story that Lexington's courthouse square tells is conveyed through what is memorialized there.

Because preservation is itself a form of memorializing and interpretive activity, preservationists might utilize the idea that meaning and value are socially constructed together with a poststructural notion of discourse to become critically aware of their own practices. James and Nancy Duncan cite preservation activity in a Vancouver neighborhood as a way of illustrating that landscapes are texts that concretize ideology. Residents there formed a neighborhood association led by individuals who did not like the changes taking place and preferred that the neighborhood continue to appear as it did historically. The group utilized standard preservation mechanisms, including a historic zoning overlay and preservation-oriented design guidelines, to halt change they found undesirable and materialize their reading of the neighborhood's original developmental model.[35] The point is that in this situation, a neighborhood association employed historic preservation as a means of making its preferred vision concrete on the landscape. If scholarship adds layers of meaning to landscapes by representing them in text and image, as the Duncans have argued, then the implication of their Vancouver example is that preservation does the same.

The more familiar example of Gettysburg, site of the national cemetery where Lincoln gave his famous address and of a highly venerated national military park, further illustrates this point. In 1959, the National Park Service commissioned the internationally renowned architect Richard Neutra to design a visitor center for the site as part of its Mission 66 program. Now, less than fifty years later, Park Service officials have elected to demolish the building in spite of its documented significance and to "restore" the battlefield vistas to their character at the time of the conflict.[36] The choice at Gettysburg is twofold. First, there is the question of whether this landscape should be restored or rehabilitated to a single point in time. A related question—and one perhaps more interesting from the standpoint of critical landscape geography—concerns the nature of the story the Park Service wishes to tell and materialize with its preferred vision of the site, and whether that story will include the federal agency as one author of Gettysburg's interpretation. Numerous memorials have been placed at the battlefield since the mid-nineteenth century; Neutra's building is far from the sole change made to the landscape since the Civil War but is among the largest, among the most conspicuously placed, and by far the most unabashedly "modern." While demolishing the building and "restoring" this landscape to its apparent mid-nineteenth-century appearance may seem contrived, from another point of view it merely shifts the landscape's materializing activity from one discourse to another, eliding the Park Service's role in interpreting the battlefield as a historic shrine. With a slight shift in perspective, we recognize that the cultural landscape of Gettysburg has long borne traces of the battle's interpretation and that this is as much part of its meaning as the battle itself. The landscape has long told the story of the memorialization and interpretation of the battle and will continue to do so whether or not a partially re-created setting replaces the Neutra building.

Geographer and historian David Lowenthal has written that "the past we know or experience is always contingent on our own views, our own perspective, and above all on our own present. Just as we are products of the past, so is the known past an artifact of ours."[37] Like other historical endeavors, preservation constructs a story of the past through the lens of the present, and the landscapes with which it is concerned make these stories concrete, seemingly natural, and true. As the narratives historic preservation constructs and materializes shape our view of the past, it accomplishes social reproduction by legitimizing landscapes that reinforce certain views of the past and elide others. Melnick reminds us so poignantly that these landscapes are central to our personal and collective identities as they create and reinforce self-images and value structures.[38] Historic preservation is thus a powerful process for designing landscapes that, while they form the "taken-for-granted" settings of daily life, silently engage in shaping who we are. This is not only the most convincing argument for preservation but also renders it a serious responsibility. The most important lesson preservationists should take from critical landscape geographers is thus a caution to consider carefully what we preserve, why we preserve it, and for whom it is preserved.

Notes

1. Charles A. Birnbaum, ed., with Christine Capella Peters, *The Secretary of the Interior's Standards for Treatment of Historic Properties with Guidelines for Treatment of Cultural Landscapes* (Washington, D.C.: National Park Service, 1996), 4; "Introduction: Why Cultural Landscape Preservation?" in *Preserving Cultural Landscapes in America,* ed. Arnold R. Alanen and Robert Z. Melnick (Baltimore: Johns Hopkins University Press, 2000), 3.

2. Carl O. Sauer, "The Morphology of Landscape," University of California Publications in Geography 2, no. 2, Berkeley, 1925; reprinted in *Land and Life: A Selection from the*

Writings of Carl Ortwin Sauer, ed. John Leighley (Berkeley: University of California Press, 1963), 315–50.

3. Ibid., 321, 343.

4. Ibid., 392–93.

5. Paul Groth and Chris Wilson, "The Polyphony of Cultural Landscape Study: An Introduction," in *Everyday America: Cultural Landscape Studies after J. B. Jackson,* ed. Chris Wilson and Paul Groth (Berkeley: University of California Press, 2003), 5.

6. Fred Kniffen, "Louisiana House Types," *Annals of the Association of American Geographers* 26 (December 1936): 79–193.

7. Peirce Lewis, "Axioms for Reading the Landscape," in *The Interpretation of Ordinary Landscapes: Geographical Essays,* ed. Donald W. Meinig (New York: Oxford University Press, 1979), 12. While Lewis did not formally study at Berkeley, he often acknowledges the influence of Berkeley-identified writers such as Sauer, J. B. Jackson, and Wilbur Zelinsky.

8. Ibid., 37, n. 47.

9. Henry Glassie, *Pattern in the Material Folk Culture of the Eastern United States* (Philadelphia: University of Pennsylvania Press, 1968), 33–34.

10. Architectural researchers of the 1890s through the 1940s, especially those working in New England and the Middle Atlantic states, produced another body of research important in influencing the contours of the comprehensive surveys conducted by state historic preservation offices in the 1970s. Though not published in book form until 1979, Abbott Lowell Cummings's work, which culminated in *The Framed Houses of Massachusetts Bay,* 1625–1725 (Cambridge, Mass.: Harvard University Press, 1979), is within this vein. Dell Upton summarizes this body of research in "Outside the Academy: A Century of Vernacular Architecture Studies, 1890–1990," in *The Architectural Historian in America,* ed. Elisabeth Blair MacDougall (Washington, D.C.: National Gallery of Art; Hanover, N.H.: University Press of New England, 1990), 199–213.

11. Groth and Wilson, "The Polyphony of Cultural Landscape Study," 14.

12. James Duncan, "The Superorganic in American Cultural Geography," *Annals of the Association of American Geographers* 70 (June 1980): 181–91.

13. Denis E. Cosgrove, *Social Formation and Symbolic Landscape,* 2nd ed. (Madison: University of Wisconsin Press, 1998), 1, 13.

14. Ibid., 18, 15.

15. Stephen Daniels and Denis Cosgrove, "Introduction: Iconography and Landscape," in *The Iconography of Landscape: Essays on the Symbolic Representation, Design, and Use of Past Environments,* ed. Denis Cosgrove and Stephen Daniels (Cambridge: Cambridge University Press, 1988), 1, 8.

16. James Duncan and Nancy Duncan, "(Re)reading the Landscape," *Environment and Planning D: Society and Space* 6 (1988): 118.

17. D. W. Meinig, "The Beholding Eye: Ten Versions of the Same Scene," in *The Interpretation of Ordinary Landscapes,* ed. Meinig, 33–48.

18. Duncan and Duncan, "(Re)reading the Landscape," 117.

19. Stephen Daniels, "Marxism, Culture, and the Duplicity of Landscape," in *New Models in Geography,* ed. Richard Peet and Nigel Thrift, 2 vols. (London: Unwin Hyman, 1989), 196–220; James Duncan, *The City as Text: The Politics of Landscape Interpretation in the Kandyan Kingdom* (Cambridge: Cambridge University Press, 1990), 11, 16. The geographer Don Mitchell has reinterpreted the idea of landscape more recently within the

"new" cultural geography. See Don Mitchell, *The Lie of the Land: Migrant Workers and the California Landscape* (Minneapolis: University of Minnesota Press, 1996), especially chapters 1 and 2.

20. W. J. T. Mitchell, introduction to *Landscape and Power,* 2nd ed. (Chicago: University of Chicago Press, 1994), 1–2; Duncan, *The City as Text,* 19; Richard H. Schein "The Place of Landscape: A Conceptual Framework for an American Scene," *Annals of the Association of American Geographers* 87 (December 1997): 664, 660, 662.

21. Mitchell, introduction to *Landscape and Power,* 1.

22. *The Secretary of the Interior's Standards for the Treatment of Historic Properties* (Washington, D.C.: National Park Service, 1995), 17, emphasis added.

23. See Bernard L. Herman, "Fleeting Landscapes and the Challenge for Historic Preservation," *Historic Preservation Forum* 8 (May-June 1994): 4.

24. "How to Complete the National Register Nomination Form," *National Register Bulletin* 16A (1991): 4, emphasis added.

25. See, for example, Kevin Lynch, *What Times Is This Place?* (Cambridge, Mass.: MIT Press, 1972); David Lowenthal, *The Past Is a Foreign Country* (New York: Cambridge University Press, 1985); and Lowenthal, *Possessed by the Past: The Heritage Crusade and the Spoils of History* (New York: Free Press, 1996).

26. J. B. Jackson, " 'Sterile' Restorations Cannot Replace a Sense of the Stream of Time," letter to the editor, *Landscape Architecture* 66 (May 1976): 194; reprinted in Helen Lefkowitz Horowitz, ed., *Landscape in Sight: Looking at America* (New Haven, Conn.: Yale University Press, 1997), 366–68.

27. Herman, "Fleeting Landscapes," 4. Although Herman was discussing a boat, it is worthwhile to consider his taxidermy metaphor with regard to landscapes.

28. Alanen and Melnick, *Preserving Cultural Landscapes,* 16.

29. "How to Apply the National Register Criteria for Evaluation," *National Register Bulletin* 15 (1991): 2.

30. Catherine Howett, "Integrity as a Value in Cultural Landscape Preservation," in *Preserving Cultural Landscapes,* ed. Alanen and Melnick, 188.

31. Catherine Bishir, "Yuppies, Bubbas, and the Politics of Culture," in *Perspectives in Vernacular Architecture, III,* ed. Thomas Carter and Bernard L. Herman (Columbia: University of Missouri Press, 1989), 8.

32. The geographers James S. Duncan and Nancy Duncan present a related argument in *Landscapes of Privilege: Aesthetics and Affluence in American Suburbs* (London: Routledge, 2003), and demonstrate that both landscape aesthetics and historic preservation are enmeshed in creating an American elite.

33. Richard H. Schein, "Normative Dimensions of Landscape," in *Everyday America,* ed. Wilson and Groth, 203.

34. Schein, "The Place of Landscape," 662.

35. Duncan and Duncan, "(Re)reading the Landscape," 121–22.

36. For further discussion, see the introduction to this volume.

37. Lowenthal, *The Past Is a Foreign Country,* 214–16.

38. See Robert Z. Melnick, "Are We There Yet? Travels and Tribulations in the Cultural Landscape," chapter 11, this volume.

2. The Politics of Preservation

Power, Memory, and Identity in Los Angeles's Little Tokyo

HILLARY JENKS

THORNY issues of "ownership" of the cultural landscape and of the relationship between ethnic identity and physical space are vividly illustrated in the evolution of what is now the Little Tokyo National Historic Landmark District, located just east of downtown Los Angeles (Figure 2.1). Little Tokyo has been dynamically created by the place-making actions of multiple groups of people. Comprehending and preserving the cultural landscapes of such urban and "ethnic" places are an especially complex and controversial undertaking due to the diversity as well as the number of concerns of those involved over time. Although the landscape of Little Tokyo may at first appear monolithic in interpretation and treatment, it is in fact the nexus of many separate communities, often with conflicting agendas. How does the landscape of a place reflect the diverse communities that have called it home? What is deserving of preservation, and who decides? How are memories and identities preserved in, and shaped by, elements of the landscape? The rehabilitation of the Far East café and redevelopment and preservation in Little Tokyo more generally afford an instructive basis for analyzing these issues.

The Transformation of Little Tokyo

Present-day Little Tokyo spans about ten square blocks, roughly bounded by Alameda, First, Third, and Main streets, just to the east of downtown and the adjacent Civic Center (Figure 2.2). Though physically small, Little Tokyo is symbolically a cultural landscape of major importance within the region. It is a place that has seen many battles—over citizenship, ethnic identity, urban redevelopment, corporate power, housing, homelessness, and most recently over exactly what type of "culture" will continue to be embodied and exhibited in the district. The theme of Little Tokyo's cultural landscape can be found in the continuing struggle of Japanese Americans for physical and symbolic control over the neighborhood's future, a struggle that is intimately tied to their solidarity and identity as an ethnic community.

Little Tokyo's beginning as an enclave for Japanese immigrants dates to 1885, when a former seaman known as Kame opened a restaurant on the west side of

Figure 2.1. Little Tokyo National Historic Landmark District, Los Angeles, view looking northwest on East First Street from Central Avenue. At right is the Buddhist temple (original location of the Japanese American National Museum and now the National Center for the Preservation of Democracy); rehabilitated Far East Building adjacent to left. Photograph by author, 2004.

Los Angeles Street.[1] In 1908, the year of the Gentlemen's Agreement limiting Japanese immigration to the United States, Japanese merchants were already running three hundred businesses in Los Angeles, mostly in the area of Little Tokyo, as well as nearly a hundred boarding and lodging houses.[2] By 1930, 35,000 Japanese and Japanese Americans lived in Los Angeles County. They carved out a niche in produce agriculture, creating a vertically integrated network of Japanese growers, wholesalers, and retailers.[3] The money earned in agriculture was spent on the Japanese goods and services—including rice, kimono silk, and bathhouses—that the *nihonmachi* (or Japan-town) ethnic enclave economy provided. James M. Omura described Little Tokyo in the 1920s and 1930s as "a jumble of poor establishments and a few nice-looking businesses like the Asia Company, and hotels on both sides, and bigger Nisei [second-generation Japanese Americans]-operated pharmacies, like Iwaki Drug and Tenshodo across the street."[4] These businesses, religious institutions, and memories constitute the immigrant, family-oriented, working-class element of the neighborhood's landscape that is preserved as a national historic landmark and remembered in the district's public art—particularly the sidewalk that is inscribed with images of

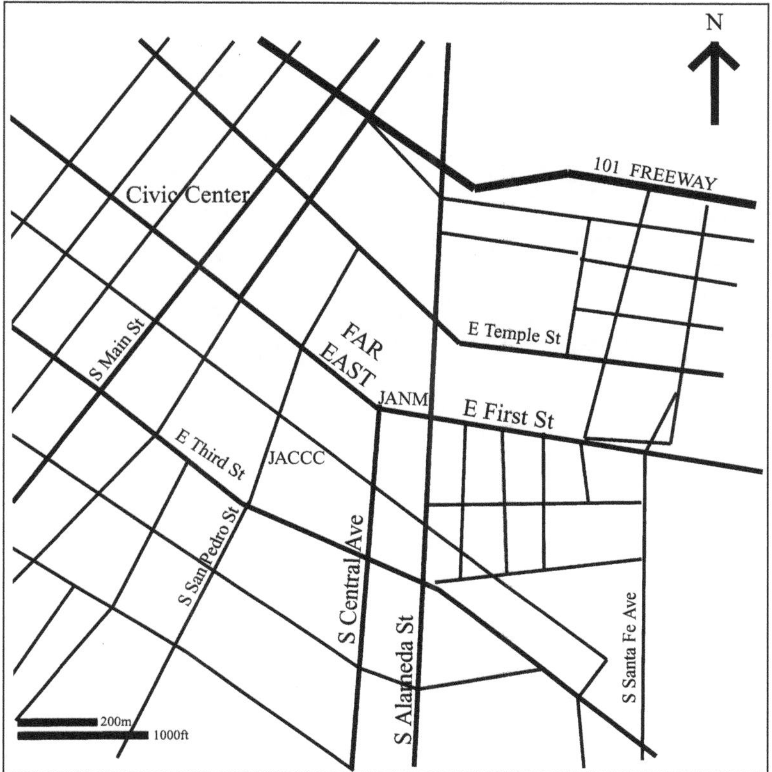

Figure 2.2. Street map of Little Tokyo. Drafted by author.

uprooting and with the locations of old stores and quotes from former residents (Figure 2.3).[5] But the Japanese American story is only one part of the neighborhood's history.

In February 1942, Franklin D. Roosevelt signed Executive Order 9066, which ordered all persons of Japanese ancestry living on the West Coast to report to "relocation centers," bringing only what they could carry. Shortly thereafter, thousands of other Americans began to enter the city for work in new wartime industries. Many were African Americans, who were barred, as the Japanese had been, from living in restricted "white" neighborhoods. Deputy mayor Orville Caldwell directed these newcomers to Little Tokyo, where they filled up the empty storefronts and hotels, causing the neighborhood to be renamed "Bronzeville."[6] By mid-1945, African American homes, clubs, and businesses were sharing the fluid and diverse cultural landscape of Bronzeville–Little Tokyo with Japanese Americans returning from the camps—an intriguing and still understudied period in the district's history. The two communities did not always coexist amicably. In 1945, for example, the Buddhist temple at First Street and Central Avenue (later

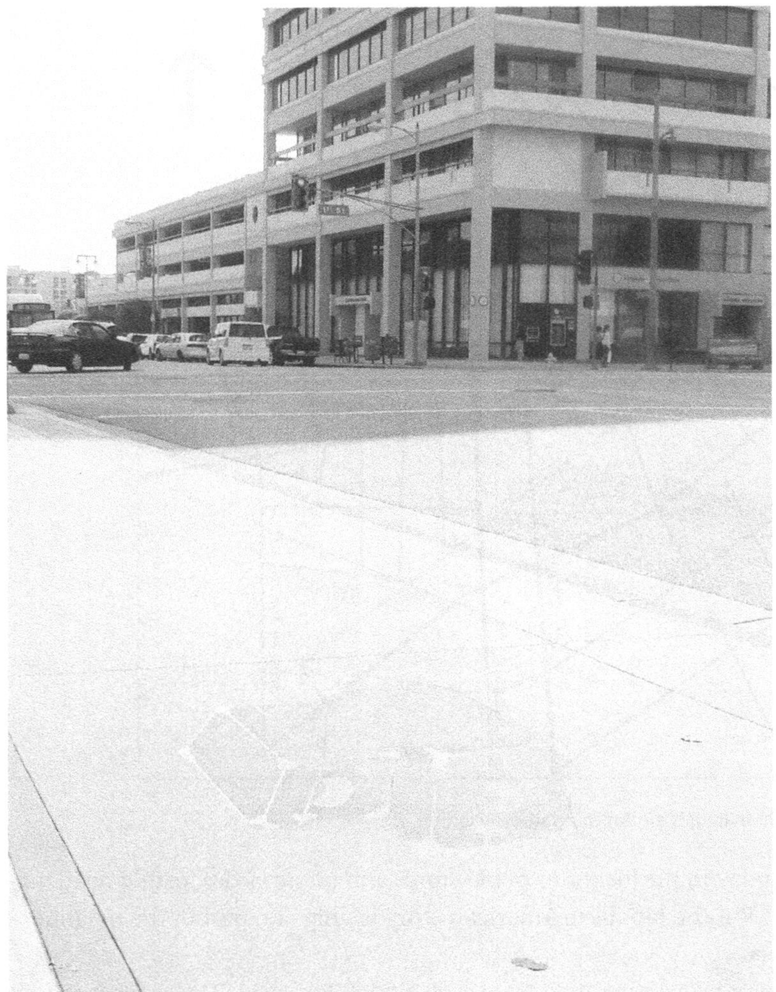

Figure 2.3. Images of suitcases from the public art sidewalk installation on East First Street in Little Tokyo. The suitcases are emblematic of the evacuation order in 1942 that instructed Japanese Americans to report for relocation with only as much as they could carry. Photograph by author, 2004.

home to the Japanese American National Museum) sheltered a black Baptist congregation of seventy-five African American war workers. Despite the fact that the church's pastor believed he had already placed a down payment on the building, returning internees began eviction proceedings.[7]

Many of the returning internees had lost their homes and businesses in Little Tokyo and were resettled throughout greater Los Angeles by the War Relocation Authority. In addition, the community had lost its prewar economic foundation in the produce industry, and wartime neglect and overcrowding had damaged the neighborhood's building stock.[8] When the Supreme Court struck down the restriction of racially exclusive housing covenants in 1948, many Japanese Americans were ready to move on residentially, though Little Tokyo retained its status as the commercial and symbolic "home" of southern California's Japanese American community. African Americans also migrated to newly available neighborhoods farther afield. Little Tokyo in the 1950s thus became a residential center mostly for elderly Issei—first-generation Japanese immigrants—as well as new immigrants and students from postwar Japan. A limited commercial strip along First Street was revived with cultural organizations and stores emphasizing traditional Japanese products.[9]

The diminished landscape of this symbolic Little Tokyo became a target for Civic Center expansion in the 1950s when a new police headquarters displaced a thousand residents. As one community activist later stated, "the fact that it was considered a deteriorated area made it very easy for the Police Administration Building to be moved in."[10] The encroachment of the Civic Center's large-scale, bureaucratic landscape caused local merchants to form the Little Tokyo Redevelopment Association (LTRA) in 1963. Its purpose, as historian Lon Kurashige has put it, was "to strengthen Little Tokyo's infrastructure so it could better resist external land grabbing."[11] Although many Japanese Americans were now building lives outside the old ethnic enclave, they still had strong emotional, not to mention financial, investments there and wanted it to *remain* Little Tokyo.

Over the next seven years, LTRA raised funds to construct a medical building on Second Street, the Merit Savings & Loan building on First Street, and the fifteen-story Kajima Building at the corner of First and San Pedro—buildings that added a new element of middle-class prosperity to the precinct.[12] The Sun Building on Weller Street became the headquarters for various social service and recreational groups aimed at the Japanese community, particularly the aging Issei. According to community historian Mike Murase, Japanese Americans resisted the idea of having to give up Little Tokyo entirely to bureaucratic expansion: "many Nikkei [Japanese Americans] continued to view Little Tokyo as a link to their past, a symbol for their ethnic identity and a convenience for practical purposes."[13]

Concerned that they lacked adequate funds, LTRA's leadership later involved the city's Community Redevelopment Agency (CRA) in its endeavors.[14] In late 1972 CRA officials announced that a group including thirty major Japanese banks and corporations would build the large, deluxe New Otani Hotel in Little Tokyo (Figure 2.4).[15] Several Japanese American groups, according to sociologist Jan Lin, "were unsettled by the entrance of the large transnational corporations and became critical of the pace and scale of redevelopment."[16] Unrest grew in 1977 when Nikkei community organizations were evicted from their offices to allow for construction of the upscale Japanese-funded Weller Court shopping mall.

Figure 2.4. East First Street between Central and San Pedro Streets, showing the New Otani Hotel and other recent construction towering over the early-twentieth-century fabric of Little Tokyo. Photograph by author, 2004.

Japanese investors seemed intent on replacing the immigrant, working-class landscape of Little Tokyo with an expensive, modern shopping district for wealthy Japanese tourists.[17] While the CRA saw Little Tokyo redevelopment as "perfectly suited to meet the growing needs of Los Angeles' trade with Japan," Kurashige noted that many Japanese Americans felt the CRA was "sacrificing ethnic community to international commerce."[18]

In addition to the hotels and malls that were constructed for visitors from Japan were projects that sought to exoticize the neighborhood in order to attract American tourists. City and corporate redevelopment emphasized the district's Pacific Rim connections and sought to represent them in the landscape. In the words of Murase, city planners intended that "Little Tokyo, along with Chinatown, Little Italy, and Olvera Street, would be an added attraction for tourists and conventioneers who visited Los Angeles, and not primarily a community for its people."[19] Since most original structures in Little Tokyo were plain, brick, two-to-three-story buildings that were typical of turn-of-the-twentieth-century American commercial districts, the CRA had to create visible signs of Little Tokyo's exotic "Japanese-ness" in order to transform it into a tourist destination.[20] The entrance to the 1978 Japanese Shopping Village, for example, was marked by a sixty-foot Japanese wooden *yagura* (or fire tower)—now the visual emblem most commonly found on tourist postcards available in the district (Figure 2.5).[21] One community organization called this scheme "redevelopment that reflects mainstream U.S. and Japanese corporate attempts to build a Japantown that looks like one."[22]

Japanese American groups fought this "Japanization" of Little Tokyo by emphasizing the specifically Japanese *American* characteristics of the landscape. The row of aging buildings on First Street, including the hotel housing the Far East café, was placed on the National Register of Historic Places in 1986, while, beginning in 1984, Nisei (or second-generation) veterans and businessmen moved to create a Japanese American museum in the district. The CRA, faced with this growing discontent in Little Tokyo, took note of the increasing popular activism centered on Japanese American memory. Japanese companies, according to Kurashige, were simultaneously "concerned by 'Japan-bashing' incidents abroad and constrained by recession at home" and "developed a new style of American investment" that projected a community-minded image.[23] The Japanese American National Museum (JANM), which opened in 1992, "attracted the same outside sources behind Little Tokyo redevelopment" (Figure 2.6). The CRA provided the site, and "Japanese multinational corporations pledged generous financial contributions."[24] Thus, in the late 1980s and the 1990s, Little Tokyo redevelopment gradually shifted in focus from eradicating the existing cultural landscape to an almost suffocating piling-on of memory artifacts and the promotion of ethnic, historic, and cultural venues in the neighborhood.

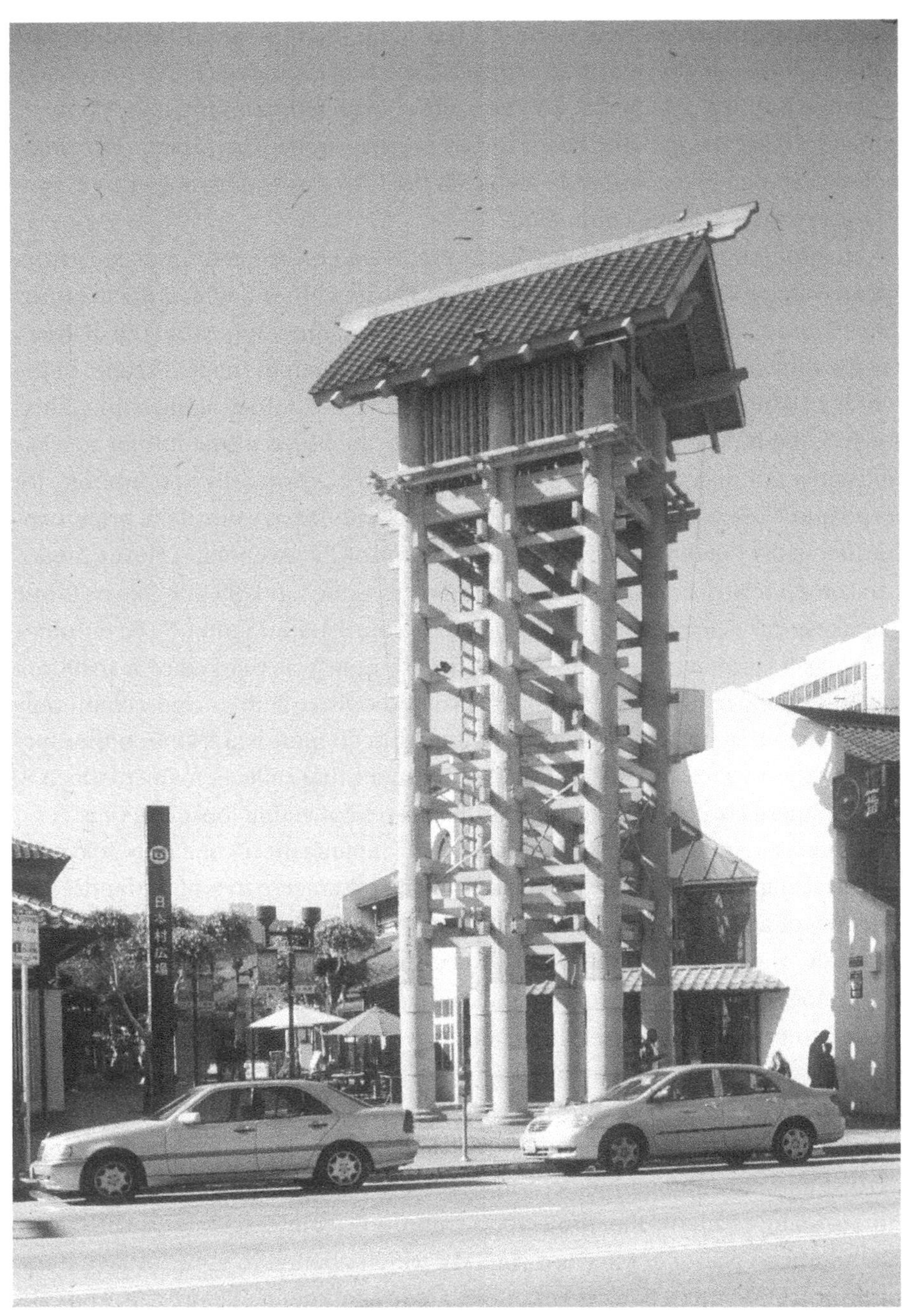

Figure 2.5. Japanese Shopping Village, East First Street and Central Avenue, with wooden *yagura* (fire tower) constructed in 1978 to make Little Tokyo look more "Japanese." Photograph by Richard Longstreth, 2004.

Figure 2.6. Japanese American National Museum, East First Street and Central Avenue, 1998–99. Hellmuth, Obata & Kassbaum, architects; Gyo Obata, principal in charge. Photograph by Richard Longstreth, 2004.

Though ceding ground to Japanese Americans' desire to maintain a connection with their symbolic home in the form of museums and memorials, the redevelopment strategy of the 1990s still focused on creating a commercial landscape to attract tourists. The CRA, for example, funded several public art works in Little Tokyo, and the City of Los Angeles has recently installed historical markers as guides for tourists at several points throughout the district (Figure 2.7). There is even a visitor center in one of the historic buildings. Many of these additions to the landscape do an excellent job of interpreting Japanese American history for visitors. The overall effect, however, is to turn the entire neighborhood into a museum, which is probably not what the initial supporters of preservation in Little Tokyo had in mind. The CRA has transformed Little Tokyo into "a national symbol and center for Japanese American history, arts, and service organizations," instead of a living site of Japanese American community.

The question of whether Little Tokyo still *is* a living Japanese American community is worth asking. The number of residents in Little Tokyo is now less than four thousand due to commercial redevelopment and the ongoing shortage of affordable housing, a situation that will soon be complicated with the completion of Trammel Crow's massive complex of luxury lofts.[25] Meanwhile, many homeless people camp on the sidewalks because of the district's proximity to

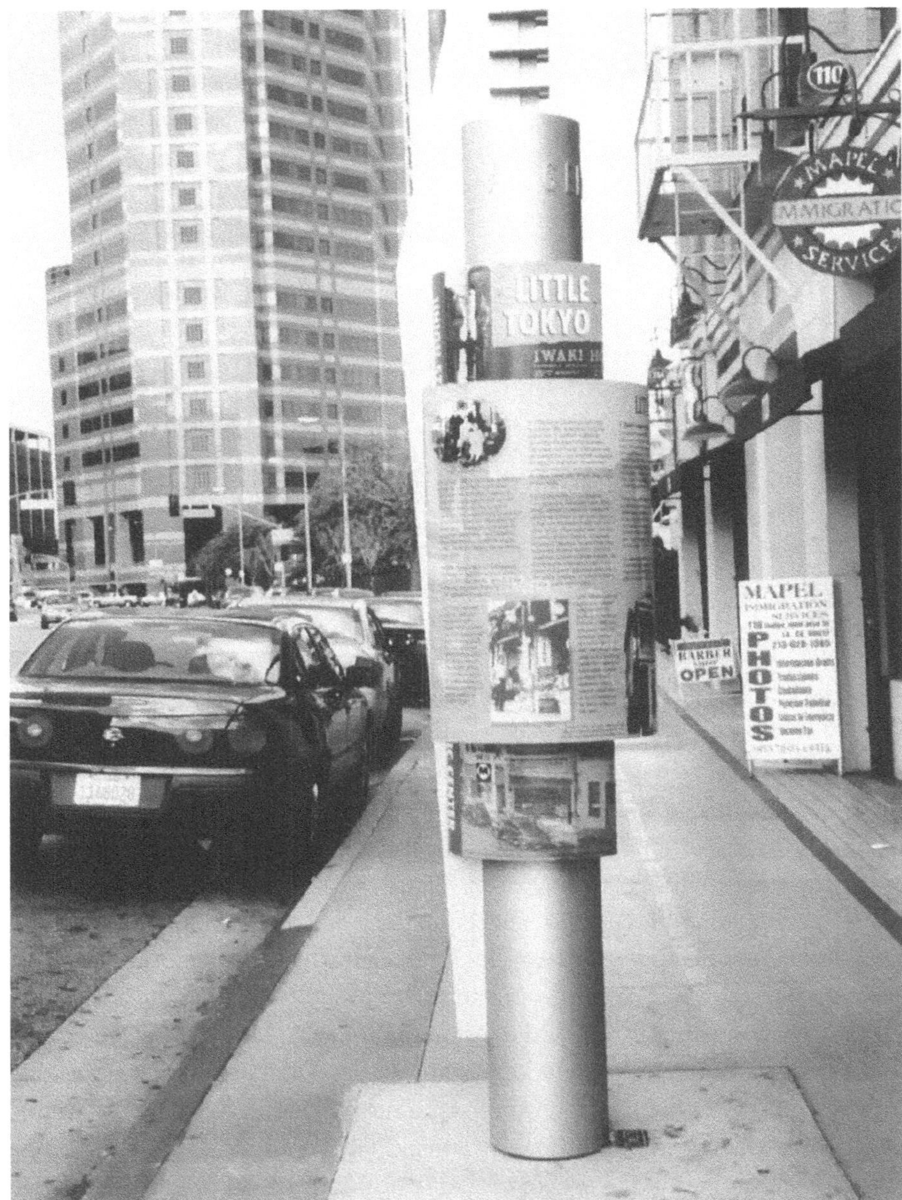

Figure 2.7. Little Tokyo tourist information kiosk, installed by the municipal government in 2003. Photograph by author, 2004.

skid row missions. The ethno-racial makeup of the district according to the 2000 census is about one-third African American, one-quarter Latino, and about one-fifth Japanese or Japanese American.[26] What does the cultural landscape of memory that has been created in Little Tokyo do for these contemporary residents? What *should* be done to maintain the neighborhood as a symbolic home for the newest generations of Japanese Americans, to explain it as a diverse and contested piece of urban ground, and to make it a livable multiracial neighborhood?

Preserving the Far East

The Far East café, a Chinese restaurant inside a turn-of-the-twentieth-century hotel within the boundaries of the Little Tokyo historic district, operated continuously from 1935 through 17 January 1994, when it was closed by the destructive power of the Northridge earthquake (Figure 2.8). During the past few years, the Far East has been rehabilitated by the Little Tokyo Service Center Community Development Corporation, a nonprofit group managing approximately five hundred units of affordable housing, as part of a project to reopen the restaurant, create a new community computer center, and turn the former hotel rooms into affordable studio apartments for seniors and members of Little Tokyo's sizable homeless population. The lobby area of the building, which stands barely fifty feet from the entrance to JANM, now houses an exhibit of photographs and artifacts detailing certain elements of the history of Little Tokyo.

The Far East stands at the nexus of Little Tokyo's conflicting cultural landscapes and exemplifies the district's complicated past and future. The Service Center along with other organizations such as the Japanese American Community and Cultural Center act as the district's symbolic bankers, managing the Japanese American cultural capital of Little Tokyo.[27] In contrast to city and corporate investment in "Japanization" of public art, these organizations reflect Japanese Americans' desire to retain control over the physical and symbolic landscape of Little Tokyo themselves and reinforce links between the space of this neighborhood and the dispersed and multigenerational ethnic community. These links take the form of stories and rituals linked to space, the invented traditions that, as architectural historian Dell Upton has stated, "reveal the process by which ethnic groups form themselves by *choosing* to commodify their identities and to attach them to equally consciously chosen material signs."[28] The role of the Far East in this imaginative structure of connection is to revive old memories and construct new ones through the reopened restaurant, while reaching out to contemporary residents through the computer center and studio apartments for the homeless.

The desire by many Japanese Americans to retain connection to and control over the form of a cultural landscape that once nurtured their traditions and protected their families from discrimination and that continues to shape their memories and understandings of their ethnic identity makes perfect sense. However, such an approach is not without its flaws and failings and thus is deserving of critical examination. Omissions and erasures have resulted from attempting to

Figure 2.8. Far East Building, East First Street, 1896; later alterations; rehabilitated 2003. Historical photographs are on exhibit in window on right. Photograph by Richard Longstreth, 2004.

define this district by identifying it solely with a single ethnic group. At the same time, opportunities have opened up for building a more dynamic, inclusive community by reaching out to other racial groups that have shared this landscape in the past and the present.

The Little Tokyo Service Center applied for grants from several organizations, including the National Trust for Historic Preservation and the Getty Conservation Institute's Preserve L.A. program, emphasizing a concern with sustaining Japanese American memory, identity, and solidarity. While the Service Center leaders celebrated cross-ethnic interaction within a pan-Asian framework—calling the restaurant "an enduring symbol of Chinese-Japanese friendship and cross-influence" and "a fond example of Chinoiserie for Japanese-American tastes"—they have ignored the impact of other racialized groups on Little Tokyo's cultural landscape.[29] For example, the Service Center–restored Union Church was an African American community center during World War II, a fact not noted in any way at the site. The Far East's exhibit on the history of Little Tokyo includes no discussion of Bronzeville or the stories of interracial conflict and cooperation that followed the war despite the fact that the restaurant, being Chinese owned, was open throughout both the Bronzeville and resettlement periods.[30] The physical and perceived landscapes that the Service Center is (re)constructing, like the museum landscape developed by the city, completely submerge the history of

Bronzeville, presenting a neighborhood to which only Japanese Americans have ever belonged. Yet the organization's affordable housing projects, as well as its art education initiatives and the computer center, are clearly directed at Little Tokyo's *current* residents, the majority of whom are black and Latino. Why then do the Service Center's overtures across class and racial lines not extend to its interpretation of the past?

Several factors may explain the exclusionary practices in presenting Little Tokyo's history. Some Japanese Americans may see the recognition of both the historic and contemporary impact of other groups on Little Tokyo's landscape as a threat to their own symbolic identification with, and thus control over, the district. The *Los Angeles Times*, for instance, recently noted that Japanese American investors have opened a new bank in Little Tokyo to "help revitalize a Japanese American community struggling to maintain its relevancy in an increasingly multiethnic world."[31] The bank has a Japanese-speaking teller but is also looking to add one who speaks Spanish. A *Times* article on a confectionary shop in Little Tokyo likewise noted that the crew making *mochi* is mostly Latino.[32]

Another possibility is that Japanese Americans are uncomfortable with their own past discriminatory practices. As historian David Hellwig has stated, Japanese immigrants often avoided African Americans out of fear of the "stigma of inferiority that whites had placed on" them.[33] In addition, Anglos, who owned much of the land in Little Tokyo (the Japanese being blocked from ownership by the Alien Land Law), preferred to rent to Japanese or Japanese American, rather than African American, tenants *even right after World War II*.[34] Japanese Americans received favorable long-term leases not offered to African Americans on condition of stabilizing the area and making it a headquarters for Japanese business: as America would rebuild Japan, so Little Tokyo could again become a profitable link between the two.

The history of ethnic interactions and the effect of racial and economic forces on postwar spatial practices are central features of the district's cultural landscape and should be an important part of the story that preservation there tells. But the national historic landmark nomination reduces this history to two lines of text: "blacks had moved into Little Tokyo during the war, when it became known as 'Bronzeville,' and the character of the community had changed drastically."[35] Discounting African American experiences in Little Tokyo and Japanese Americans' own discriminatory attitudes allows the preservation narrative to maintain Japanese American primacy in the cultural and imaginative landscape of Little Tokyo and thus the moral and symbolic power to make overtures to other people of color in the district—*on Japanese American terms*. In other words, community initiatives in Little Tokyo come from and are controlled by Japanese American organizations—symbolic power stays with the historic Japanese American community rather than with the current multiracial one. This dynamic tends to play into the hands of the city's representation of Little Tokyo as a landscape of exotic, but safe, ethnic difference.

Historian Thomas Holt has pointed out that in the contemporary, global marketplace, "all commodities are cultural, and they thrive on real and simulated differences—on containable signs of difference, on distinction."[36] One of these containable signs of difference is ethnicity, and it can be a valuable commodity in our economy of symbols. The CRA has supported the preservation and rehabilitation of the Far East and other historic properties remaining in Little Tokyo in general because the "different-ness" of its cultural landscape makes such an investment worthwhile. According to the CRA, the rehabilitation of the Far East helps make Little Tokyo a "vibrant, destination neighborhood" on the basis of its ethnically defined attractions (as well as improving the district's image as a center for museums and high culture by moving several homeless persons from the streets into the building's affordable housing units).[37] However, in order to be, as Holt puts it, "containable," the narrative the district tells must be limited to a single ethnic group, following a predictable storyline of immigrant struggle followed by successful assimilation. Including the complexity of Bronzeville does not increase the district's marketability.

However well the Far East project seems to fit into the CRA's strategy of recreating Little Tokyo as one big indoor-outdoor museum (visitors can get food *and* history in one-stop shopping, just steps from JANM), the building's rehabilitation is supported by Japanese Americans for completely different reasons. The Far East is not intended to market Little Tokyo's past to tourists, rather it is meant to interpret that past for Japanese Americans. The goal is to preserve the memory of Japanese Americans' collective experience and to make new memories that bolster Japanese American identity, solidarity, and connection to Little Tokyo. Because the Far East was next door to the Buddhist temple at First and Central streets, the restaurant hosted banquets after wedding and funeral services for sixty years. The Mar family, the Chinese Americans who ran the café, provided free meals to penniless Japanese Americans returning from the internment camps. It is a site of strong emotional attachment for many Japanese Americans. According to the Service Center, "details of life at the Café are well-known to virtually *every* member of Los Angeles' Japanese-American community whose relatives lived through relocation."[38]

A woman's letter to the *Times* supporting the rehabilitation project recalled Sunday dinners at the restaurant and her grandfather's wake in the banquet room; she could not wait "to return with [her] family to share more Sunday dinners, retell all the old stories."[39] The Far East is one of the spaces of Little Tokyo through which Japanese Americans seek to name and define both what it meant to be Japanese American in the past and what it means today. The rehabilitation of the Far East building in effect creates an alternative to the landscape "of tourist-dependent restaurants and gift shops" by generating new traditions around which Japanese American identities—fractured by class, generation, place of residence, gender, and the like—can coalesce and solidify.[40] Though in some ways intended to reach out to the current residents of Little Tokyo by offering a new affordable housing option, the real engine driving the building's rehabilitation is the desire to return a cherished site of Japanese American memory-making to active operation and to perpetuate Little Tokyo as a Japanese American cultural landscape.

Maurice Halbwachs, the sociologist who first laid out a framework for theorizing the social nature of memory, argued that memories place us in society, and "through them, as by a continual relationship, a sense of our identity is perpetuated."[41] Remembering the past is particularly vital for Japanese American identity because of the traumatic experience of internment. People of Japanese *ancestry* were removed from the West Coast in 1942, regardless of whether they had been born in the United States or were American citizens. Thus, although Japanese Americans have taken steps toward "assimilating" into mainstream American life, their identity remains hyphenated because they know, through bitter experience, that the American half can be tenuous. This is why Japanese Americans had previously tended to support the city's museum strategy in Little Tokyo: where the city saw opportunities for ethnic tourism and cultural prestige, Japanese Americans saw new venues for constructing and reinforcing their identity, maintaining a connection with their symbolic home by remembering and passing on that collective memory and hyphenated identity.

The Far East exemplifies the point at which the unity between city planners and Japanese American community builders breaks down: while Japanese American Angelenos focus on *personal* memories in the lobby exhibit and create new traditions linking past and future through the reopened restaurant, the city has expanded outward from the specificity of JANM and memory-related public art projects into support for the creation of a literal museum district, including making the Los Angeles Museum of Contemporary Art's Geffen Contemporary (Figure 2.9) next door to JANM a permanent feature and backing a proposed, bitterly contested Children's Museum.[42] To the city, Little Tokyo should be a zone of historical and cultural tourism and postindustrial leisure and consumption that attracts both tourists and luxury loft development, but for Japanese Americans, it must be what French historian Pierre Nora has called a "*lieu de memoire,*" a site of memory.

Nora's work on memory and history in France can be adapted to a discussion of the break between the living memory of the Issei and Nisei, discriminated

Figure 2.9.Geffen Contemporary (formerly the Temporary Contemporary), Los Angeles Museum of Contemporary Art, Central Avenue, early-twentieth-century warehouse remodeled 1982–83. Frank Gehry & Associates, architects. Located adjacent to Japanese American National Museum. Photograph by author, 2004.

against on a racial basis and segregated in Little Tokyo, and attempts by their more "assimilated" and dispersed children and grandchildren to re-create (or, as Upton would have it, "commodify") historical memory as collective identity by controlling the district's physical and cultural landscapes. Nora emphasized:

> The defense, by certain minorities, of a privileged memory that has retreated to zealously protected enclaves in this sense intensely illuminates the truth of *lieux de memoire*—that without commemorative vigilance, history would soon sweep them away. We buttress our identities upon such bastions, but if what they defended were not threatened, there would be no need to build them.[43]

Recent articles in the *Times* have made clear that some Japanese Americans feel that their symbolic control over Little Tokyo, and thus their ability to foster ethnic solidarity and shape a collective identity for themselves through remembering and memory-making tied to specific places, is threatened. Besides Japanese Americans' fear of decreasing relevance, they also fear becoming too "American," forgetting the Japanese roots that internment demands they remember. The article on the candy shop, for example, noted that the store was now less profitable than in the past because "as Japanese Americans become more assimilated, they are buying less *mochi.*"[44] Another article on attempts to build a

Little Tokyo gym for Japanese American adolescent basketball leagues quoted Little Tokyo Service Center executive director Bill Watanabe: "We need a place for all generations of people. . . . If we miss that, and we miss a whole generation of people who don't connect to Little Tokyo, then we will lose them forever, and Little Tokyo will just become a façade or a shell of what it used to be."[45] Faux-Japanese tourist shops provide no usable framework for continuing the formation of a Japanese American collective memory, so the Far East must be returned to operation as a site of *living* memory that represents and restores Japanese American collective identity and demonstrates their symbolic connection to a particular place and history. If that process involves removing stories—like that of Bronzeville—from the cultural landscape, distorting our understanding of the past and erasing some of its lessons, it is a price even the well-intentioned Service Center leaders seem willing to pay.

Conclusion

How, then, as people passionately interested in preserving the past, in retaining and interpreting cultural landscapes in all their difficult complexity, do we attempt to understand and resolve the multiple conflicting claims to physical and symbolic ownership that mark this place? How can we move beyond linking identity to control over a particular space and instead connect it to shared experiences, positive *and* negative, both within and across space? An answer to these questions may be found in a strategy just making itself visible in Little Tokyo, a strategy that moves beyond remaking the cultural landscape in a singularly Japanese American image and instead links Japanese American remembering and memory-making to those processes among other people of color on terms of cooperation and equality. This nascent strategy is best exemplified by two recent exhibits at JANM: Boyle Heights—The Power of Place, which highlighted a landscape of interethnic and interracial friendship, collaboration, and respect in an early Los Angeles suburb; and Finding Family Stories, a collection of works by Los Angeles–based visual artists of various ethnic, racial, and cultural backgrounds that rotated between JANM, Self-Help Graphics (a Latino organization), the Chinese American Museum at El Pueblo Art Gallery, and the California African American Museum. Accompanying these exhibits were workshops drawing different communities together to share their stories and represent their histories in artistic media. These exhibits seem to reinforce Upton's call to "step away from the commodified notion of culture for a minute and understand ethnicity as a synthesis of imposed and adopted characteristics that is forged through contact and conflict."[46] They are a recognition that the category of "Japanese American" was not formed in isolation from those of, for example, "African American" or "Chinese American," and that a willingness to share both spaces and memories across the dividing lines of race, class, and ethnicity points to a new and more complicated story for the cultural landscape of Little Tokyo to tell.[47]

While this emerging strategy is in danger, like any other, of being appropriated by the city marketers for economic gain or cultural distinction—perhaps as part of Los Angeles's image as multicultural mecca, or to attract urban pioneers to all those new loft developments—it is still a promising path for Japanese Americans attempting to preserve Little Tokyo as both their symbolic "home" and as a distinctive and contested cultural landscape in the postmodern, postindustrial metropolis. By symbolically uniting Little Tokyo with other neighborhoods and communities in the metropolitan area, including East Los Angeles, Chinatown, South-Central, Monterey Park, Little India in Cerritos, and Westminster's Little Saigon, Japanese Americans place their own experiences within the context of those of other people of color and other immigrants, both past and present. They help demonstrate that all neighborhoods are complicated cultural and ethnic landscapes and thus increase opportunities for cooperation among constituencies that question the destruction of place by municipal authority, by corporate redevelopment, or by the more deadening effects of ethnic tourism. This approach succeeds at expanding enthusiasm for preservation and "telling family stories"—stories that need to be heard and incorporated as part of the meaningful experience of cultural landscapes.

Notes

1. Ichiro Mike Murase, *Little Tokyo: One Hundred Years in Pictures* (Los Angeles: Visual Communications, 1983), 6.

2. Ibid., 8.

3. John Modell, *The Economics and Politics of Racial Accommodation: The Japanese of Los Angeles*, 1900–1942 (Urbana: University of Illinois Press, 1977).

4. Gail Dubrow and Donna Graves, *Sento at Sixth and Main: Preserving Landmarks of Japanese American Heritage* (Seattle: Seattle Arts Commission, 2002), 162.

5. Dolores Hayden, *The Power of Place: Urban Landscapes as Public History* (Cambridge, Mass.: MIT Press, 1994), 218–25.

6. Kariann Akemi Yokota, "From Little Tokyo to Bronzeville and Back: Ethnic Communities in Transition" (master's thesis, University of California, Los Angeles, 1996), 48.

7. "Japs Plan Return to 'Little Tokyo,'" *Los Angeles Times*, 31 December 1944, 1.

8. Little Tokyo National Historic Landmark District nomination (hereafter NHL nomination), 1993, 19.

9. Hayden, *Power of Place*, 216.

10. Murase, *Little Tokyo*, 19; Jim H. Matsuoka, "Little Tokyo: Searching the Past and Analyzing the Future," in *Roots: An Asian American Reader*, ed. Amy Tachiki et al. (Los Angeles: Asian American Studies Center, University of California, Los Angeles, 1971), 329.

11. Lon Kurashige, *Japanese American Celebration and Conflict: A History of Ethnic Identity in Los Angeles, 1934–1990* (Berkeley: University of California Press, 2002), 187–88.

12. Murase, *Little Tokyo,* 20.

13. Ibid.

14. Jan Lin, "The Reclaiming of Asian Places in Downtown Los Angeles," *HCM, A Journal of Asian American Cultural Criticism* 5 (spring 1998): 12.

15. Murase, *Little Tokyo,* 23; Ray Hebert, "Little Tokyo Renewal Under Way as Work Begins on $24 Million Hotel," *Los Angeles Times,* 30 September 1974, II-1.

16. Murase, *Little Tokyo,* 23; Lin, "Reclaiming of Asian Places," 12.

17. Kurashige, *Japanese American Celebration and Conflict,* 193.

18. Ibid., 191, 196.

19. Murase, *Little Tokyo,* 23.

20. NHL nomination, 4.

21. Murase, *Little Tokyo,* 24; Lynn Simross, "Little Tokyo Image Slowly Changing," *Los Angeles Times,* 6 March 1977, VII-1.

22. Little Tokyo Service Center, American Architectural Foundation Accent on Architecture grant application (hereafter AA application), 2 October 2001, 5.

23. Kurashige, *Japanese American Celebration and Conflict,* 208.

24. Ibid., 209.

25. Ronald D. White, "Little Tokyo Project Raises Big Expectations," *Los Angeles Times,* 22 September 2003, C1. One of the selling points for these lofts is their proximity to Little Tokyo's "cultural attractions." Given the explosion in market-rate housing in downtown Los Angeles over the past five years, the city is now selling the district's historical and cultural amenities to developers and renters as much as to tourists.

26. For 2000 census figures on the tract encompassing Little Tokyo (Tract 2062), see http://www.census.gov/main/www/cen2000.html.

27. This is an adaptation of Diane Barthel's description of preservation professionals as "symbolic bankers." See Diane Barthel, *Historic Preservation: Collective Memory and Cultural Identity* (New Brunswick, N.J.: Rutgers University Press, 1996), chapter 2.

28. Dell Upton, "Ethnicity, Authenticity, and Invented Traditions," *Historic Archeology* 30 (June 1996): 5.

29. Little Tokyo Service Center, National Trust for Historic Preservation grant application (hereafter NTHP application), 25 February 2002, 2; AA application, 4.

30. Kelli Ann Nakayama, the Museum Studies intern who created the exhibit, is aware of the Bronzeville era but chose to focus almost exclusively on the 1930s "golden age" and Nisei organizations such as the Oliver Club as the subjects of the photographs and artifacts included in the exhibit. A planned historical marker at the southeast corner of First and San Pedro streets, denoting the former location of the Cobra Club and the famous jazz musicians who played there, is the only recognition of the Bronzeville period of which I am aware.

31. Evelyn Iritani, "Japanese American Group Opens Bank in Little Tokyo," *Los Angeles Times,* 11 November 2002, D2.

32. Julie Tamaki, "New Year's Delicacy Is Bittersweet for Family," *Los Angeles Times,* 30 December 2002, B1.

33. David J. Hellwig, "Afro-American Reactions to the Japanese and the Anti-Japanese Movement, 1906–1924," *Phylon* 38 (March 1977): 103; quoted in Yokota, "From Little Tokyo,"

66. Of course, several scholars have pointed out the rich tradition of African American–Japanese American coalition and cooperation. See, for example, Vijay Prashad, *Everybody Was Kung Fu Fighting: Afro-Asian Connections and the Myth of Cultural Purity* (Boston: Beacon Press, 2001); Laura Pulido, "Race, Class, and Political Activism: Black, Chicano and Japanese American Leftists in Southern California, 1968–1972," *Antipode* 34: 4 (2002): 762–88; and Scott Tadao Kurashige, "Transforming Los Angeles: Black and Japanese American Struggles for Racial Equality in the Twentieth Century" (Ph.D. diss., University of California, Los Angeles, 2000).

34. Yokota, "From Little Tokyo," 76–77.

35. NHL nomination, 19.

36. Thomas C. Holt, *The Problems of Race in the Twenty-First Century* (Cambridge, Mass.: Harvard University Press, 2000), 107.

37. "Little Tokyo Five Year Implementation Plan (FY 2000–04)," Community Redevelopment Agency of Los Angeles, 5 October 2000, 2. An excellent examination of ethnic commodification, racial exclusion, and historic preservation in Tampa can be found in Susan D. Greenbaum, "Marketing Ybor City: Race, Ethnicity, and Historic Preservation in the Sunbelt," *City and Society* 4 (1990): 58–76.

38. NTHP application, 2.

39. Kaz Baba, "Far East Café's Timeless Memories," *Los Angeles Times*, 23 March 2002, B22.

40. David W. Chen, "Charting Revival through Basketball," *Los Angeles Times*, 5 November 2001, A15.

41. Maurice Halbwachs, *On Collective Memory*, ed. and trans. Lewis A. Coser (Chicago: University of Chicago Press, 1992), 47.

42. K. Connie Kang, "Backers of Little Tokyo Gym Decry Museum Plan," *Los Angeles Times*, 18 July 2000, B1.

43. Pierre Nora, "Between Memory and History: *Les Lieux de Memoire*," *Representations* 26 (spring 1989): 12; trans. Marc Roudebush.

44. Tamaki, "New Year's Delicacy."

45. Chen, "Charting Revival."

46. Upton, "Ethnicity, Authenticity," 4.

47. Another excellent example of this realization being put into action to envision a better Los Angeles is Nina Revoyr's novel *Southland* (New York: Akashic Books, 2003), in which African American and Japanese American Angelenos rediscover their kinship by examining their intertwined heritage in the multiracial Crenshaw district.

3. Cross-Bronx

The Urban Expressway as Cultural Landscape

MICHAEL CARATZAS

URBAN expressways have earned a reputation for destroying historic buildings and damaging neighborhoods among their other professed ills.[1] But because many of these highways are now at least half a century old, they beg reexamination in a more historical framework as features of the urban landscape.[2] New York's Cross-Bronx Expressway is a revealing example in several respects. It is historically significant, making it an important part of the city's cultural landscape. But it is also a cultural landscape in its own right, showcasing the values of an era. In addition, it is significant experientially, serving as an urban gateway into Manhattan. Finally, it acts as a viewing platform from which travelers enjoy wide-ranging vistas of the Bronx, getting an introduction to the places that surround them.

New York City has many public works, such as the subway system and Central Park, that are recognized as pioneering achievements nationally, symbolizing the city's greatness. The Cross-Bronx Expressway, which is a six-mile, six-lane trench carved through about a dozen Bronx neighborhoods between 1948 and 1963, symbolizes something very different. Although it is a considerable engineering achievement, the Cross-Bronx is now seen as an example of almost everything that was bad about urban planning in the 1950s and 1960s. Ask any New Yorker with an interest in the city's history and you will probably hear that the Cross-Bronx represents the arrogance and elitism of highway planners and the callousness with which expressways were rammed through neighborhoods after World War II, with little concern for their buildings or for the people who lived in them. As the recent television documentary *New York* put it, none of the other projects built by the powerful and influential "master builder" of public works, Robert Moses, "would have more devastating consequences for the city and its people, or instill more rage against its executor, than the Cross-Bronx Expressway... [which] would carve a path of destruction New Yorkers would never forget."[3]

While that assertion may be true, in assessing the significance of early expressways, we must look beyond their role in destroying buildings and carving up neighborhoods without glossing over that major component of their history. Postwar expressways, for better or worse, have had a profound effect on American society and on our cities, suburbs, culture, and landscape; their construction has been called the nation's "most important public works project since the Erie Canal."[4] To paraphrase a criterion of the National Register of Historic Places, expressways have made a significant contribution to the broad patterns of our history, and the Cross-Bronx, which is a particularly early and complete expressway, is an excellent, historic example of its kind.

Historical Significance

The Cross-Bronx Expressway is locally significant for being among the first expressways planned and designed for New York City.[5] Initially proposed in the groundbreaking *Regional Plan of New York and Its Environs* (1929) as part of a "Metropolitan Loop" that would circumnavigate the city at a distance of about twelve miles from City Hall, its route was laid out in 1944, more than a decade before work would begin on the Interstate Highway System (Figure 3.1).[6] The Cross-Bronx, with other proposed expressways, was unveiled to the public in a 1945 magazine article written by Moses, who declared, "The great need . . . which we are at last ready to meet . . . is for mixed traffic expressways right through town. These are prodigious undertakings, the full extent and nature of which the average city dweller does not yet grasp."[7] Many of the Cross-Bronx's overpasses were designed within months of World War II's end. Because it was such an early expressway not only for New York but for the entire country, and because of New York's widespread reputation at that time as a leader in highway construction, the Cross-Bronx arguably has national as well as local significance.

At the start of World War II, New York was unique among American cities in having already constructed an extensive limited-access highway system. That network was composed primarily of several bridges and parkways built by Moses in the 1930s, and it was the envy of the nation, admired for both its utility and aesthetics. No other city in the country had anything like it: of the five American cities in 1946 with populations of more than one million, New York was the only one with a limited-access highway system that was approaching an integrated network.[8] A glowing account of Moses's parkways appeared in a "special American issue" of a venerable British art magazine, *The Studio,* in 1944. Likewise an article in a 1938 issue of *Fortune* declared that Moses's parkways and bridges exhibited "the high standard of distinction and beauty on top of utility that set apart almost every project [he] has laid his magic fingers on. . . . Thanks to him, [New York's] parks and parkways now rank with the tall buildings as things that every outlander simply must see. . . ."[9]

Significantly, during the 1930s and 1940s, Moses and his engineers exported their knowledge in building highways to other American cities, including Pitts-

THE CITY OF NEW YORK
PRESIDENT OF THE BOROUGH OF THE BRONX

ROUTE STUDY FOR DEVELOPMENT PLAN

CROSS-BRONX THRUWAY

Figure 3.1. Map of projected route of Cross-Bronx Expressway (1944), juxtaposing the nearly straight route with the existing street grids. Cover of *Route Study for Development Plan: Cross-Bronx Thruway* (Bronx, N.Y.: Borough President's Office, 1944).

burgh, Baltimore, and New Orleans. Los Angeles traffic engineers traveled to New York to study its parkways as they planned their own celebrated highway network.[10] Moses would ultimately have a strong influence on the Interstate Highway System: Bertram D. Tallamy, its first administrator, told Moses's biographer, Robert Caro, that "the principles on which the System was built were principles that . . . Moses taught him in a series of private lectures in 1926."[11] Moses claimed to have influenced the design of Germany's autobahns, writing in 1940 that he had once hosted German counterparts "who came to this country while studying preliminary plans for their autobahn system and we showed them what had been done here. . . . The engineering design principles used in the autobahn system were in a large measure copied from the work done in the New York area."[12] As one of the earliest urban expressways to be planned in the United States and as one of the initial expressway projects of Moses—who was internationally recognized by the late 1940s for building highways to their highest standards—the

Cross-Bronx Expressway possesses historical significance. Adding to its importance, nearly all of its original features remain today, a rare feat for a fifty-year-old urban expressway.

The Cross-Bronx as a Cultural Landscape

Beyond its precedent-setting role, the Cross-Bronx is historically significant as a cultural landscape in itself, shaped by humans and communicating what a broad segment of society considered important, and unimportant, at the time of its planning and construction. The people who directly and indirectly supported its construction—everyone from highway builders and politicians to average car-owning Americans who simply wanted bigger, faster, and straighter roads—so valued this expressway that they saw it through to completion despite its tremendous cost.

Many Americans badly wanted urban expressways in the mid-twentieth century. In 1949, cheerleading editors of the *New York Times* wrote that

> the prospect opened up by the thought of the Cross-Bronx Expressway and its tributaries is a pleasant one. For one thing, the city does not have adequate east-west express routes. It is good to know that this situation will soon be improved. . . . The possibilities are many. They will be eagerly anticipated.[13]

Even Boston's infamous Central Artery—now considered such a hopeless mistake and blight on its city that, at fifty years of age, it has been replaced by an astronomically expensive tunnel—was so popular when it was built that politicians were eager to take credit for its construction. At the Central Artery's opening, Democrats chafed at Republican efforts to claim responsibility for it, parking a truck near the dedication ceremony that sported a large billboard reading, "Men of character and ability: Central Artery . . . planned and built by Democrats; music and speeches by Republicans."[14] If it is true that a society expresses its hopes, desires, and convictions through the things on which it spends money, then at least some of the values of postwar American society are manifested in the fabric of the Cross-Bronx Expressway—in its asphalt, concrete, stone, and steel.

The Cross-Bronx Expressway is essentially a trench, blasted at its deepest through more than forty feet of rock. The buildings on either side of the expressway meet it at odd angles, giving the Cross-Bronx the appearance of a scar, of a drastic landscape intervention that disrupted the evolutionary qualities typical of an old neighborhood's buildings and blocks (Figure 3.2). These characteristics begin to explain what a challenge constructing the highway was: little more than six miles long, the Cross-Bronx took fifteen years to complete, longer than it took to construct the entire Erie Canal in the early nineteenth century. The express-

Figure 3.2. Cross-Bronx Expressway, aerial view ca. late 1950s, looking east from the Bronx River Parkway interchange, showing the disjuncture between the highway and the urban fabric through which it passes. Courtesy of MTA Bridges and Tunnels Special Archive.

way's construction was made difficult by rugged topography and by the need to shoehorn the route into an area that had been densely developed over the preceding half century, with apartment houses and all kinds of infrastructure, including elevated and subway lines, water mains, gas lines, and sewers. Even today, the driver using the Cross-Bronx gets a sense of this channeling, if only implicitly, through the road's roller-coaster grade. Repeatedly dipping, particularly under cross streets, then rising, the highway communicates both the need to accommodate itself to the urban fabric, however disruptive the impact may seem, and also the difficulties inherent in that process.[15]

The expressway's tall rock walls, left bare and rough faced in many places, are among its most impressive features. These natural walls inspired Moses to hail the highway's "monolithic landscaping, [which] will show no scars and will seem always to have been there," but they also emphasize the violence that was done to the Bronx landscape in building the expressway.[16] Raw, exposed rock is strikingly displayed at the Grand Concourse tunnel, which was especially difficult to

Figure 3.3. Cross-Bronx Expressway, looking west at tunnel beneath the Grand Concourse and the Concourse subway line, an especially difficult passage to construct. Photograph by author, 2001.

create, and where the highway is threaded *below* a Depression-era subway line, which itself is sixty feet beneath the street (Figure 3.3).

Largely because the Cross-Bronx was so hard and time-consuming to construct, its cost, especially relative to its length, was enormous: roughly $130 million, or the equivalent of five Shea Stadiums.[17] There was, of course, a human cost as well: approximately five thousand people were displaced by the expressway in East Tremont alone, one of about a dozen neighborhoods through which it passes.[18] In East Tremont, residents famously fought against Moses. Their efforts, while ultimately unsuccessful, spurred unusually contentious city council hearings on the Cross-Bronx's route and represent what was probably the first organized, grassroots effort against highway construction in New York City and possibly the United States.[19] Significantly, the neighborhood-based nature of the East Tremont protests and the protestors' techniques anticipated much more fruitful anti-highway demonstrations in San Francisco, in Boston, and elsewhere in New York, where protestors succeeded in derailing a Lower Manhattan Expressway that would have displaced thousands of residents and many businesses and would have destroyed much of the city's incomparable collection of cast-iron architecture.[20] No marker has been erected to commemorate the Bronx protestors' important historical role. All that exists to remind us that they and others once lived in the expressway's path is the gaping void that the highway creates and the way in which it cuts cleanly through the old urban grid, implicitly devaluing, like many urban planning projects of the time, what had come before it.

The Cross-Bronx is primarily a straight road, interrupted by occasional curves. This configuration is noteworthy because the expressway's predecessors—the revolutionary New York parkways—typically featured gently curving alignments inspired by the pathways of picturesque English gardens. Swiss architectural historian Sigfried Giedion celebrated this quality of the parkways, writing that their curves "humanize[d] the highway by carefully following and utilizing the terrain, rising and falling with the contours of the earth, merging completely into the landscape."[21] By the time the Cross-Bronx was laid out in 1944, however, the ideas of the French architect Le Corbusier and American industrial designer Norman Bel Geddes held sway. Bel Geddes—who designed the influential General Motors Futurama at the 1939 World's Fair, which envisioned a future of multilane highways crisscrossing the country—argued that safety, comfort, speed, and economy were the key principles of future highway design, that "a properly designed highway follows the most direct route that is available from one point to another; it obeys the old geometric axiom that a straightest line is the shortest distance between two points." In his 1940 book, *Magic Motorways,* Bel Geddes humorously illustrated his argument by juxtaposing a photo of tightrope walkers with one of a car swerving along a curvy mountain road.[22] Bel Geddes's work followed by a decade Le Corbusier's pronouncement that "a city made for speed is made for success," and that the modern city "lives by the straight line. . . . The circulation of traffic demands the straight line; it is the proper thing for the heart of the city. The curve is ruinous, difficult, and dangerous; it is a paralyzing thing."[23] Although hardly known as a forum for avant-garde architects, the planning magazine *American City* publicized Le Corbusier's arguments in 1930, explaining that to "M. Le Corbusier . . . whose theory of modern planning as embodied in 'The City of Tomorrow,' presupposes not a poet, but a staff of mathematicians on the job, 'the straight road gives a good sense of direction, while the winding road destroys all sense of direction.' " In designing expressways, the straight line would become an inspiration in and of itself.[24]

Straight horizontal alignment is important in demonstrating that a shift had taken place, that after the war, in planning limited-access highways, speed, directness, and efficiency had trumped the sense of leisure and recreation that the parkways had represented. It has also provided evidence of Moses's callousness and a lack of respect for the Bronx. Political scientist Marshall Berman remarked that the Cross-Bronx's builders never asked, "Can we work this highway into existing life? They had the power to build in straight lines, and they just did."[25] The "humanizing" quality and respect for the surrounding landscape that were typical of the parkways are not typical of the Cross-Bronx. Its engineers saw the highway primarily as a means to get through the borough as quickly as possible, and the highway's design shows it.

Thus, the Cross-Bronx has come to symbolize many attitudes that today seem astonishingly deficient, including callousness toward neighborhood buildings and their residents, an antagonistic approach to the environment, and a cold valuing of efficiency and speed over other human concerns. These may be seen in the expressway's straightness and in its bare, blasted rock walls, and by its appearance as a scar on the landscape. But there are other ways of interpreting the expressway's features as well. Bare rock that symbolizes damage to the environment also recalls the substantial engineering challenges overcome in building the highway and the persistence and know-how of engineers and construction workers alike. In fact, the expressway's blasted-out, below-grade alignment was likely seen by its builders as a *good* thing, as a feature that would cause the fewest long-term problems for the highway's neighbors. At that time, engineers felt that although depressed expressways—as opposed to surface or elevated ones—were the most expensive and difficult to build, they gave the most benefits. The landmark 1944 U.S. government publication *Interregional Highways* concluded that depressed highways "may be considered by many, more pleasing to the eye and more consonant with a gracious improvement of the urban environment than any other solution of the express-highway problem."[26] Eight years later, Glenn C. Richards of the Detroit public works bureau explained that "depressing opens up an expressway to light and air, makes it attractive, enhances property values. That seems well settled, by experience in other cities. . . . Exhaust fumes, being heavier than air, tend to stay below the surface. There the swift movement of cars sets up air currents which prevent the fumes from accumulation."[27] Where today we see in the Cross-Bronx Expressway's trench an assault on the urban and natural environments with dynamite and backhoes, highway engineers half a century ago saw long-term public benefit and a progressive solution to a difficult problem.

The Cross-Bronx has additional significant characteristics, among which are features that carry over from the earlier parkways. Granite-veneered, concrete, rigid-frame bridges were a parkway staple, as were curbing and granite-veneered retaining walls. The Cross-Bronx's post-and-rail steel railings recall the parkways' timber fencing (Figure 3.4). In addition, there is at Crotona Avenue a monumental, granite-veneered concrete arch that recalls similarly impressive arches on

Figure 3.4. Cross-Bronx Expressway, looking west from Boston Road, showing granite-veneered concrete bridges carrying Southern Boulevard and Marmion Avenue, Belgian block safety walks and curbing, exposed rock walls, and railings—all features rooted in earlier parkway construction. Courtesy of MTA Bridges and Tunnels Special Archive.

New York's Hutchinson River and Henry Hudson parkways (Figure 3.5). Moses's description of the Cross-Bronx as "metropolitan architecture in its finest sense" may be stretching things, but with its miles of exposed rock walls, brick and stone veneer, and Belgian block, the expressway does recall an era in which it was considered necessary to give civic works a sense of permanence and monumentality, to decorate a type of infrastructure that we have come to associate with spare functionalism (Figure 3.6).[28]

In the parkway tradition of integrating highway construction with recreational amenities, the Cross-Bronx's builders included numerous playgrounds near the expressway.[29] The most unusual of these is one over the highway at East 176th Street, which was designed in 1946 and probably represents the first planned effort, locally or nationally, to cover an expressway with recreational space.[30] It is significant in representing a very early effort to accommodate an expressway to its urban environment and seems to indicate that in the 1940s highway builders understood that the impact of their works on adjacent communities was large and that it would somehow have to be mitigated.

Figure 3.5. Stone-faced, concrete arch bridge carrying Crotona Avenue on Cross-Bronx Expressway. Photograph by author, 2002.

The Cross-Bronx as an Urban Gateway

While I was researching the Cross-Bronx, one of my professors surprised me by relating his fondness for the expressway. Recalling his arrival in New York many years before, he said that his first trip to Manhattan on the Cross-Bronx was unforgettable: noisy, congested, overwhelming, and slightly chaotic, it was a fitting entrance to a city that is world famous for those traits. Indeed, it is not a stretch to liken driving the Cross-Bronx to scrambling and fighting one's way across Grand Central Terminal at rush hour or through Macy's Herald Square store on the day after Thanksgiving. All of these experiences give a strong flavor of life in the nation's most crowded city.

The Cross-Bronx's importance goes beyond its design and history. It is also a cultural experience, providing a unique gateway to the iconic Manhattan skyline. Nearly every major city in the United States has a skyline view that appears from the highway, providing a welcome beacon, showcasing the city's power, and beckoning the motorist to stop and explore. Each skyline is monumental but unique, much like the train stations that were the urban portals of the past. In the 1950s and 1960s, as expressways began to replace train stations as America's

Figure 3.6. Cross-Bronx Expressway at Jessup Avenue, showing forty-foot brick veneered and bare rock walls, an example of Robert Moses's "monolithic landscaping." Photograph by author, 2001.

urban front doors, the experience of approaching the city from the expressway began to be depicted in post cards, joining the city halls, stadiums, parks, and other urban landmarks that were considered the city's most important places.[31]

New York, of course, has some of the world's most famous skyline views. The Henry Hudson Parkway in Manhattan, the Bruckner and Major Deegan expressways and Bronx River Parkway Extension in the Bronx, the Long Island Expressway in Queens, Brooklyn's Belt Parkway, the Brooklyn-Queens Expressway, as well as the Verrazano-Narrows, Triborough, Bronx-Whitestone, and Throgs Neck bridges provide numerous views of Manhattan's skyscrapers that convey a sense of the city's rapid approach. Berman recognized this attribute, writing that Moses's highway and bridge projects "helped . . . give [the] region a unity and coherence it never had. They created a series of spectacular new visual approaches to the city, displaying the grandeur of Manhattan from many new angles . . . and nourishing a whole new generation of urban fantasies."[32]

But New York's highways do more than simply provide romantic views of the Manhattan skyline. For example, a trip along the Brooklyn-Queens Expressway, which is elevated for most of its length, provides a primer on Brooklyn's built environment, a thumbnail sketch of the borough's building stock, topography,

Figure 3.7. Cross-Bronx Expressway, looking east at Webster Avenue viaduct, showing an assortment of typical Bronx buildings, including schools, commercial buildings, prewar tenements, and postwar housing projects. Photograph by author, 2004.

industrial past and present, major infrastructure, and relationship to the harbor and to Lower Manhattan, the core of the metropolitan region. Viewing Brooklyn from the approach of the Verrazano Bridge, one begins to appreciate its vastness. On the Brooklyn-Queens Expressway, the traveler sees block upon solid block of row houses, tenements, and housing projects, the backbone of Brooklyn's residential stock; the Statue of Liberty, visible beyond the old factories and warehouses along Brooklyn's industrial waterfront; billboards advertising everything from local carpet stores to Japanese restaurants; large, dormant neon signs hinting at Brooklyn's faded manufacturing greatness; elevated subway lines, passing high in the sky, in the distance; close-up views of the great Brooklyn and Manhattan bridges; and the Manhattan skyline, rising at different times from a foreground of ordinary Brooklyn backyards, or waterfront docks, or church steeples, or drab industrial lofts. On this trip, the traveler gains an introduction to the environment in which more than two million Brooklynites live.[33]

Upon entering Queens on the Brooklyn-Queens Expressway, motorists again see the towers of Midtown Manhattan, but here these features appear from the highway to grow from the enormous, dark cemeteries in the foreground. In 1965, famed photographer Evelyn Hofer captured this view, and the English writer V. S. Pritchett described it in telling about New York's "road from the airport":

What one wants is the city. And here, as one comes in from the airport, is another startling view, one that is palatial, ethereal, and also macabre. For coming across the hills of Queens

> one enters the huge estates of the city's cemeteries. Their stones are black. A few miles away, beyond the hills falling to the East River, is the desired apparition of Manhattan . . . a string of faraway diamonds . . . but before one gets there, there is this glum, black parody of life. . . . [C]onscious or unconscious as the makers of this place may have been, and of what they were contributing to arrival, they did something immensely dramatic, and in some moods I find this the most impressive approach to the city.[34]

Pritchett's words get at one of the essential elements of the urban landscape: the strange visual juxtapositions that often occur in crowded, dense urban environments such as New York's. They also remind us that in urban cultural landscapes the most impressive, memorable, and important views are often not planned; instead, they are the happenstance products of the growth and change of diverse, dynamic cities over time.

Driving the Cross-Bronx, like the Brooklyn-Queens Expressway, is a cultural experience. Driving in from the north, the Cross-Bronx provides an evolving urban gateway journey from the suburban, low-scale East Bronx, through an increasingly congested and built-up environment, to the towers of Manhattan. In two locations, the Cross-Bronx rises out of its trench, offering panoramic views that give an overview of the Bronx's built fabric. Here, the traveler sees the borough's own cultural landscape, from its Art Deco apartment houses, prewar walk-ups, wood-frame houses, and postwar housing projects, to its houses of worship, warehouses, elevated subway lines, and old brick school buildings (Figure 3.7). In

Figure 3.8. Alexander Hamilton Bridge, Cross-Bronx Expressway, view from Washington Bridge looking south to Manhattan skyline. Photograph by author, 2001.

the early 1980s, city government recognized how the view from the Cross-Bronx practically dictated public perceptions of the borough, which were awful. After many apartment houses near the expressway had become conspicuously abandoned, the city slapped cheery decals over the windows to make things in the Bronx seem better than they were.[35]

At the Harlem River crossing, the Manhattan skyline glitters in the distance, like the city of Oz (Figure 3.8). Being on the Cross-Bronx at this point recalls another of Berman's observations:

> The big thing about any New York neighborhood is its relationship to the center. The city center in Manhattan, with its spectacular cluster of big buildings and bright lights, has a magical aura. It is the focal point of every New Yorker's primal dream. This dream unfolds itself like a giant panorama. The picture's foreground is the dreamer's neighborhood.... Over the roofs, over the water, at the picture's center, our eyes meet the prize: Manhattan's skyscrapers and skyline, bathed in sunshine or radiating electricity and neon light.... As it reaches for the sky, this complex of buildings beckons to us a life of passionate striving, feverish intensity, and expressive fullness, and it seems to deny that there are any limits on what human beings can do.[36]

The Cross-Bronx, like many of New York's other highways, generates this panorama. Travel Moses's parkways and expressways, and it is impossible to deny that they have created some of the most remarkable urban vistas in New York and the nation. As such, they are more than highways or historical artifacts—they are important components of the contemporary urban experience and thus are culturally valuable.

Conclusion

The Cross-Bronx Expressway is a complex resource. Historically significant, it is an important component of New York's cultural landscape. But it is also a multifaceted cultural landscape in its own right. Depending on your perspective, the Cross-Bronx may be the "heartbreak highway" that evicted you from your home or a necessary public benefit, an environmental despoiler or an awesome public work, a symbol of arrogance or a symbol of protest, an engineering triumph or a cannonball shot straight through the heart of the Bronx. It may be where you go to the playground or an unforgettable urban gateway. It may be a symbol of the "layers of complex engineering that hold the city together," as one critic has written about a painting by Rackstraw Downes, which shows the Cross-Bronx and its monumental, complex interchange near the Harlem River.[37] The Cross-Bronx is all of these things.

But whatever the Cross-Bronx represents to a given individual or group, the questions that it raises cannot be tucked away safely in the past. How much of the environment do we despoil to feed our appetite for rapid movement and cheap goods? Who should bear the greatest burden for public works that benefit society as a whole? What are the long-term implications of cheap and easy automobile use? The importance we place on efficiency should come at what expense relative to other values? These are issues with which society continues to grapple. Maybe these issues will make the Cross-Bronx's preservation more difficult. After all can we accept something as historic if the issues it raises are so much a part of the present? Perhaps we will never be able to accept the expressway as historic until the idea of building and enlarging expressways becomes clearly part of the past in the public's mind.

Notes

1. The views expressed herein do not necessarily reflect those of the New York City Landmarks Preservation Commission, where I am employed. This essay is adapted from my "Cross-Bronx, Trans-Manhattan: Preserving a Significant Urban Expressway and Its

Megastructure" (master's thesis, Columbia University, 2002). I wish to thank my advisers at Columbia, Carol Clark and Elliott Sclar, as well as Marie Helms Gardiner, who was of invaluable help in researching the thesis and editing this essay.

2. Historical studies focusing on the physical characteristics of limited access highways are rare. The most attention of this kind has been given to parkways; see, for example, Harry Jolley, *Painting with a Comet's Tail: The Touch of the Landscape Architect on the Blue Ridge Parkway* (Boone, N.C.: Appalachian Consortium, 1987); Bruce Radde, *The Merritt Parkway* (New Haven, Conn.: Yale University Press, 1993); Timothy Davis, "Rock Creek and Potomac Parkway, Washington, D.C.: The Evolution of a Contested Urban Landscape," *Studies in the History of Gardens and Designed Landscapes* 19 (summer 1999): 123–237; Timothy Davis, "'A Pleasant Illusion of Unspoiled Countryside': The American Parkway and the Problematics of an Institutionalized Vernacular," in *Constructing Image, Identity, and Place: Perspectives in Vernacular Architecture, IX*, ed. Allison K. Hoagland and Kenneth A. Breisch (Knoxville: University of Tennessee Press, 2003), 228–46; Hoagland, Breisch, et al., eds., *America's National Park Roads and Parkways: Drawings from the Historic American Engineering Record* (Baltimore: Johns Hopkins University Press, 2004); and Hoagland and Breisch, "The American Motor Parkway," *Studies in the History of Gardens and Designed Landscapes* 25 (October-December 2005): 219–49. The pioneering study of expressways is David Brodsly, *L.A. Freeway: An Appreciative Essay* (Berkeley: University of California Press, 1981). Pictorial histories may also be useful; see, for example, Yanni Tsipis and David Kruh, *Building Route 128* (Charleston, S.C.: Arcadia, 2003). A small sampling of the numerous important period documents includes Jean Labatut and Wheaton J. Lane, eds., *Highways in Our National Life* (Princeton, N.J.: Princeton University Press, 1950); Christopher Tunnard and Boris Pushkarev, *Man-Made America: Chaos or Control* (New Haven, Conn.: Yale University Press, 1963); and Michael Rapuano et al., *The Freeway in the City: Principles of Planning and Design* (Washington, D.C.: U.S. Government Printing Office, 1968).

3. "Episode Seven: The City and the World," *New York: A Documentary Film* (Steeplechase Productions, 2001) plays up the Cross-Bronx's negative aspects. The most famous critique of the highway is by Robert Caro in *The Power Broker* (New York: Vintage Books, 1974). The popular urban planning critic James Howard Kunstler exaggerated the highway's impact in writing that the Cross-Bronx "all but destroyed the life of its borough" in *The Geography of Nowhere* (New York: Simon and Schuster, 1993), 100. For a more positive assessment, see "Catalog of Built Work and Projects in New York City, 1934–1968," in *Robert Moses and the Modern City: The Transformation of New York*, ed. Hilary Ballon and Kenneth T. Jackson (New York: W. W. Norton, 2007), 217–20.

4. "Episode Seven: The City and the World."

5. Expressways, as opposed to other types of roads, are limited-access highways that carry both trucks and cars.

6. Committee on the Regional Plan of New York and Its Environs, *Regional Plan of New York and Its Environs, Volume I: The Graphic Regional Plan* (Philadelphia: Fell Co., 1929), 210–305; "Route Study for Development Plan: Cross-Bronx Thruway," Bronx Borough President's Office, 1944.

7. Robert Moses, "New Highways for a Better New York," *New York Times Magazine*, 11 November 1945, 10–11.

8. Gano Dunn et al., *Selected Measures for the Partial Relief of Traffic Congestion in New York* (New York: Steidlinger Press, 1946), 40. For recent discussions, see Owen N. Gutfreund,

"Rebuilding New York in the Auto Age: Robert Moses and His Highway," in *Robert Moses*, ed. Ballon and Jackson, 86–93; and Gutfreund, "Catalog of Built Work," in ibid., 204–41.

9. Cleveland Rogers, "Highways and Parkways," *The Studio* 127 (June 1944): 204–8; "Robert (Or-I'll-Resign) Moses," *Fortune* 17 (June 1938): 70–78.

10. Robert Moses, "Arterial Plan for Pittsburgh," 1939; Robert Moses, "Baltimore Arterial Report," 1944; and Robert Moses, *Arterial Plan for New Orleans* (New York: Steidlinger Press, 1946). "The construction of a freeway system to answer the needs of urban transportation was an American innovation whose first realization came in New York City. . . championed by Robert Moses," according to Brodsly, *L.A. Freeway*, 97. See also Phil Patton, *Open Road: A Celebration of the American Highway* (New York: Simon and Schuster, 1986), 72.

11. Caro, *The Power Broker*, 11.

12. "Vital Gaps in New York Metropolitan Arteries," Triborough Bridge Authority, New York, 1940.

13. "Harlem River Bridge," editorial, *New York Times*, 13 June 1949, 18.

14. "Democrats Hop Ride on G.O.P. Highway Ceremony," *New York Times*, 30 October 1954, 11. For a pictorial history of the freeway, see Yanni Tsipis, *Boston's Central Artery* (Charleston, S.C.: Arcadia, 2001).

15. Caro, *The Power Broker*, 840, offers an excellent account of the difficulty of constructing the Cross-Bronx.

16. "Cross-Bronx Expressway, Alexander Hamilton Bridge, George Washington Bridge Bus Station," Triborough Bridge and Tunnel Authority and Port of New York Authority, commemorative booklet, 17 January 1963.

17. Joseph C. Ingraham, "Cross-Bronx Road Gets Revised Plan," *New York Times*, 27 November 1958, 31. Shea Stadium, which opened in 1964, cost $28.5 million, according to numerous sources, including *Ballparks by Munsey & Suppes* (http://www.ballparks.com).

18. Caro, *The Power Broker*, 850–79; *The World That Moses Built* (Obenhaus Films Production for the American Experience, 1988).

19. Charles G. Bennett, "Bronx Expressway Dispute Has Estimate Board Fuming," *New York Times*, 24 April 1953, 1.

20. Jane Holtz Kay, *Asphalt Nation: How the Automobile Took Over America, and How We Can Take It Back* (New York: Crown, 1997), 250–54; Robert A. M. Stern, Thomas Mellins, and David Fishman, *New York 1960: Architecture and Urbanism between the Second World War and the Bicentennial* (New York: Monacelli Press, 1995), 259–61; and Tom Lewis, *Divided Highways* (New York: Viking, 1997). For other case studies, see Zachary Schrag, "The Freeway Fight in Washington, D.C.: The Three Sisters Bridge in Three Administrations," *Journal of Urban History* 30 (July 2004): 648–73; and Raymond A. Mohl, "Stop the Road: Freeway Revolt in American Cities," *Journal of Urban History* 30 (July 2004): 674–706.

21. Sigfried Giedion, *Spaces, Time and Architecture: The Growth of a New Tradition*, 5th rev. ed. (1941; Cambridge, Mass.: Harvard University Press, 1967), 728.

22. On the importance of the General Motors Futurama, see Patton, *Open Road*, 120; and Norman Bel Geddes, *Magic Motorways* (New York: Random House, 1940), 22–23, 35.

23. Le Corbusier, *The City of Tomorrow and Its Planning*, reprint ed. (1929; New York: Dover, 1987), 192.

24. "Which—or Both? Geometrically Designed Highways, or 'Winding Countrified Walks'?" *American City* 42 (June 1930): 148. In the 1940s and 1950s, the image of two straight

lines receding into the distance became an icon for the new, modern highways, as shown on the cover of New York State's "Co-Operative Highway Needs Study," 1950.

25. "Episode Seven: The City and the World."

26. U.S. National Interregional Highway Committee, *Interregional Highways* (Washington, D.C.: U.S. Government Printing Office, 1944), 80.

27. "Special Report: How to End Traffic Jams; Detroit's Sunken Roads Speed Cars Fivefold," *U.S. News and World Report*, 22 February 1952: 44–48.

28. "Cross-Bronx Expressway," commemorative booklet.

29. "New Parkways in New York City," New York City Department of Parks and Recreation, 1937, 17.

30. The 1946 date comes from the bridge files at the New York State Department of Transportation's Region 11 office in Long Island City, N.Y. A better-known example of putting recreational space over an expressway, the cantilevered Brooklyn Heights Promenade over New York's Brooklyn-Queens Expressway, was not designed until 1947, according to Steve Anderson, *New York Area Roads, Crossings, and Exits* (http://www.nycroads.com).

31. Postwar postcard views of urban skylines are easy to find on the online auction site eBay; I have collected several, including views of Boston, Philadelphia, Atlanta, and Dallas.

32. Marshall Berman, *All That Is Solid Melts into Air: The Experience of Modernity* (New York: Penguin, 1982), 301.

33. Editor's note: Drivers may appreciate these landscapes when traffic is highly congested; otherwise only passengers can partake in the scene given the vagaries of negotiating high-speed roadways of any sort.

34. V. S. Pritchett, *New York Proclaimed* (New York: Harcourt, Brace and World, 1965), 9.

35. Edward I. Koch, "Of Decals and Priorities in the South Bronx," *New York Times*, 19 November 1983, 24.

36. Marshall Berman, "Views from the Burning Bridge," in *Urban Mythologies: The Bronx Represented since the 1960s*, ed. John Alan Farmer (Bronx, N.Y.: Bronx Museum of the Arts, 1999), 70.

37. Grace Gleuck, *New York: The Painted City* (Salt Lake City, Utah: Peregrine Smith, 1992).

4. The American Summer Youth Camp as a Cultural Landscape

COURTNEY P. FINT

The summer youth camp movement emerged during the late nineteenth century in response to a growing concern among parents, educators, and civic leaders in the United States that the purported vagaries of the industrial age threatened traditional values and the positive development of children. Much as with the maturation of the suburban ideal and of landscape design in the decades immediately previous, the creation of the summer camp was spurred by the pursuit of a more "authentic" life—physically, morally, and socially—through contact with nature. The setting created for this experience was viewed as an essential tool for furthering the character and development of youth. The ways in which summer camps were developed physically as landscapes, incorporating both natural and man-made features, bears direct correlation to the values, beliefs, and goals of the sponsoring organizations and often to the personal vision of an organization's leader.[1] In contrast to a college or university campus, where professional designers have played a major role in giving form and expression to administrators' wishes, the summer camp tends to be more a product of the client, sometimes aided by an architect or landscape architect, but seldom, if ever, dominated by them. Jackson's Mill State 4-H Camp in Weston, West Virginia, affords an excellent case study of such an institution, both in terms of its generic and distinctive qualities. To understand those qualities fully, the summer camp is best examined as a cultural landscape, to which the development and change of numerous components over time significantly contribute to the meaning of the whole. This understanding, in turn, is crucial to creating an effective preservation strategy for such places.

The first summer camps were founded in the 1880s in New Hampshire by New Englanders for sons of well-to-do urban families. These places emerged in large part out of fear that city life, particularly during the summer vacation months, was producing listless and amoral young men. In 1892, Winthrop T. Talbot of Boston summarized the problem in the *Journal of Social Science:*

What shall the boys do during the long vacation? Where shall they go, and how best care for them? The question has presented itself to many an anxious parent who realizes all too helplessly the increase in nerve tension, the pallor and languor of a naturally healthy son,

> but does not appreciate or cannot remedy the complex cause of the altered conditions,—long indoor confinement, late hours, smoking, hurried eating, and the deadening mechanism of ordinary school life.

For more than twenty years Talbot was the director of Camp Asquam, a prestigious New Hampshire summer camp, and fostered the popular belief that contact with nature was essential to producing mentally and physically healthy boys. "The subtle charm of beautiful, natural surroundings," he wrote, "will help in a marvelous degree to bring out the truest and best side of the boyish nature."[2]

Across the country, many groups that catered to a broader segment of society soon embraced the concept of the summer camp. The YMCA, YWCA, and other religious organizations, as well as the Boy Scouts, Girl Scouts, Campfire Girls, and 4-H clubs, were among those that adapted the camp idea to fit their individual objectives. By the 1920s, summer camps were a national phenomenon—widely appreciated and recognized for their educational and character-building values. Harvard president Charles Eliot called summer camps "the most important step in education that America has given the world."[3] Numerous educational journals hailed the health benefits of summer camp as extremely effective in increasing mental capacity. Indeed, summer camp integrated education with recreation and daily life in an unprecedented way. Campers were fully immersed in the routine, day and night, and were required to live cooperatively, assume leadership roles, and learn skills not taught in the classroom or even at home. This creative fusing of instruction, recreation, and social interaction—all conducted in an informal, open-air, and largely natural environment—was indeed a significant part of America's contribution to the education field.

The physical environment of the summer camp was central to the transformative experiences of those who attended. The natural surroundings, including topography, vegetation, and views; the arrangement and character of buildings; the scope and placement of outdoor facilities; the historical associations the site and/or region carried; and the ways in which these facets related to one another—all had an impact on camp life. Campers also could be profoundly affected by the removal from their domestic environments. The novel camp setting, almost its own universe, apart from the outside world, helped frame the new experiences and friendships acquired there. As places imbued with the ideals and objectives of the sponsoring group, as well as a backdrop for significant personal growth and memories, summer camp landscapes often became beloved, even sacred, places to many of the people who partook in them.

Underpinning the entire summer camp phenomenon was the longstanding popular belief in the Arcadian myth, described by historian Peter J. Schmitt as an "urban response [that] valued nature's spiritual impact above its economic importance."[4] This idea began to gain strength in the mid-nineteenth century as a result of the growing dichotomy between urban and rural environments. Though many camp operators stated that their camp philosophies were based on allowing "savage" freedom and manliness in nature, in truth camps were highly structured communities placed in natural settings. It was sometimes difficult to reconcile the back-to-nature wildness with the need to retain some measure of cultivation and the fundamental goal of camp to inculcate particular values in the campers. Historian John Higham observed: "The emergent culture of the Strenuous Age had an ambiguous relation to its institutional matrix. In some measure a rebellion against the constraints of a highly organized society, it was also an accommodation to those constraints, a way of coming to terms with them."[5] Regardless of this conflict, however, children were affected by the separation from conventional society and participated in most camp activities with enthusiasm, even if the camp programs were simply disguised reflections of mainstream culture. Furthermore, activities such as Indian play allowed youth to change their identities and liberate themselves from their regular routines of action and thought. Away from family and school, young people at camp could reinvent themselves temporarily, guided by adults with a formulated set of goals.

Jackson's Mill State 4-H Camp, established in 1921 as the first statewide 4-H camp in the United States, embodied prevailing trends in the development of such compounds, but did so in some unusual ways. 4-H emerged in the late nineteenth century as a program dedicated to improving practical education for rural children by providing them with hands-on learning opportunities. West Virginia's 4-H program was administered by the state university's Extension Department. William H. ("Teepi") Kendrick was one of the first persons appointed as a 4-H administrator in the state program and was influential in its development. The son of a minister, Kendrick had a close relationship with the founders of the American Youth Foundation, a religious organization concerned with elevating the morals and character of young people. With them, Kendrick refined his ideas about a fourfold approach to youth development, focusing on religious, physical, mental, and social pursuits. When summer camps began to be held on a county level in West Virginia, Kendrick saw the value of creating a statewide camping center. He developed Jackson's Mill according to his personal vision as a place for rural children to learn and grow. Serving as camp director from 1921 until his death in 1937, Kendrick believed that the goals of 4-H should be character and leadership development rather than simply dissemination of practical agricultural and domestic knowledge, as was standard in other states. The 4-H program had the potential to empower rural youth to set and achieve higher goals. Kendrick and his colleagues created Jackson's Mill as the training center that would provide an ideal environment for furthering the development of the four "Hs"—head, heart, hands, and health—in new ways. As a state institution, moreover, the camp was to extend its leadership programs to West Virginia citizens beyond 4-H members, including those in other youth organizations and adults.[6]

In winter 1921, Kendrick, as state 4-H Club agent leader; Charles H. Hartley, an assistant club leader; and T. D. Gray, West Virginia University Extension landscape architect, set out in search of a site for what was to be "the great hope of West Virginia farm youth."[7] The state legislature had already passed a bill that called for the establishment of a 4-H camp "at some suitable location."[8] Mrs. Arthur Rhodes of the Stonewall County Life Club in Weston, West Virginia, suggested Jackson's Mill, the boyhood home of Confederate General Thomas J. ("Stonewall") Jackson, who had lived there from 1831 until 1842. The three men inspected the site, which lay on a bend of the West Fork River (Figure 4.1). The property had been neglected for some years, yet it was well suited to the camp's purpose and carried valued historical associations. A commemorative stone marked the site of the Jackson house, and the grist mill built for the family in 1837 still stood nearby.

Kendrick and his associates recognized several advantages of the site. Besides being near the geographic center of the state, Jackson's Mill lay only five miles from the county seat of Weston and was accessed by good roads and an interurban car line. The example of Stonewall Jackson could serve as an inspiration to 4-H'ers. Finally, businessmen in Weston and nearby Clarksburg had volunteered their financial support of the project.[9] Kendrick, Hartley, and Gray returned to the state 4-H headquarters in Morgantown and recommended Jackson's Mill as the site of the state 4-H camp. The Monongahela West Penn Service Corporation (later the Monongahela Power Company), which owned the property, promptly agreed to donate the five acres on which the mill was located to the University Extension, with the stipulation that the Jackson homestead marker remain. Soon thereafter, the Weston Chamber of Commerce and the Lewis County Farm Bureau provided funds to acquire thirty additional acres. In 1922 the state purchased several more parcels, increasing the total acreage threefold. Over the years, gradual acquisition of land by the state brought the camp to its current size of 523 acres.

After securing the site, Kendrick, Hartley, and others began an intense campaign to fashion the camp as an institution and as a physical reality. The first encampment, a training conference for adult 4-H leaders, took place in summer 1921, with seventy-five participants sleeping in tents and in the old mill, cooking outside over an open fire. By the next summer, a mess hall and several small cabins had been built. Camps, which generally lasted one week each, included the state 4-H boys' and girls' camps, coed county camps, and non–4-H gatherings for

Figure 4.1. Jackson's Mill State 4-H Camp, near Weston, West Virginia, general view looking north across West Fork River, interurban car line in foreground, grist mill at right, and dining hall at center, rear. Postcard, ca. 1930. Author's collection.

such groups as the Farm Women and the West Virginia University football team.[10] 4-H campers ranged in age from nine to the late teens.

The following year, Kendrick and his colleagues in the University Extension commissioned the Pittsburgh engineering firm of Morris Knowles to create a master plan for the camp. Tell W. Nicolet, a Harvard graduate, was the landscape architect in charge of the design and later became an associate landscape designer for the National Park Service, overseeing the plans for Catoctin Mountain Park in Maryland and Gettysburg and Antietam national military parks.[11]

Not long after developing the master plan for Jackson's Mill, Nicolet discussed his views on planning and landscape design:

> Beauty is a real asset and is essential to all of us because it makes for a better place in which to live. It adds to the value of our properties, it denotes thrift and energy, and it makes other people want to live in our community. . . . Beauty without utility is expensive and wasteful. But beauty arising out of a well-solved problem is the kind of beauty most desirable.

As an example, he used school grounds, an environment somewhat comparable to camp grounds as facilities for young people's education. Some of these ideas, particularly respect for the natural environment and the value of landscape as a teaching tool, no doubt helped shape Nicolet's design for the 4-H camp:

> We send our children to school each day that they may learn to be better citizens. Their environment while at school has just as much to do with their learning as their books, teachers, or fellow pupils. If children are accustomed to playing on dirty, ill-kept playgrounds, or in the street . . . or are accustomed to seeing unsightly things, they have no way of learning [about beauty].[12]

The plan for Jackson's Mill was an imaginative response to the natural landscape. Large, rounded mountains divided by flat and fertile river valleys typify the topography of central West Virginia (Figure 4.2). The camp's location at a bend in the West Fork River placed it on a relatively flat tract of land that minimized traversing steep grades and was conducive to construction of the extensive recreational facilities proposed in the master plan. Over the course of development, parts of the camp were leveled further through grading and filling ravines, while the gently rolling hills were retained in places such as the western cottage area.[13] Taking advantage of the terrain, the plan included forty-eight residential cottages along the main drive and along curving secondary drives with culs-de-sac in the wooded acreage to the west of the dining hall. Other buildings, particularly the dining hall, with its expansive front porch, partook of the broad views of the mountains and valleys.

The sharp river bend that defined a major portion of the site's boundaries also formed the basis for Nicolet's master plan. The location was chosen for the Jackson homestead in the early nineteenth century because of its usefulness in attaining water for power as well as for irrigation and because its peninsular configuration was a safeguard against Indian attack. The river bend continued to serve as an important feature once the camp was established. In the master plan, the large central green, containing the playing fields, paralleled the river's path. The dining and assembly halls were placed at prime locations facing the green, capturing views of the river and mountains beyond. Athletic facilities lined the riverbank behind the assembly hall, with an unbroken view of the water. The assembly and community hall complex possessed a sightline across the river to a clearing labeled "View" on the master plan. Likewise, the campfire circle and "All-Star Shrine," a meditation garden, were aligned on a more isolated axis, with a direct view of the river, in accordance with their special roles as sites of reflection.

Rather than an extension of the agrarian home environment or a rustic forest outpost, Nicolet's plan was more akin to that of an idealized small town—one that would provide for all the anticipated needs of campers. Each aspect of activity—sleeping, eating, classroom learning, recreation, assembly, religious worship—had its distinct place within the scheme. Nicolet's design reflected influences from both picturesque suburban and town planning of the period and the more formally structured City Beautiful plans. Instead of the then conventional

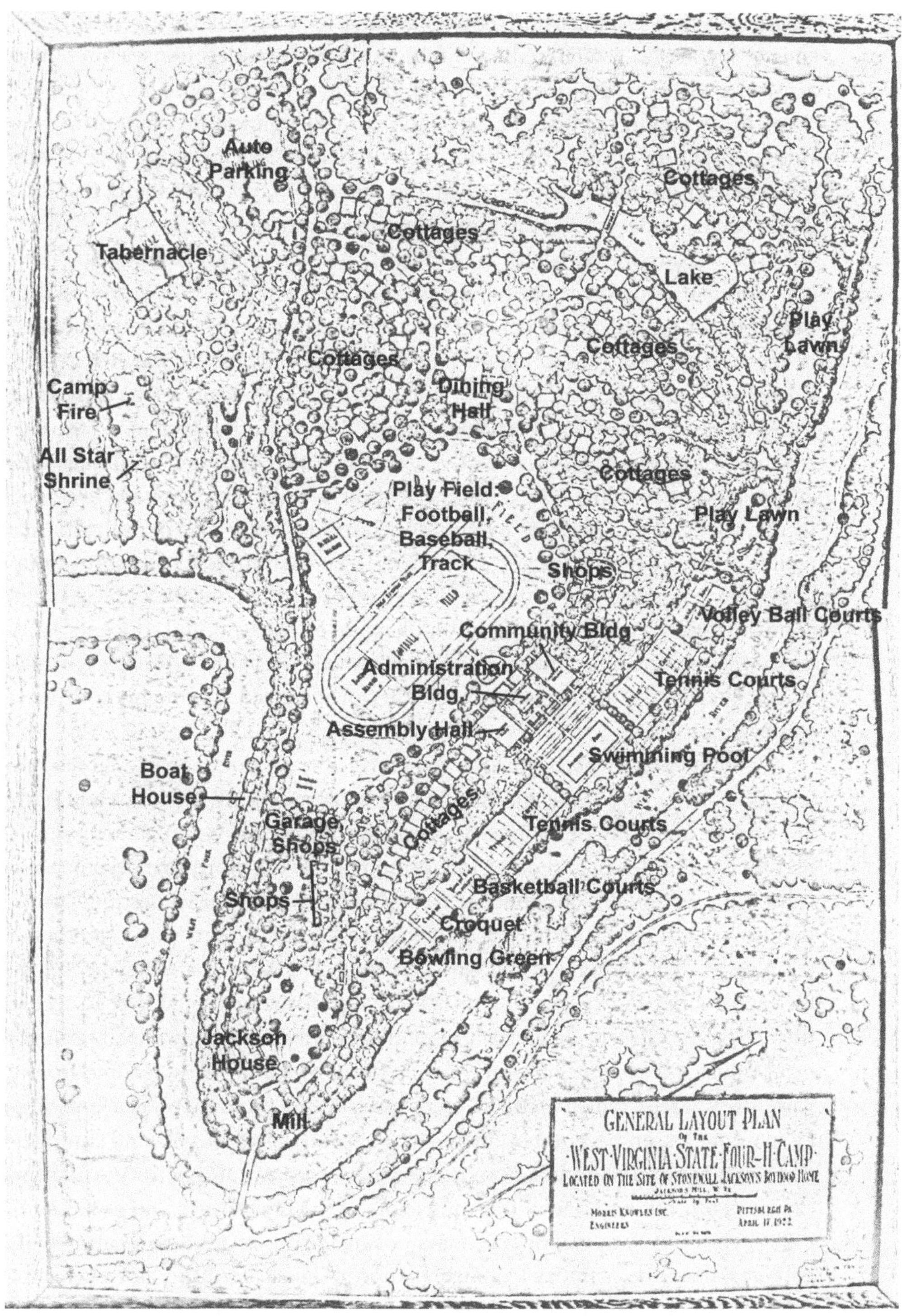

Figure 4.2. Jackson's Mill, "General Layout Plan," 1922. Tell W. Nicolet, landscape architect for Morris, Knowles, Inc. Drafted by author after plan in Jackson's Mill Archive.

reliance on simple cabins, bunkhouses, or tents for residential quarters, the plan called for cottages, which in their realized form were modest houses built in an array of stylistic modes then popular. Informally arranged along curving roadways, these buildings created a sense of enduring community, supporting the values of "family, pride of ownership and rural life."[14] Each cottage was slightly different, representing individualism and ownership, yet was clearly part of a larger whole, underscoring the importance of shared ideals.

In contrast to the cottage layout, the arrangement of the camp's main buildings and gathering places in the master plan was strongly influenced by City Beautiful concepts—an aspect of the master plan that was far less pronounced in the realized compound (Figure 4.3). The dining hall, which was inspired by George Washington's Mount Vernon, anchored an axial crossing.[15] One axis linked the campfire area, meditative shrine, and the river; the other connected the recreation areas along the river with the assembly hall, community building, and administrative building. The latter three edifices were symmetrically arranged facing the flagpole, perhaps to impart a sense of order and organization as campers arrived, registered, and got settled. The most important centers of group activity for the camp were almost all placed on axes, reflecting their places in the camp hierarchy. Furthermore, in the application of City Beautiful concepts, Jackson's Mill's planners may have sought to challenge the status of West Virginia as a poor, backward mountain state by creating an advanced, thoroughly conceived statewide institution.

While the master plan of Jackson's Mill was the product of professional collaboration between Nicolet and University Extension officials, Kendrick and Hartley worked diligently to include participation from West Virginia citizens, 4-H members, volunteers, and other interested parties, transforming Jackson's Mill from a professionally designed matrix to an array of local values and tastes. Kendrick's enthusiasm and energy motivated adults and youth from a number of counties to erect permanent cottages. Eventually, the camp was to have a cottage for each county, in which residents from that jurisdiction would live. To secure the necessary support, Kendrick appealed to county and state pride, traditional rural values, and the promise of a lasting heritage. Funds were secured from a variety of sources, which included local and state government offices, individuals, companies, and events conducted by 4-H youth, as well as in-kind contributions of labor and materials from the private sector. According to Pete Hartley, Charles's brother and one of the counselors at the first boys' camp at Jackson's Mill, each county was responsible for choosing the design and the location of its cottage.[16] That the counties were truly autonomous is doubtful, however, considering the locational correspondence between many of the buildings and those in the master plan. Rather, Kendrick appears to have worked closely with repre-

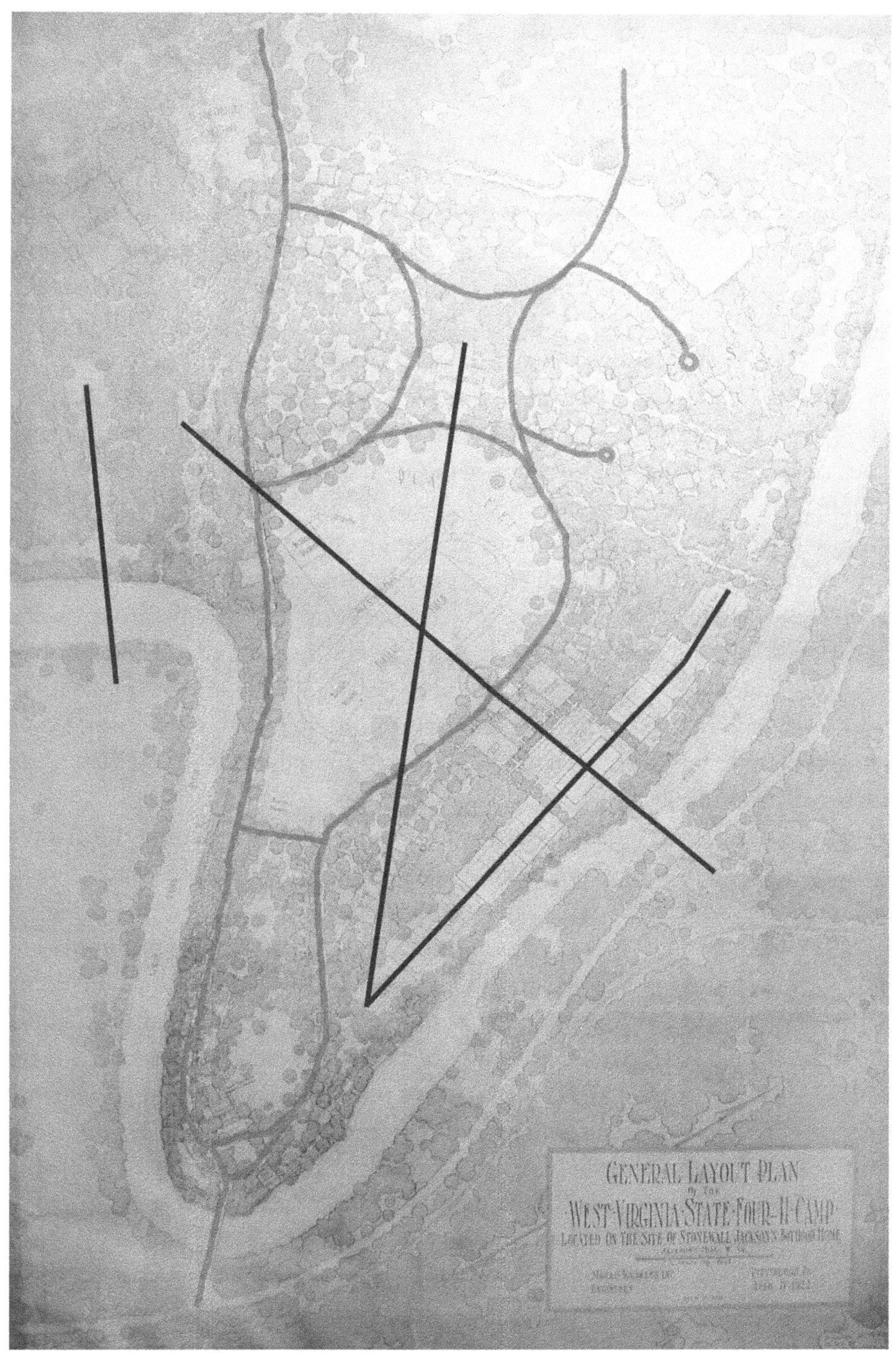

Figure 4.3. “General Layout Plan,” overlay showing axes and drives. Diagram by author.

sentatives of each county on a personal basis, entertaining their ideas as well as providing suggestions. Ralph Myers, the camp's caretaker, also played a role in the final siting and construction of facilities, in all likelihood to ensure the practicality and economy of those endeavors.[17]

Many of the cottages possess symbolic features that were planned by county sponsors with Kendrick's input. An early history of the camp, attributed to extension director Nat T. Frame, emphasized the underlying motivation behind the design of the cottages. "The great challenge," he intoned, "is to build so that each structure will stand for an ideal in the lives" of the campers, concluding that the "fundamentals of American civilization should be brought out in buildings which would challenge the best there was in boys and girls."[18] Weston Chamber of Commerce chairman F. R. Yoke was no less effusive when he opined in 1922 that "Jackson's Mill is going to be one of the showplaces of the state and a project of considerable national interest and publicity."[19] Sponsors considered the planning of a cottage an opportunity to represent the positive attributes of their county at a state level. In many cases, the facilities were better appointed and more up-to-date than the campers' rural homes. Most of the early cottages were bungalows, a form prevalent in many West Virginia communities. Other county sponsors built representations of what they considered typical dwellings in their respective locales—log cabins, for example, or simple frame farmhouses. However, even these folk-inspired cottages were larger and more finished than most prototypical examples.

The first cottage was built in 1922 by sponsors from Lewis County, the camp's home base. Lewis Cottage, as it was called, was clearly a bungalow, built of "everlasting cypress which represents the 'never-say-die' spirit of successful club members."[20] Other counties' sponsors soon followed, each group balancing individuality with overarching 4-H camp ideals. Recurring symbolic themes included achievement, pride in one's county, patriotism, perseverance, and Christian morals. Upshur Cottage (1923) was built of stone because a "stone cottage is as solid as the 4-H ideals themselves, and meets the challenge of our great National Leader, Theodore Roosevelt, who loved to sing in his youth the old song, 'How Firm a Foundation.'"[21] Many cottages employed materials native to the home county, including Webster Cottage, which was built of logs to represent the major industry there and "the pioneering spirit of 4-H club members" (Figure 4.4). Cottage locations were also chosen for symbolic and aesthetic value: Barbour County cottage planners chose to site their building on a sharp curve of a drive, which was said to represent the "turning point in the lives of boys and girls" when coming to camp.[22] Webster, Randolph, and Monroe cottages were sited in a sequestered, wooded area compatible with their log construction or shingle veneers. The more urban-looking bungalows were located along the main camp road.

Figure 4.4. Webster Cottage, Jackson's Mill, 1923, construction photograph. Courtesy of West Virginia University Jackson's Mill, West Virginia University Extension Service.

Campers often remarked on the isolation of the rustic cottages and the long walk to the dining hall from them, although in reality the distances were no farther than from those that seemed more centrally placed, demonstrating the effects that naturalistic landscape planning can have on human perceptions. Additionally, there was a recognizable division at the dining hall between cottages located along the main drive and those located in the western portion of the camp. This bifurcation was convenient for keeping girls' and boys' quarters well removed from one another and even allowed two discrete camps to be conducted simultaneously.

Many components of Nicolet's plan were realized over the following decade (Figure 4.5). The assembly and dining halls were built on their designated sites. Only fourteen of the intended forty-eight cottages were erected, but the location of each roughly corresponded to those stipulated in the plan. Fulfillment of the plan was probably first a matter of priorities, then of economics. The principal goal of the early years was to provide shelter and essential group facilities for campers. By 1930, Jackson's Mill boasted its dining and assembly halls as well as twelve cottages (Figure 4.6). The Depression severely hindered fund-raising efforts. Kendrick's death in 1937 robbed the camp of the man who held the vision and was its most active promoter.

A major part of Kendrick's youth development philosophy was religion and the strengthening of the "Heart H." Key components of Jackson's Mill included

Figure 4.5. Jackson's Mill, aerial view showing main green, dining hall, and some cottages. Postcard, 1949. Author's collection.

Figure 4.6. Jackson's Mill, general view from water tower in 1930, showing cottages *(center and left)* and camp green. Courtesy of West Virginia University Jackson's Mill, West Virginia University Cooperative Extension Service.

places for meditation, vespers, and nurturing of interpersonal relationships. At the first volunteer leaders' camp in 1921, an impromptu vesper service was held at sunset. Thereafter, at all state camps, campers attended daily vesper services at sunset—a time for quiet reflection and prayer.[23] For many years, vespers were held at an outdoor site overlooking the river called Vesper Knoll. After a chapel was built there in 1960, services were held at a variety of places around camp. Today, groups of campers plan meditation programs together and choose their own sites in clearings, groves, gardens, and other outdoor spaces throughout camp—the spaces that in many cases are never recognized with a name or marker but that are remembered for the deeply moving experiences that occur there. These places are, in effect, created and maintained by the campers themselves.

Camp programs likewise enjoyed a harmonious relationship with the site. With up to four hundred campers at a time, many activities—including talent shows, lectures, and group meditations, as well as games of all kinds—were held outdoors. The amphitheater (1939–40) afforded a primary staging ground for such gatherings. The location selected lay along the riverbank, with a gentle slope that required minimal grading. Rough-hewn stone retaining walls, a stage, and wings for dressing and storage rooms, as well as tall arborvitae that served as a stage backdrop, complemented the natural setting.

Many camp activities, such as classes and discussion groups, that were conducted on a smaller scale also took place outside, using a wide variety of spaces. Most cottages had large porches, which were frequently employed for such purposes and served as a link between building and landscape. Each porch afforded a view that could extend to the distant mountains, other camp buildings, or outdoor activity areas.

As they were realized, recreational facilities were not formally arranged as stipulated in the master plan but instead were scattered around the camp. The swimming pool lay not by the river but directly in front of the dining hall. Built in 1926, the pool was the work of male campers, manifesting Kendrick's hands-on teaching method and also probably a cost-saving measure. Volleyball courts and a softball field were placed on the camp green, while tennis and basketball courts were constructed in a somewhat remote location. The dispersal of these and other recreational facilities ensured that they were an integral part of the entire compound rather than clustered in a discrete zone.

Roads were recognized as important contributors to collective identity. Most followed the master plan, although several of the proposed culs-de-sac were never realized. As in a village, roads, not paths, connected all the cottages and other buildings, underscoring the idea of Jackson's Mill as a community. That tie was reinforced by inclusion of male campers in the workforce and also by the addition of sidewalks, which were installed in 1940 by the Works Project Administration, with concrete pavers cast in an abstract pattern designed to resemble the four-leaf clover symbol of 4-H.[24]

Jackson's Mill also included landscape elements appropriate for individual exploration and contemplation. The "Informal Garden," for example, was designed by T. D. Gray around 1934 and soon became a favorite retreat. Flowers from the garden were used in awards ceremonies recognizing outstanding 4-H members. Completed in 1949 as a memorial to Kendrick, the "Teepi Shrine" was situated in the wooded area at the northern end of the camp—reputedly a favorite place of its honoree. From this sunken, circular, stone terrace extended over four miles of paths that surrounded wooded wetlands and included rustic stone bridges and steps.

One of the most sacred places at Jackson's Mill was the campfire circle, known as the Council Circle. In its early years, West Virginia 4-H camping integrated a program of Native American tradition and imagery. This practice was influenced by Kendrick's association with Ernest Thompson Seton, a naturalist and Native American enthusiast who was influential in youth organizations such as the Boy Scouts and Camp Fire Girls. To Seton, youth could benefit from modeling themselves after the "Ideal Indian," who "stands for the highest type of primitive life. He was a master of woodcraft, and unsordid *[sic]*, clean, manly, heroic, self-controlled, reverent, truthful, and picturesque always."[25]

The Council Circle, like all such facilities at 4-H camps in West Virginia, was constructed around 1926 according to Seton's specifications, with a diameter of twenty-four feet, concentric rows of rising benches, and a rustic outer railing made of branches (Figure 4.7). The site was determined not by the master plan but, reputedly, by the original group of young adult campers sent to survey the grounds for an ideal council circle location. They found the "perfect" natural hollow in the woods, but a giant, ancient tree occupied the center of the site. Shortly thereafter, the tree was struck during a thunderstorm, clearing the way for construction.[26] Whether one chooses to believe in divine intervention or coincidence, the site remains the spiritual center of camp. The nightly campfire program at 4-H camps is an immensely important time of bonding and unification for campers and staff. Singing, storytelling, games, commentary on the day's events, comic skits, and traditional rituals help campers feel connected with each other, as well as to those who in the past engaged in the same activities in that very place.

By 1952, when Northern Panhandle Cottage was built, the camp had a capacity of 300 to 350 people, which 4-H administrators agreed was an ideal and realistic number based on their experience. When asked a few years before he died what he and Kendrick hoped Jackson's Mill would look like, "Uncle Charlie" Hartley replied, "About like it does now. Teepi had visions far ahead of his time."[27] Beyond Kendrick's role, however, Jackson's Mill was molded by thousands of West Vir-

Figure 4.7. Council Circle, Jackson's Mill, ca. 1926, general view after removal of outer railing. Photograph by author, 2003.

ginians who believed that it would indeed challenge young people to become better versions of themselves through education, fellowship, and special programs. Under the guidance of Kendrick and his colleagues, the physical environment at Jackson's Mill was crafted over time to represent myriad values, from stewardship of nature to patriotism, from spirituality to a strong work ethic. The many generations of 4-H'ers and other youth who continue to attend camp at Jackson's Mill year after year reveal the deep significance the site carries as a place of memory and heritage. Though its physical qualities are different from those of many camps, Jackson's Mill has associational significance comparable to that of many summer camps throughout the United States, each of which has its own story to tell.

After World War II, the master plan ceased to have the relevance it had possessed for Kendrick's generation. Development also occurred at a slower place than it had in the 1920s. A chapel, a health center, and three modest, corporate-sponsored classroom buildings were erected in the 1950s along existing drives in a manner complementary to the cottages. During the following decade, the camp director, Harley V. Cutlip, sought to increase the comforts of the camp and increase its use. A camp advisory board was appointed in 1966 to assist in reaching these objectives. The changes that ensued did not significantly alter the qualities that distinguished the camp. Jackson Lodge, a twenty-room motel, was constructed between a camp entrance and one of the cottages. While its modernist design set the building apart from its predecessors, its edge location and low-key character ensured an unobtrusive relationship with the main body of the camp. To provide even more private housing, some cottage spaces were converted to hotel-like rooms. Yet these facilities were not usually occupied when camps were in session, minimizing their impact on traditional programs. During the 1970s, the swimming pool was replaced by a new one in a more remote location. When the health center was converted to the camp headquarters in 1992, an addition was built in the same manner as the original building.

A more substantial change occurred in the 1980s when a plan was devised to "restore" the area surrounding the 1837 mill to its mid-nineteenth-century appearance.[28] The "Historic Area," as it was designated, initially included the mill and a log cabin that had been moved to the property in 1926. As plans progressed to create a museum enclave, a 1795 mill and an 1845 cabin were moved to the precinct. Conjectural reconstruction of a blacksmith shop and other supporting buildings were completed soon thereafter. A new pond, created to power the relocated mill, flooded the "Formal Garden," a landscape feature developed in the 1920s.

In 2001 West Virginia University commissioned a misguided master plan delineating a blueprint for a new Jackson's Mill. Citing a $500,000 annual deficit, the authors posited the goal of expanding year-round operations and attracting a higher-paying clientele outside the summer camping season. Plans to increase the number of private rooms and dining facilities included additions to the dining hall and Jackson Lodge, a project that required relocation of one of the cottages and destruction of the "Informal Garden," as well as expansion of the lodge to as much as six times its original size. Each cottage was to be renovated to meet access and safety codes and to "refresh [its] 'look.'"[29] While historic preservation was one of the principal goals stated in the master plan, little sensitivity to preservation practices is in evidence in the contents.

The significance of Jackson's Mill lies in its nurturing of rural West Virginian and American values through an extraordinary program of fourfold youth development—intangibles fully revealed in the physical environment. Kendrick's vision for a character education program to create a new philosophy of personal growth went beyond typical 4-H goals. Jackson's Mill was conceived as the setting in which 4-H'ers embarked upon their own journeys of self-discovery. Thousands of youth have attended camp there, many of them returning year after year and sending their children and grandchildren as well. The camp continues this vital function today. The landscape of Jackson's Mill is central to communicating the institution's core values of community, appreciation of nature, and personal improvement. A radical altering of scale and destruction of key landscape elements, as proposed in the 2001 master plan, eroding the intimate sense of community that the camp has long fostered, would undermine both the quality of the setting and the ideas upon which it was developed. Unfortunately, economic pressures and competition from more upscale conference centers have left many summer camps with few options besides attempts to update facilities to attract more business. Working against Jackson's Mill, and all summer camps, is a lack of study and analysis of the architectural and cultural meanings of summer camp and a corresponding poor awareness of applicable preservation tools.

The placement of Jackson's Mill on the National Register of Historic Places in 2004 increased awareness and appreciation of the camp as a historical cultural landscape. To their credit, the University Extension managers have advanced a new development plan that includes sensitive rehabilitation and restoration of existing buildings and thoughtful addition of new landscape elements. Any development plans in the future should continue to focus on rediscovering the conceptual framework that Kendrick advanced and build upon it in ways suitable to future needs. This approach can include marketing the traditional 4-H values of personal and leadership development, community, and service to user groups looking for a values-based approach to training that is integrated with the site's physical environment. 4-H clubs, corporations, service and professional organizations, and other user groups should be encouraged to contribute to the physical setting through maintenance of existing components and through adding new, compatible ones, just as an array of individuals and groups contributed to the camp's development during its first forty years. Recognizing Jackson's Mill and other summer camps as historic places that are rich cultural landscapes does not preclude development but rather can help define future directions in ways that underscore the enduring message they have to offer to youth and to the public at large.

Notes

1. This essay draws from Courtney P. Fint, "Jackson's Mill 4-H Camp: The Summer Camp as a Cultural Heritage Site" (master's thesis, Columbia University, 2003). Pioneering studies of the subject include W. Barksdale Maynard, " 'An Ideal Life in the Woods for Boys': Architecture and Culture in the Earliest Summer Camps," *Winterthur Portfolio* 34 (spring 1999): 3–29; and Abigail A. van Slyck, "Kitchen Technologies and Mealtime Rituals: Interpreting the Food Axis at American Summer Camps, 1890–1950," *Technology and Culture* 43 (October 2002): 668–92. Abigail A. van Slyck, *A Manufactured Wilderness: Summer Camps and the Shaping of American Youth, 1890–1960* (Minneapolis: University of Minnesota Press, 2006) affords an essential, in-depth view of the subject nationally.

2. Winthrop T. Talbot, "Summer Camps for Boys," *Journal of Social Science* 29 (August 1892): 1, 2.

3. Marie M. Ready, "Organized Summer Camps for Children Have Proved Their Worth," *School Life* 12 (October 1926): 25.

4. Peter J. Schmitt, *Back to Nature: The Arcadian Myth in Urban America,* reprint ed. (1969; Baltimore: Johns Hopkins University Press, 1990): xix.

5. Quoted in Maynard, "'An Ideal Life,'" 20.

6. Guy Stewart, *A Touch of Charisma,* reprint. ed. (1969; Morgantown: West Virginia 4-H All-Stars, 2000), 39, 43.

7. I. B. "Tubby" Boggs, *Wa-Kon-Da Dhe-Dhu* (Morgantown: West Virginia 4-H Club Foundation, 1957), 114.

8. West Virginia Senate Bill No. 289, 1, Jackson's Mill archives, Weston, W.Va. (hereafter cited as "archives").

9. Stewart, *Touch of Charisma,* 39.

10. Ibid., 45–46.

11. Telephone interview with Etta Nicolet, 13 April 2003.

12. Tell W. Nicolet, "Improvement of Grounds for Town Betterment," *Presbyterian Banner,* 24 June 1926, 23.

13. Michael Meador, *Historic Jackson's Mill: A Walking Tour* (Parsons, W.Va.: McClain Printing, 1991), 34.

14. Robert A. M. Stern, ed., *The Anglo-American Suburb* (London: Architectural Design, 1981), 5.

15. Att. Nat T. Frame, "History: State 4-H Camp," typescript, 1935, 32, archives.

16. Interview with L. S. ("Pete") Hartley, Morgantown, W.Va., 27 July 2002.

17. Stewart, *Touch of Charisma,* 78.

18. Frame, "History," 30.

19. Stewart, *Touch of Charisma,* 46.

20. Frame, "History," 31.

21. William H. Kendrick, *The Four-H Trail* (Boston: R. G. Badger, 1926), 110.

22. Frame, "History," 33, 34.

23. Stewart, *Touch of Charisma,* 45.

24. Ibid., 47.

25. Seton was author of several widely read books on nature and camping activities, most notably *The Book of Woodcraft* (1921).

26. Brad Davis, *The Nature of Jackson's Mill* (Wilmington, Del.: by the author, 1982), 73.

27. Stewart, *Touch of Charisma,* 140; Davis, *Nature of Jackson's Mill,* 19.

28. Meador, *Historic Jackson's Mill,* vii.

29. "Master Plan Summary, WVU Jackson's Mill, The West Virginia Center for Lifelong Learning," West Virginia Cooperative Extension Service, Morgantown, October 2001, 4, 9–10.

5. Wild Lands and Wonders

Preserving Nature and Culture in National Parks

BONNIE STEPENOFF

NATURAL areas may be significant for historical reasons as well as for biological, geological, and aesthetic ones. As an open glade in a secluded valley shelters species of wildflowers, insects, and animals that would not thrive in an altered environment, so a clear spring gushing from a rocky bluff possesses visual qualities we admire. The ecological and scenic values of natural areas deserve protection, but so do the historical qualities that arise from connections between the land and human activities. A preservationist's first impulse might be to treat wild areas as we do cultivated landscapes, buildings, structures, and objects, but we must recognize an important principle: because natural landscapes change over time, their physical characteristics often should not, and perhaps cannot, be controlled in order to preserve what we may value as long-term attributes.

Suppose "Old Faithful" stopped living up to its name. After all, "faithfulness" is a human value, and a geyser, even in Yellowstone National Park, is a geological phenomenon, subject only to natural laws. In the 1870s, admirers praised the great waterspout for its punctuality, comparing it to the pulse of the human heart and also to a powerful mechanical force, thereby transforming a natural wonder into an icon of the industrial age.[1] If eventually the geyser lets us down, should we intervene with engineering technology to keep it on schedule? The National Park Service has built a landscape around it, blending the natural and the artificial, for the enjoyment of tourists. There are many such landscapes created by humans to highlight natural wonders.

Where does nature end and culture begin, and how can we preserve the beauty that lies in the places where human contrivance meets untamed land? Two settings in the Missouri Ozarks afford useful insights on the question. Roaring River Hills Wild Area, a state park in the southeastern part of that region, is significant as an open glade that is home to a vast array of wildflowers. The issue facing park officials is whether or not to intervene with tractors and chain saws to remove the cedar trees that threaten to reduce biodiversity in the area. The second example, the former Big Spring State Park, now under Park Service management in Ozark National Scenic Riverways, showcases a spectacular spring that surges from a dolomite bluff and empties into the free-flowing Current River. Over the past eighty years, state and federal officials have made decisions that have altered the spring and its physical setting, creating a historic landscape that in itself deserves protection. How can preservationists help to establish policies that will adequately safeguard the natural and man-made characteristics of these areas?

To address these questions, preservationists need a working definition of the word *wilderness*, a concept that has changed markedly over time. Preindustrial Americans tended to view wilderness as a treacherous, dark, and godless wasteland. Yellowstone, for instance, appealed to most visitors only after the railroads and a national advertising campaign converted it from an ostensibly dismal hellhole to an accessible and reliable theater of wonders.[2] As the country industrialized, the wilderness became an exploitable commodity, yielding raw materials as well as salable attractions. In the late nineteenth and early twentieth centuries, as the tourism industry developed, railroads yielded to automobiles, road building opened remote corners of the land, and scenic attractions lost their integrity. In postindustrial America, wild places have become fragile reminders of an increasingly distant past.

Landscape historian John R. Stilgoe has defined wilderness as the antithesis of landscape, which he identified as "the land shaped by men."[3] But Stilgoe was looking backward. Clearly, in America in the twenty-first century, the human imprint is everywhere on the land, and wilderness will cease to exist without human protection. As early as 1925, ecologist Aldo Leopold defined wilderness in human terms as "a wild, roadless area where those who are so inclined may enjoy primitive modes of travel and subsistence."[4] While stressing that humans could not create a wilderness as they could a city, he insisted that people must learn to understand and manage wild places.[5]

In the late 1920s, the Park Service began designating wilderness areas within the parks, and in 1964 the Wilderness Act required federal agencies to identify areas for inclusion in a national wilderness preservation system. This legislation asserted the need for active protection of areas "where man himself is a visitor who does not remain."[6] As environmental historian William Cronon recently pointed out, the Wilderness Act posited a rigid boundary between natural and cultural landscapes. With this distinction in mind, Park Service managers have engaged in a process of "rewilding" certain areas by removing traces of human activity, demolishing historic buildings, and failing to interpret the cultural connections of these places for park visitors.[7] Ironically, the tendency to elevate ecological over human values also leads park managers to intervene in natural processes that, over time, would change the character of the land.

Roaring River Hills is a useful case study for examining the question of when it is proper for humans to intervene to preserve or restore an area's "wildness." In the 1980s, Missouri state parks director John Karel implemented a policy for designating and protecting wild areas on parklands throughout the state. Prior to that time, officials had viewed state parks as places for intensive visitation and recreation. Karel believed that certain areas within the parks were more valuable for their pristine beauty than for their recreational potential. One of these was Roaring River Hills, a secluded area within Roaring River State Park. Karel's wild area policy prohibited paved roads, motorized vehicles, power tools, or machines of any kind in Roaring River Hills.

Problems developed when cedar trees threatened to overrun the wild area, producing shady conditions and reducing the number of sun-loving plant species that grew there. After a program of controlled burning failed to halt the growth of cedar trees in the area, a new generation of park administrators proposed using heavy equipment to remove the invaders and protect the area's biodiversity. Karel protested vigorously, arguing that there was another, more important value to protect: the area's wildness. The succession from open glade to shady grove was a natural, biological process, he argued, and humans should let nature take its course.[8]

In an impassioned essay titled "The Hills of Roaring River: How Shall We Love Them?" Karel placed the idea of wildness in a historical context. He argued that wilderness preservation served the purpose of protecting ecological systems that existed before European Americans settled the land. In this characterization he echoed Leopold, who argued in the 1940s that "wilderness is the raw material out of which man has hammered the artifact called civilization." Therefore, Leopold reasoned, the remnants of wilderness should be preserved as "museum pieces," for those who want to study the origins of their culture.[9] In the United States, Karel agreed, the desire to save remnants of untouched wilderness arose "from our American cultural experience of encountering the original untamed landscape—an encounter that was in part, to be sure, a confrontation, but was also a profound and satisfying engagement."[10] The major characteristic of this original landscape was its wildness, by which Karel meant its freedom from human intervention. Protection of wild lands, he insisted, required a hands-off policy rather than aggressive management. Humans could protect these areas best by leaving them alone.

When the focus is on buildings, preservation generally implies protection from incompatible alteration, but the most salient characteristic of natural lands is the fact that they change over time. Wildlife populations fluctuate. Birds nest and migrate; insects propagate and pollinate. Seeds move with the wind; plants grow and die. There is a natural succession of species that, in the absence of lightning fires or controlled burning, turns sunny glades into shadowy groves of cedars. Geysers are not attached to clocks set to go off at specified intervals. The idea of preserving tracts of wild land in some permanent and unchanging state of existence makes no sense because the very essence of wildness is the capacity for continual change directed entirely by natural forces.

Karel's question about the Roaring River Hills—"How shall we love them?"—may seem naive, but it is in fact quite profound. He again echoed Leopold, who wrote that "it is inconceivable to me that an ethical relation to land can exist without love, respect, and admiration for land, and a high regard for its value."[11] The word *love* places management questions in the ethical and moral realm and expresses the need to honor, as well as understand, wild places. The decision to intervene or not may come down to our scientific understanding of the succession of species and our technological ability to change the course of nature. But morally and ethically, we may recognize an issue larger than that of biodiversity or efficient land management. If places that experienced minimal human intervention of any kind are truly disappearing from the earth, then the value of "wildness" may supersede other considerations. The fact that we can does not necessarily mean that we should use modern technology to alter the course of nature.

The question of when and how to intervene in natural events is not a new one. Big Spring, near Van Buren, Missouri, is a case in point. In the 1920s, this natural wonder, which had never been developed for commercial purpose, became the centerpiece of a state park. By the early 1930s, periodic flooding threatened to submerge the spring under a channel of the Current River. The Van Buren *Current Local* reported that past floods "played havoc with the park grounds, spring branch, bridge and some of the buildings," and a spring flood in 1933 could potentially "cut in on the big spring" (Figures 5.1, 5.2).[12]

The matter was of sufficient regional concern to prompt an editorial in the *St. Louis Globe-Democrat* that called for action. The

> . . . Current River, now in flood, is said to be threatening to cut a new channel to the face of the bluff and thereby submerge the outlet permanently, . . . transforming a gushing spring into an underwater . . . , bubbling one, which makes all the difference in the world in [the] spring['s] character and beauty, even though it changes the flow of water not at all.
>
> So if this gusher is really threatened . . . , if there is [the] possibility of this sparkling gift of nature being smothered, something really should be done about it. The Current River should be made to follow the course it has followed, even if we have to stake her in the man-driven piles. As much as we love Current River, we love Big Spring more.[13]

The plea spoke volumes about contemporary attitudes toward nature. In the writer's view, the scenic value of the gushing spring clearly overrode the natural value of a free-flowing river. The editorial demanded human restrictions on natural processes.

Historical events facilitated a massive public works project that saved the spring. During the early 1930s, the Park Service supervised many construction

Figure 5.1. Big Spring emerging from dolomite bluff, Current River, Big Spring, Ozark National Scenic Riverways, Missouri. Photograph by author, 2002.

projects in Missouri state parks, employing workers in the Civilian Conservation Corps (CCC) and Works Progress Administration programs.[14] In June 1933, Company 1710 of the CCC arrived at Big Spring. Initially, federal work crews focused on flood control and fire prevention. As soon as they settled in a tent camp, the men began cutting a fire safety zone and clearing out fallen timber.[15] But their most pressing job during that summer was to build a set of large earthen dikes to block the channel and prevent the river from inundating the spring.[16]

Fortunately, the CCC worked under the supervision of Park Service architects, who were imbued with respect for the natural landscape.[17] In 1917, the renowned landscape architect Frank Albert Waugh, whose philosophy was embraced by the Park Service Landscape Department, stated that park planners should "greatly reverence the native landscape, should seek to conserve it for human use and enjoyment, should endeavor to make it physically accessible to all, should try to make it intelligible to all, [and] should work to open up for it the way to men's hearts."[18] Clearly, he believed, as Leopold did, that the natural landscape deserved our affection. However, he was willing to alter it respectfully in order to open it up to human enjoyment. In the 1930s, articulating the values adopted by the Park Service, Waugh wrote that "artificial structures in wild park lands should be made as inconspicuous as possible, and should be constructed of native materials such as local stone, peeled logs, etc."[19]

In fall 1933, J. S. Hazelton, a federal construction engineer assigned to the CCC project at Big Spring, made a field survey of the Current River drainage area and planned a system of permanent dikes to protect the spring. The Park Service obtained easements from the adjacent landowner to enable construction and

Figure 5.2. Big Spring flowing into the Spring Branch of Current River. Photograph by author, 2002.

maintenance.[20] CCC worker Floyd Downey remembered constructing the dikes by driving posts into the riverbed

> like telephone poles with a pile driver. . . . And we drove spikes into that and then we took guy wire which is like your strands going down from telephone poles and we wrapped it around that in such a manner that the idea was that your, and I hope they did, brush and dirt and silt coming down would collect and make a natural dike.[21]

By May 1934, the CCC had constructed five of these water control structures, which Hazelton called "rock-filled timbered dikes or jetties, located at intervals across the old channel bed." They had

> . . . two rows of piling, 10 feet, center to center, and tied together with heavy planks. The cribbing thus formed is stabilized by rock weighted mattress work hurdles. Pile clusters tied together with heavy cable are interspersed in the area between the dikes.
>
> At the point where the dikes are tied into the high bank or hillside, an area extending forty feet each way from the center of the dike is built with an apron of rip rap on each side . . . to prevent scour at this point.[22]

Each dike was wide enough for automobiles to drive over it but also blended into the landscape, resembling natural formations of flowing water and soil (Figure 5.3). The dikes altered the setting but protected the aesthetic qualities of the spring.

Figure 5.3. Dike #5, Big Spring, ca. 1934. Courtesy of the National Park Service, Ozark National Scenic Riverways.

Figure 5.4. Tourist cabin, Big Spring, ca. 1935–36. Donald Blake, architect. Photograph by author, 2002.

Three CCC companies also provided a number of recreation-oriented visitor facilities. After completing the dikes, Company 1710 began constructing buildings in a rustic vein typical of Park Service architecture during the interwar decades. Architect Donald Blake designed several of these buildings in an "Old English," or Tudor, mode, utilizing heavy oak timbers and local cut stone.[23] To supervise the stonework, the Park Service engaged Leo Anderson as a Local Experienced Man—a position created to secure needed expertise that could be provided neither by CCC workers nor by Park Service personnel readily at hand. A veteran stonemason, Anderson moved to the Ozarks from St. Louis during the Depression. Under his supervision, inexperienced recruits learned to cut, dress, and lay stone.[24] With the help of two other companies (743 and 1740) for brief periods, Company 1710 built fourteen stone and timber tourist cabins, a museum, service buildings, picnic shelters, bridges, trails, culverts, a fire tower, and many other structures in the park (Figures 5.4, 5.5). All this work was designed to harmonize with its natural environment.

In setting the national standard for park infrastructure, the Park Service helped ensure a widespread reverence for the natural landscape. Stone construction was particularly appropriate for Big Spring because, according to project superintendent N. Curtis Case, "the Ozark uplift, which exposes the oldest geological formations of the earth's crust, contains some of the most beautiful and unique building rock that can be found anywhere in America."[25] Locally, builders had already used these rocks to create commercial buildings and small houses. According to Case, this vernacular replaced the frontier log cabin as an

Figure 5.5. Museum–Interpretative Center, Big Spring, ca. 1935–36. Donald Blake, architect. Photograph by author, 2002.

expression of Ozarks culture. For constructing the buildings at Big Spring, he proposed to use

> . . . irregular rocks, placed with the smooth cleavage outside, and with a shade of cement not too pronounced, but that would blend with the color of the predominate rocks used, wiping back this cement between the rocks to give depth of pattern, and therefore without a bead, or a bold outline. We wish to group the rock colors, utilizing their own natural beauty and blending these colors in a pattern if possible.[26]

Easily the most spectacular accomplishment of the CCC at Big Spring was the dining lodge, designed by Blake and completed in 1936, with an addition in 1942 (Figures 5.6, 5.7). This rambling stone building, set into the hill overlooking the confluence of the Spring Branch and the Current River, resembled a large rock outcropping on an Ozark hillside. Besides its obvious Tudor references, the design may have been in part inspired by the Prairie School tradition of horizontal buildings that abstractly responded to the expanses of flat land in the central United States. By September 1936, the Van Buren newspaper reported that Company 1710 was completing the lodge's interior, setting the flagstone floor in the entrance lobby and the hardwood floors in the kitchen and dining room. Behind the lodge, enrollees built a heavy rock retaining wall and a narrow flagstone terrace. A convoy of seven men traveled to Pacific, Missouri, to obtain the flagstones.[27]

A spectacular portal to the park was provided by the Entrance Building (1935–36), consisting of a picturesque gatehouse flanked by two forty-foot stone walls, each with an arched culvert. Great effort went into dressing the stone. According

Figure 5.6. Dining lodge, Big Spring, 1935–36. Donald Blake, architect. Photograph by author, 2002.

Figure 5.7. Dining lodge, entrance detail. Photograph by author, 2002.

to the *Current Local*, "It takes one man one day to complete one of these stones."[28] Excellent design and careful craftsmanship using natural materials paid tribute to the park's scenic qualities.

Inspired by the dramatic Ozark spring, the Park Service created a memorable landscape of its own, which did not preclude altering natural features. For instance, CCC enrollees dramatically changed the appearance of the Spring

Figure 5.8. Big Spring, bank improvements and deepening of pool, ca. 1934–35. Courtesy of the National Park Service, Ozark National Scenic Riverways.

Branch, through which the churning waters of the spring found their way to the Current River (Figures 5.8, 5.9). Using heavy machinery, federal workers deepened the channel, preventing the surging water from spreading over the land. CCC men also built "natural" structures meant to contain the course of the water. Of particular note are thirteen rock ledges constructed along the western bank of the Spring Branch just upstream from the lodge. These ledges, designed to curb flooding, were made of rough quarried stone with no mortar, stacked to resemble natural formations. Completion of the ledges in 1937 marked the last major accomplishment of Company 1710 at the park.[29]

Federal workers left an enduring legacy at Big Spring, with an infrastructure that has become an integral, indeed seamless, part of the park experience and to which we now ascribe historical as well as aesthetic value. In his widely read book *State Parks: Their Meaning in American Life* (1962), the popular author Freeman Tilden included a special section on Big Spring. He described the spring itself as "a spectacle that has no rival in any other state."[30] The surrounding five thousand acres of parkland, he said, were well wooded with oaks, hickories, and other hardwoods, although much of the native pine had disappeared during an early-twentieth-century lumber boom.[31] After acknowledging the park's natural features, Tilden praised the placement of housekeeping cabins in the shade of these trees: "Who was the forgotten landscape artist who spaced these cabins so judiciously that no occupant feels elbowed and yet the most timid, when night comes on, have a sense of neighborship *[sic]*?"[32]

Figure 5.9. Spring Branch, showing clear waters resulting from CCC improvement. Photograph by author, 2002.

After World War II, local officials and businessmen discussed the possibility of damming the spring-fed Current River to generate power.[33] Missouri conservationists and their federal allies defeated this effort with a counterproposal to create a federally managed corridor along the Current and its tributary, the Jack's Fork River. Under this plan, the State of Missouri conveyed title to Alley Spring, Big Spring, and Round Spring state parks to the Park Service in 1969. Under Park Service auspices, this acreage was christened Ozark National Scenic Riverways.[34] In 1976, Big Spring Historic District was listed on the National Register of Historic Places. More than twenty-five years later, just before the CCC's seventieth anniversary, the Park Service commissioned a cultural landscape report, documenting the features of the district that embodied Depression-era ideals of landscape conservation.[35]

To preserve Big Spring, the Park Service must pay attention to the historical as well as the natural features of a dramatic Ozarks landscape. Until the 1930s, Big Spring had never been developed for residential or commercial use. In an attempt to preserve the spring, federal relief workers blocked the flow of a river, channeled the Spring Branch, and created a mountain retreat for tourists. Clearly, they did not take a "hands-off" approach to preservation of wild lands. Equally clearly, the architects and engineers who planned the CCC projects demonstrated respect for the natural landscape. The placement of buildings and structures, the use of native materials, and the insistence upon high ideals of craftsmanship all testified to their outlook. New generations of park designers and managers could do much worse than to follow the example of their predecessors.

Old Faithful, Roaring River Hills, and Big Spring provide compelling examples of the ways in which natural landscapes enrich our human experience and stimulate our imagination. In the 1870s, the reliable geyser became an icon of the engine-driven, clock-regulated emergence of a great industrial nation. Roaring River Hills remained blessedly obscure and unappreciated until ecologists perceived a threat to the many species of plants and animals that thrived there. Big Spring acquired its special character in an era of cheap labor and ambitious public works programs. Now they have histories of their own that deserve to be recognized and preserved, but this will require an understanding of their cultural no less than their natural qualities.

Three important principles should guide the preservation of wild and scenic places. First, as Frank Waugh urged, we must strive to treat the natural landscape with reverence. Second, we should take a cue from the federal definition of wilderness as those places "where man himself is a visitor who does not remain."[36] We should behave like guests in these areas, remembering that polite guests do not invade someone else's home and start moving the furniture. Third, we need to accept the fact that the natural world inevitably evolves with the passage of time. Whenever possible, we should follow a hands-off policy, even if it means that time-honored views and other scenic qualities may disappear. Old Faithful may stop following our artificial schedule. Roaring River Hills may become a cedar grove until a lightning fire burns off the trees and re-creates an open glade. Similarly, the Current River may eventually leap out of its banks and cover Big Spring, but in this case we should respectfully maintain the park created by our forebears until that natural event occurs.

There is a saying in the Ozarks: "This axe has been in our family for four generations. We only replaced the handle five times and the blade twice." In a throwaway society, this viewpoint strikes people as odd. Why not just buy a new axe? But the problem lies with the throwaway society, not with the Ozarkers' notions of conservation and continuity. A preservationist might argue that after the handle has been replaced, the axe lacks integrity, and any real connection with the past has been broken. But the family truly believes, and with some justification, that the axe connects them with their roots.

This mountain homily provides the basis for a workable theory of landscape preservation. Traditional notions of saving original fabric and preventing future alterations might reasonably apply to a building or a work of art but cannot apply to a living landscape. The idea of restoring a piece of wild land back to a particular historical period and expecting it to remain there in a condition of stasis is absurd on the face of it. But landscapes, even wild ones, need our protection. If we cannot prevent them from changing, we can minimize human impacts upon them. Where humans have already encroached, we can try to understand the dialectic between the cultural and the natural world. We can respect the legacy of previous generations and pass it along, like the Ozarkers' axe, to those who come after us. A conflict between nature and history need not exist.

Notes

1. Cecelia Tichi, "Pittsburgh at Yellowstone: Old Faithful and the Pulse of Industrial America," *American History* 9 (fall 1997): 531.

2. Ibid., 522–23.

3. John R. Stilgoe, *Common Landscape of America, 1580 to 1845* (New Haven, Conn.: Yale University Press, 1982), 12.

4. Aldo Leopold, "Wilderness as a Form of Land Use" (1925), in *The River of the Mother of God and Others Essays by Aldo Leopold,* ed. Susan L. Flader and J. Baird Callicott (Madison: University of Wisconsin Press, 1991), 135.

5. Ibid.

6. Linda Flint McClelland, *Building the National Parks: Historic Landscape Design and Construction* (Baltimore: Johns Hopkins University Press, 1998), 474–75.

7. William Cronon, "The Riddle of the Apostle Islands," *Orion* 22 (May-June 2003): 39–40.

8. John Karel, "The Hills of Roaring River: How Shall We Love Them?" Missouri Parks Association, *Heritage* 19 (November 2001): 3–6.

9. Aldo Leopold, *A Sand County Almanac with Other Essays on Conservation from Round River,* rev. ed. (1949; New York: Oxford University Press, 1966), 264–65.

10. Karel, "The Hills of Roaring River," 4.

11. Leopold, *Sand County Almanac,* 261.

12. "Reforestation Unit to Camp at Big Spring," *Current Local* (Van Buren, Mo.), 25 May 1933, 1.

13. "Is Our Greatest Spring Endangered?" *St. Louis Globe-Democrat,* 29 May 1933, reprinted in the *Current Local,* 1 June 1933, 1.

14. James M. Denny and Bonnie Wright (Stepenoff), "E.C.W. Architecture in Missouri State Parks, 1933–1942," thematic nomination, National Register of Historic Places, 1985.

15. "Reforestation Coming to Big Spring State Park," *Current Local,* 15 June 1933, 1.

16. "Reforestation Unit Like Big Spring as Camp Site," *Current Local,* 22 June and 27 July 1933, 1, 2.

17. McClelland, *Building the National Parks,* provides a comprehensive account of the history and philosophy of the Park Service regarding the natural landscape.

18. Frank A. Waugh, *The Natural Style in Landscape Gardening* (Boston: Richard G. Badger, 1917), 28. Concerning Waugh, see Charles A. Birnbaum and Robin Karson, eds., *Pioneers of American Landscape Design* (New York: McGraw-Hill, 2000), 434–36; and Katherine Crewe, "The Rural Landscapes of Frank Waugh," *Landscape Journal* 22: 2 (2003): 126–39.

19. Frank A. Waugh, *Landscape Conservation* (Washington, D.C.: National Park Service, 1935), 2.

20. "Big Spring State Park, Semi-Monthly Progress Report," 13 October 1933, CCC File #25; "Easement for the Purpose of Erecting and Maintaining Dikes for the Protection of the Big Spring Park," 16 December 16, 1933, both National Park Service, Ozark National Scenic Riverways, Van Buren, Mo. (hereafter ONSR).

21. Floyd Downey, interview by Warren Snyder, Van Buren, Mo., July 1981, ONSR.

22. "Dikes Nearing Completion," *Current Local,* 10 May 1934, 1.

23. "Old English Architecture for Big Spring State Park," *St. Louis Post-Dispatch,* 19 June 1934.

24. Leo Anderson, interview by Warren E. Snyder, 5 March 1979, transcript, ONSR.

25. "NPS, Big Spring State Park, Monthly Progress Report," 13 October 1933, file #25, ONSR.

26. Ibid.

27. "News from Company 1710," *Current Local,* 17 September 1936, 1, and 15 October 1936, 1.

28. "News from Company 1710," 17 September 1936.

29. Bonnie Stepenoff, "The Big Spring Historic District: The Civilian Conservation Corps Builds a State Park to Last," National Park Service Ozark National Scenic Riverways, Van Buren, Mo., 2003, 17.

30. Freeman Tilden, *State Parks: Their Meaning in American Life* (New York: Alfred A. Knopf, 1962), 263.

31. Ibid., 267.

32. Ibid.

33. Joseph Jaeger, interview by author, Jefferson City, Mo., 1 October 2002.

34. On 27 August 1964, President Johnson signed the law establishing the ONSR. Five years later, in 1969, the Missouri State Park Board signed documents giving the three parks to the Park Service. The story of the creation of the ONSR has been told several times in print. See Stephen N. Limbaugh, "The Origin and Development of the Ozark National Scenic Riverways Project," *Missouri Historical Review* 91 (January 1997): 121–32; Will Sarvis, "A Difficult Legacy: Creation of the Ozark National Scenic Riverways," *Public Historian* 24 (winter 2002): 31–52; and Donald L. Stevens Jr., "Ozark National Scenic Riverways: Another Perspective," *Public Historian* 24 (spring 2002): 83–88.

35. Stepenoff, "Big Spring Historic District," 1–26.

36. McClelland, *Building the National Parks,* 474–75.

PART II

Balancing Change and Continuity

6. Mediating Ecology and History

Rehabilitation of Vegetation in Oklahoma's Platt Historic District

HEIDI HOHMANN

OVER the past decade, the National Park Service's *Guidelines for the Treatment of Cultural Landscapes* has defined landscape preservation methodology.[1] Despite the advancement in historic landscape preservation that this document represents, challenges remain in effectively bridging the gap between nature and culture and in incorporating ecological principles into landscape treatment. In their current form, the guidelines contribute to those challenges.

One area in which the problem is particularly apparent is the guidelines' approach to vegetation. Following general landscape preservation practices, they focus primarily on vegetation from a structural standpoint (vegetation as physical fabric), not an ecosystem standpoint (vegetation as living material, dependent on other systems). The prevailing practice is partly due to the limitations of using "character-defining features" as a theoretical base for treatment. A feature by definition is a "structure, form, or appearance," a definition that does not accommodate the more complex systematic relationships of nature. The guidelines also offer few large-scale examples, focusing instead on smaller, designed landscapes, where concerns of ecology are less important. In addition, the guidelines are biased toward propagation or additive actions. This premise comes from the historical orientation of historic preservation practice, where removal is equivalent to a loss of fabric. When dealing with living systems, however, there may be situations where wholesale removal is required. Yet another problem is the guidelines' apparent prejudice toward change for human needs such as access, use, or understanding. However, the guidelines rarely address change in response to biotic needs or ecosystem health. Finally, the guidelines seldom address ongoing management in terms of ecological process. Rather, they reveal an architectural legacy of replace-in-kind, ignoring processes such as growth and death. If, as ecologist Joan Nassauer states, "[l]andscapes are more like children than works of art. They require tending, not making," then preservationists need to focus less on one-time repair and more on cyclical replacement and management.[2] In addition, landscape preservationists might also consider for what ends they are managing: historical accuracy, visual appearance, ecosystem health and structure, or something else entirely.

Granted, some strides have been made toward addressing ecology in landscape preservation, primarily through Ian Firth's *Biotic Cultural Resources* (1985).[3] However, this short document focuses on evaluation of integrity and does not address treatment in a substantive way. Only six pages of text are devoted to management and maintenance, with much of that text describing agricultural systems, not naturalized or wilderness landscapes. In 1999, Firth created an eighteen-page addendum, but again little of this text is devoted to treatment standards.

A recent planning project at the former Platt National Park in Oklahoma provides an instructive case study by which to explore some of these "natural" problems in cultural landscape preservation and to examine how we might revise treatment practices to encompass and integrate ecological ideas more effectively.

The Platt Historic District

The Platt Historic District is a 928-acre historic designed landscape located in the Chickasaw National Recreation Area (CNRA) in south-central Oklahoma (Figure 6.1). Located near the town of Sulphur, Platt National Park was initially known as Sulphur Springs Reservation, which was established in 1902 through an agreement with the Chickasaw and Choctaw nations as a means to protect the area's mineral springs. Until 1932, development of the park focused on building springhouses, campgrounds, and comfort stations to accommodate visitors' use of the healing waters. Then, during the Depression, the park was almost completely remade by the Civilian Conservation Corps (CCC), following the tenets of rustic design propagated by the Park Service between the world wars (Figure 6.2). Completed around 1940, the project included spring pavilions constructed of local stone, automobile campgrounds, roads and trails, elaborate picnic areas, dams, waterfalls, and naturalistic swimming holes. After World War II, park use shifted from visitors' appreciation of the medicinal springs to more active recreation, and in 1976 the park was united with the Arbuckle Recreation Area to become the CNRA.

Today, the Platt District is considered primarily significant under National Register criterion C as a distinctive example of Park Service rustic architectural and landscape design, with a period of significance of 1932 to 1940. The Platt District has been well maintained and retains a relatively high degree of integrity. All major historic structures are extant, and the only substantial changes were the addition of several Mission 66 structures, including a nature center and new comfort stations. In contrast, less attention has been paid to the park's vegetation, perhaps because of ongoing assumptions about its historical vegetation patterns.

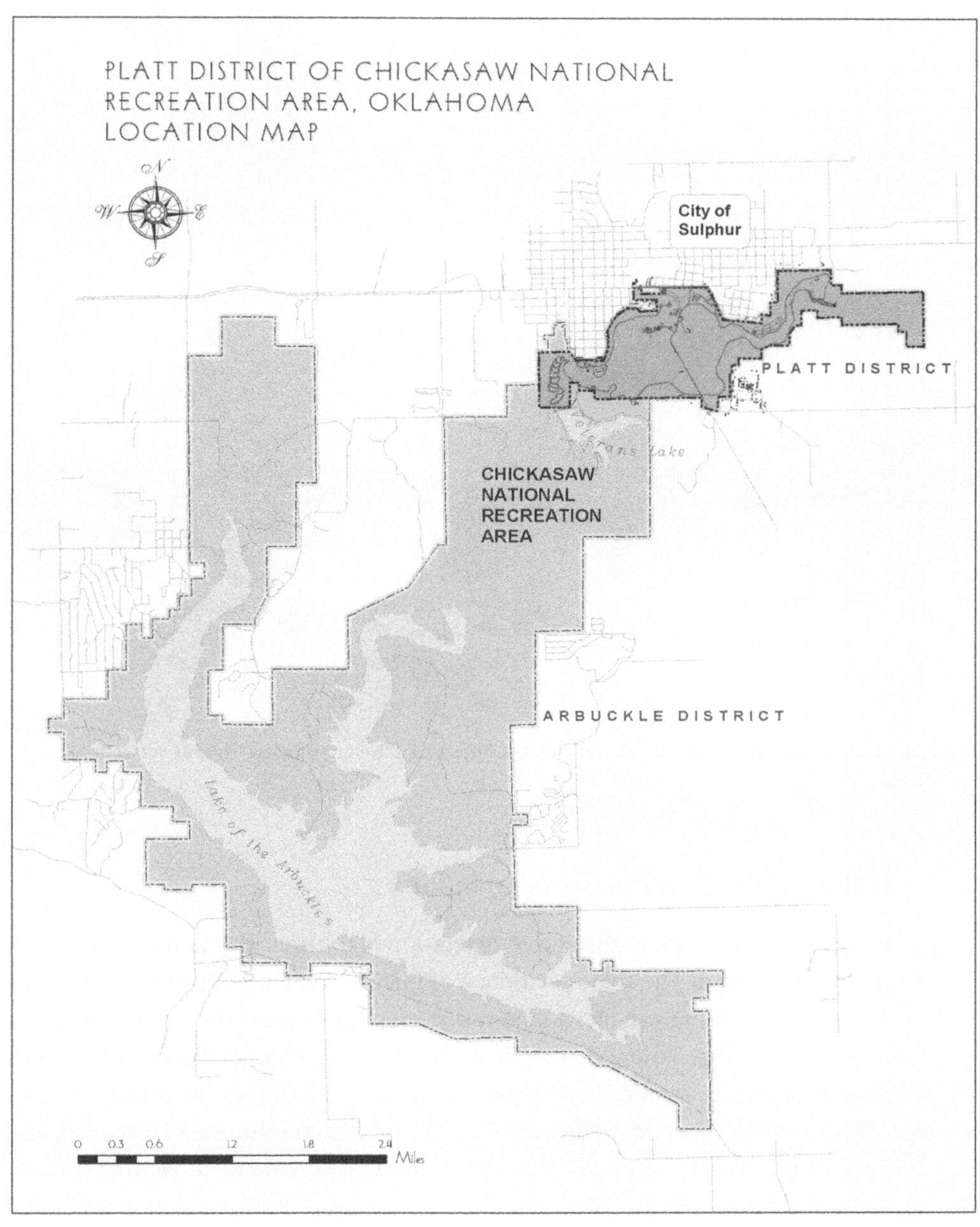

Figure 6.1. Map of Chickasaw National Recreation Area (CNRA), near Sulphur, Oklahoma, showing Platt Historic District. Drafted by author.

Figure 6.2. Picnic shelter, Platt Historic District, ca. 1936. Photograph by author, 2001. Courtesy of National Park Service.

History of the Platt District's Vegetation

Early information about the native vegetation of the area now known as the Platt District is limited. The major evidence of historic vegetation prior to the park's designation comes from 1871 and 1897 plat maps and surveyors' notes from work conducted by the General Land Office. The plat maps generally show the area's stream valleys as wooded and depict the balance of the area as grassland. Surveyors' notes further describe the district's timber as composed of red, post, and black oaks; elms; sycamores; hickories; and ashes. Upland areas were characterized as "rolling," "rocky," "first-rate," or "second rate" prairie. Such graphic and written descriptions indicate that the early, and perhaps pre-European, settlement vegetation of the area was a combination of wooded ravines and upland savanna landscape. Savanna grasslands are transitional ecosystems existing between deciduous forests and grasslands, in which understory grassland exists with overstory climax species. The earliest photographs of the site, made around 1900, also typically depict a savanna landscape of open prairie with scattered trees (Figure 6.3).

Figure 6.3. Platt Historic District, showing large oaks that once comprised part of the park's original oak-hickory savanna landscape. Photograph ca. 1920. Courtesy of National Park Service.

Detailed, site-level evidence of early maps and photographs also corresponds with regional floristic studies of the nearby Arbuckle Mountains. For example, ecologist W. E. Bruner located the Arbuckle Mountains region within the oak-hickory savanna, a region "characterized by a scrubby growth of oaks usually associated with hickory."[4] A description written six years after the park's establishment indicated that out of the then 848 acres, woodland constituted 200 acres, and grassland 500 acres. The major woodland species included a rich mix of oak, elm, hickory, black walnut, persimmon, hackberry, box elder, willow, redbud, cottonwood, sycamore, plum, ash, acacia, pecan, linden, bois d'arc, red cedar, black locust, honey locust, mulberry, wild cherry, black haw, red haw, and dogwood.[5] Though grassland clearly constituted the dominant vegetation cover, there is no accompanying description of its various species or their character or distribution in the park.

Early park management was limited and focused on protecting the existing forest, probably due to the high aesthetic and cultural values associated with trees. Techniques included fire suppression and exclusion of livestock. In 1909, the first of many recommendations to reforest the park was made. Both deciduous and, interestingly, given their absence from early plant surveys, evergreen (red cedar) trees were used, but the results were poor due to vandalism.[6] At the same time, some natural regeneration of oak, walnut, ash, and elm began to occur, and it was hoped that the "denuded" areas would be "reforested without further efforts." Such statements would seem to indicate that from the early years of the park establishment reforestation was a primary vegetation management goal.

By the 1930s, however, management had created a park landscape that was "overgrown with weeds, vines, brush and trees, some . . . dead and dying, presenting a very untidy . . . appearance."[7] In response to these conditions, the CCC established a vegetation management program with two major objectives: "first, the protection and rejuvenation of the existing vegetation insofar as possible," and second, "to replenish and re-establish the deforested areas," this latter goal despite the fact that the "deforested areas" were likely originally grasslands.[8]

To improve "the general conditions of the park vegetation," five types of new plantings were implemented: reforestation plantings, ornamental plantings, nursery plantings, boundary plantings, and protective plantings. Reforestation plantings, with the intent to return the park to its "original conditions" and to "strengthen the design," were the top priority.[9] Park officials never strictly defined their notions of the park's "original" conditions, likely because the landscape had sustained enough change that its pre-park state was difficult to determine. However, it appears that managers believed that the park had been considerably more wooded than it was in the early 1930s.

As a result, between 1933 and 1935 alone, over 500,000 trees and shrubs were planted as part of reforestation efforts (Figure 6.4). Red cedar was the major species used, yet it is unclear why. Although red cedar is native to the region, it was not common in the park, and its use may have been dictated by low cost and ready availability from local farmers. At carefully designed spring pavilions, cedars were primarily used to create a sense of spatial enclosure. On the steepest slopes, erosion control plantings of red cedar were made because of the presence of several large existing cedars and an unsubstantiated idea that "at one time this whole area was covered with large cedars." Cedars were also planted as a fire control method. Because the designers thought that grass fires were dangerous, difficult to control, and "very detrimental to the natural growth in the park," cedars were planted to divide broad grassland areas.[10]

In 1937, park managers undertook a comprehensive vegetation survey, revealing that both woodland and grasslands were important cover types at that time. Maps and aerial photographs reveal that in 1940 there were approximately 240 acres of woodland and 680 acres of grassland (Figure 6.5).[11] Yet, pride was taken in efforts "to return much of the open area to what is probably very like its original condition by planting many seedlings of eastern red cedar."[12] By 1940, grassland possessed little economic or aesthetic value to park managers; rather, it was seen as hazardous and unwanted. Fire was suppressed and reforestation encouraged. These ideas, commonly accepted in the 1930s, indicate a lack of understanding of ecological processes in prairie communities and resulted in the gradual decline and loss of grassland within the district.

Figure 6.4. CCC crew planting trees and shrubs in the park's prairie uplands. Photograph ca. 1933. Courtesy of National Park Service.

World War II ushered in years of benign neglect for the Platt District. With minor exceptions, virtually no widespread vegetation management was undertaken after 1940. In the 1950s, fire suppression and the elimination of other natural disturbances began to cause prairie degradation, and by 1965 the slow invasion of woody vegetation into the grassland was noted (Figure 6.6)[13] Thirty-five years

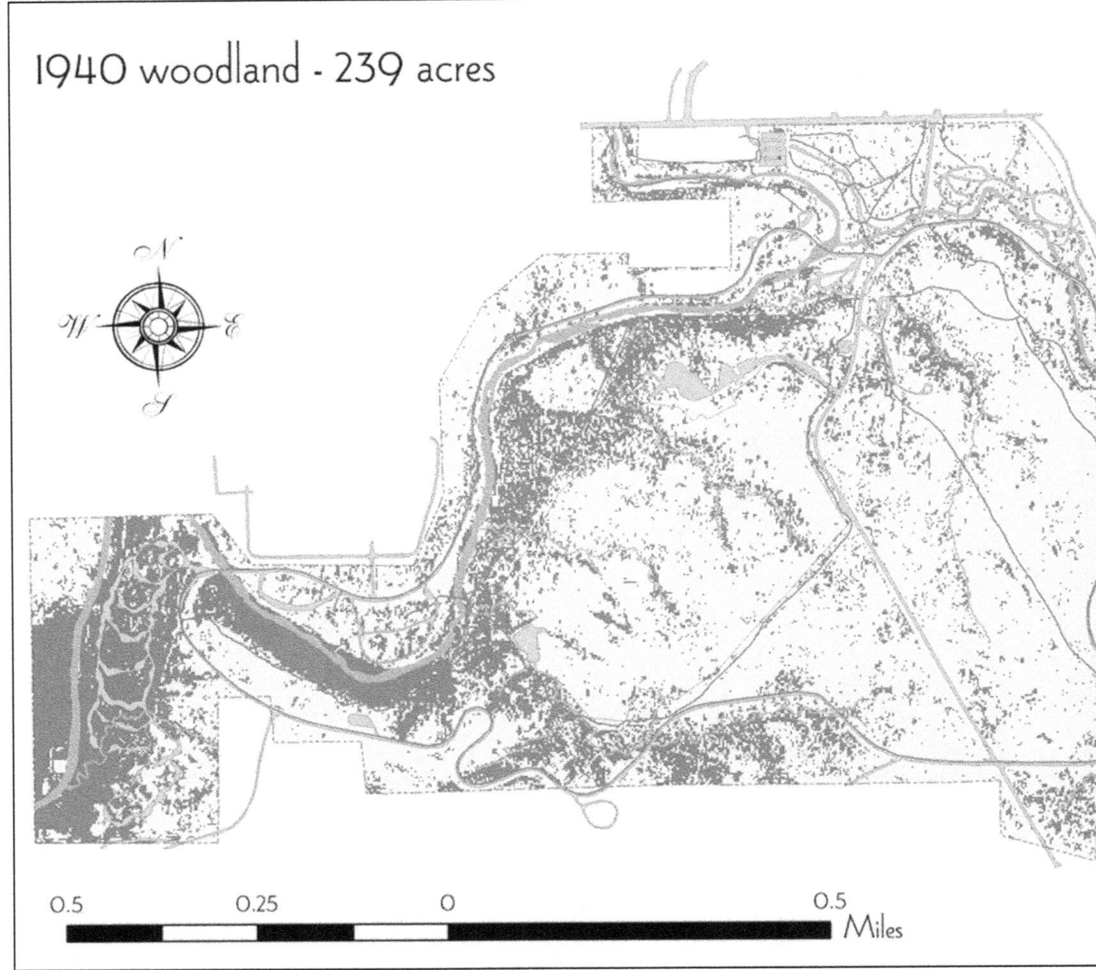

Figure 6.5. Map of Platt Historic District, showing vegetative cover as of 1940, based on aerial photograph analysis. Image by author.

later, policies of minimal management and fire suppression resulted in a significant loss of grassland within the park, as evident through a Geographic Information Systems (GIS) analysis of plant cover, based on aerial photographs dating to 1940 and 1999. Today grassland covers approximately 180 acres, and forest about 740 (Figure 6.7). Grasslands are small and weedy, and much of the park's forest is invasive red cedar, the offspring of the original "conservation" plantings. This forest, which appears "natural," expands rapidly, lacks ecological diversity, forms a visually dense and aesthetically unappealing environment for visitors, and poses fire control issues for the adjacent community. There has, in general, been a loss of the presumed climax forest species (oak and other hardwood) in favor of cedar and weedier colonization species such as sugarberry *(Celtis laevigata)*.[14]

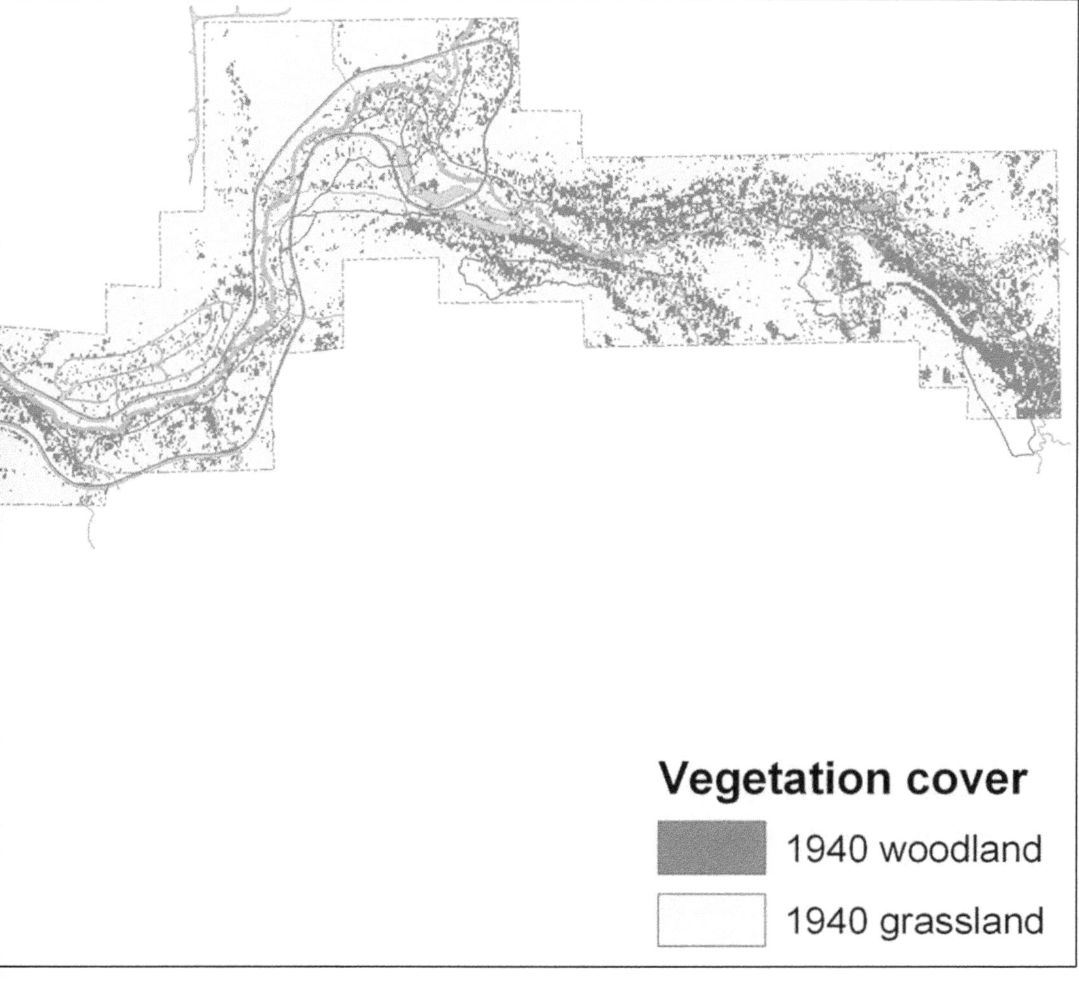

Yet, regardless of its ecological "unsuitability" or "infidelity," the extant forest might be considered historically significant as the manifestation of the retrospectively misinformed idea to reforest the park.

Preservation Treatments

In 2000, I began a cultural landscape report for the Platt District.[15] Given the high integrity of the historic district and given park officials' desire to depict the ongoing evolution of the property over time, "preservation"—in the strict sense of that term, as defined by the Park Service—was recommended as the basic treatment for the district as a whole.[16] "Preservation" is an appropriate choice since

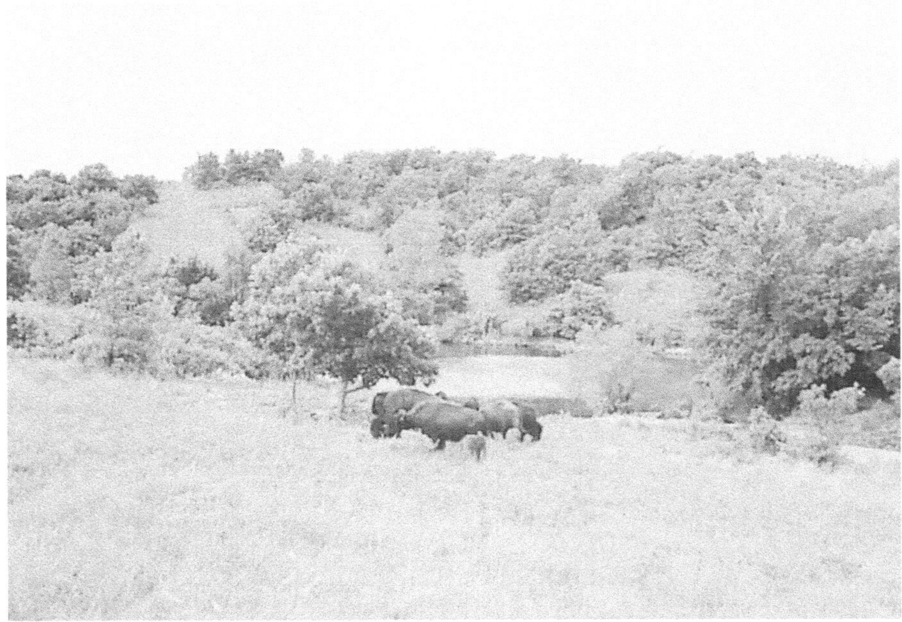

Figure 6.6. Early encroachment of vegetation into open grasslands in the park. Photograph ca. 1940. Courtesy of National Park Service.

features, materials, and spaces are intact. At the same time, focusing just on the period of significance is not desirable, because changes made since that time are considerable. Bringing the district's infrastructure back to its 1940 state would require both significant reconstruction of features as well as demolition of others. However, within the overall preservation treatment, it is possible to restore some individual features, an important consideration for some of the significant CCC structures in the park.

At the request of park officials, vegetation management in the district was addressed separately, primarily because of perceived degradation of forest and grassland resources. This degradation was distinguished by visual density, reduced vigor of climax species, and a lack of species diversity in forest areas, as well as by the loss of grassland and the loss of ornamental plantings.

Historical research revealed that the five types of vegetation described above were implemented during the period of significance. Treatments for ornamental plantings, such as foundation plantings and significant specimen trees, and for structural plantings, such as boundary screens, were easily accommodated within the existing framework set up by the *Guidelines for the Treatment of Cultural Landscapes.* The guidelines generally treat vegetation as built form, making it easy to formulate recommendations for vegetative features that create spatial or decorative effects in the landscape. On the whole, significant extant ornamental plantings—foundation plantings, flower beds, specimen trees in park-like areas—were addressed as features within individual component landscapes "nested" in the district. They are therefore generally proposed to be retained and rejuvenated through pruning and fertilizing. Conversely, severely degraded plantings were generally proposed to be replaced in kind, but only if documentation exists to replace them.

Making a decision on the treatment best for "naturalized" woodland and grassland vegetation was more difficult. Given the extent and history of the site's vegetation and poor health, it was not clear how existing treatment definitions would apply. The project team initially examined two options: either restoration or preservation, both based on federal standards.

Restoration, of course, is based on substantial documentary evidence to return a landscape to its appearance and condition at a specific point in time, and is undertaken when the historical significance of the landscape at that period in time considerably outweighs the loss of material from other periods. When applied to the Platt District, restoration would dictate returning the vegetation to its 1940 conditions, when grassland dominated. It appears that sufficient evidence (1940 aerial photographs, still photographs, and the 1937 vegetation documentation) exists to do so. A restoration to 1940 conditions would require the removal of hundreds of acres of existing cedar forests to create open grassland areas. In addition, restoration would necessitate retaining or replanting the red cedar buffers originally planted to screen boundaries and create firebreaks.

While restoration would presumably create a historically accurate physical appearance, it is problematic from other standpoints. First, a restoration to 1940 conditions does not consider the designers' intent to create a forest and an enclosed landscape and would institute a far more open and different landscape than the designers sought with their interventions. Of course, replanted vegetation such as screens and buffers could be allowed to grow, but that choice poses difficult issues: At what point should the vegetation be arrested? And how does this point of time and appearance relate to the period of significance? In other words, a restoration treatment would not just simply "turn back time," but would also "restart the clock," beginning again the cycle of historical growth. While such a treatment might be appropriate for replanting a hedge on a twenty-year cycle, its appropriateness for the Platt District's extensive naturalized vegetation is less clear. Reliving the great "sixty-year cedar invasion" does not seem to be productive either in terms of re-creating historic appearance or in terms of a functioning ecological grassland and forest mosaic. Of course, this conundrum is intensified by the fact that the original desire to create forest across the park landscape was misguided, based on a subsequently invalidated idea of what "natural" or "original" conditions were.

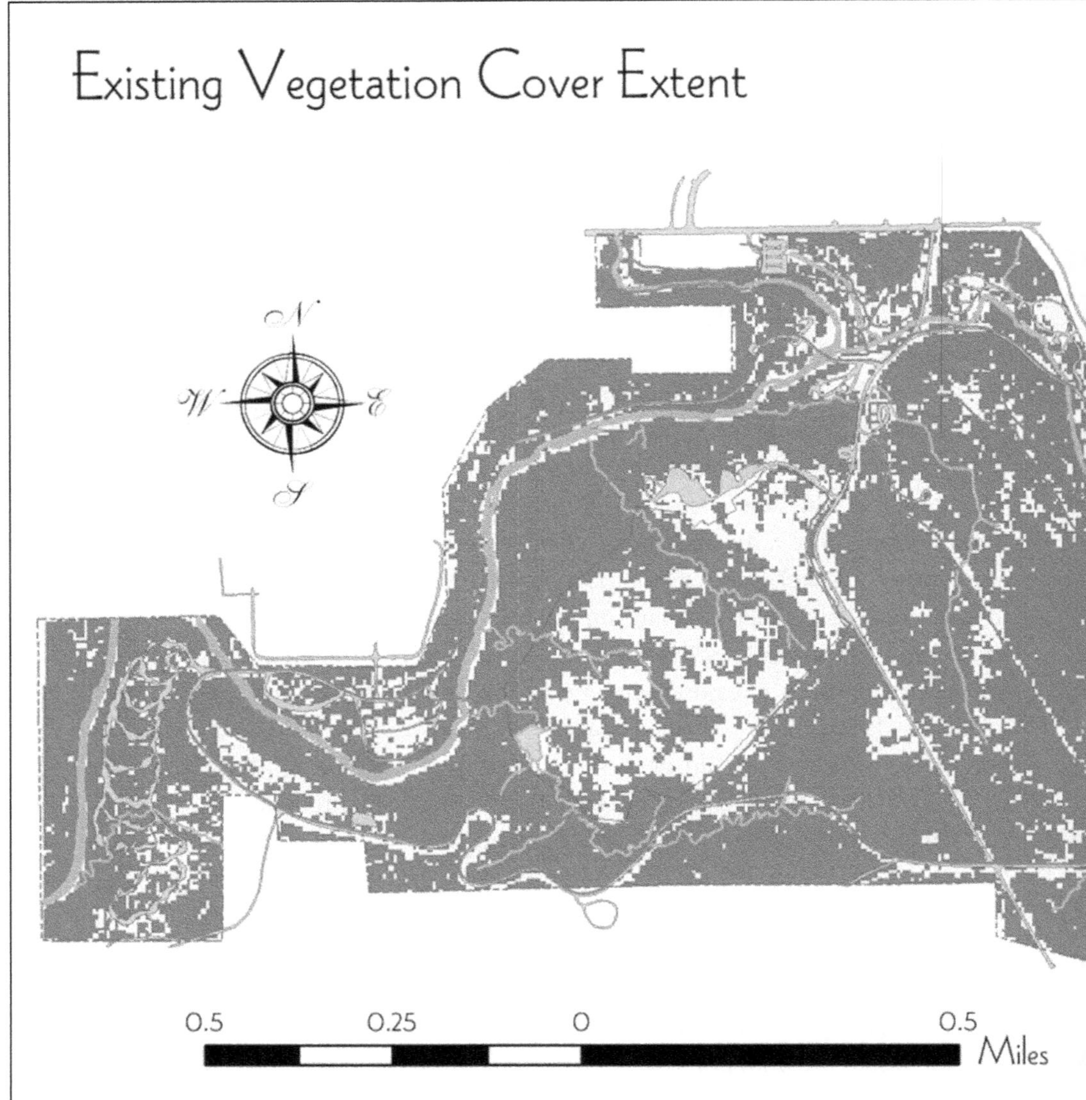

Figure 6.7. Map of Platt Historic District as of 1999, showing increase of woodlands to 81 percent of land from 26 percent in 1940. Image by author.

Preservation of the vegetation—keeping forest and grassland in their current configuration and conditions—might also seem appropriate, especially given the proposed overall preservation treatment for the landscape. Despite the fact that preservation of vegetation (a living, growing entity) seems to be a contradiction in terms, one interpretation of preservation for the Platt District would be simply to arrest vegetation in its current state.[17] This approach would require extensive pruning, future monitoring, and cutting of new seedlings in order to

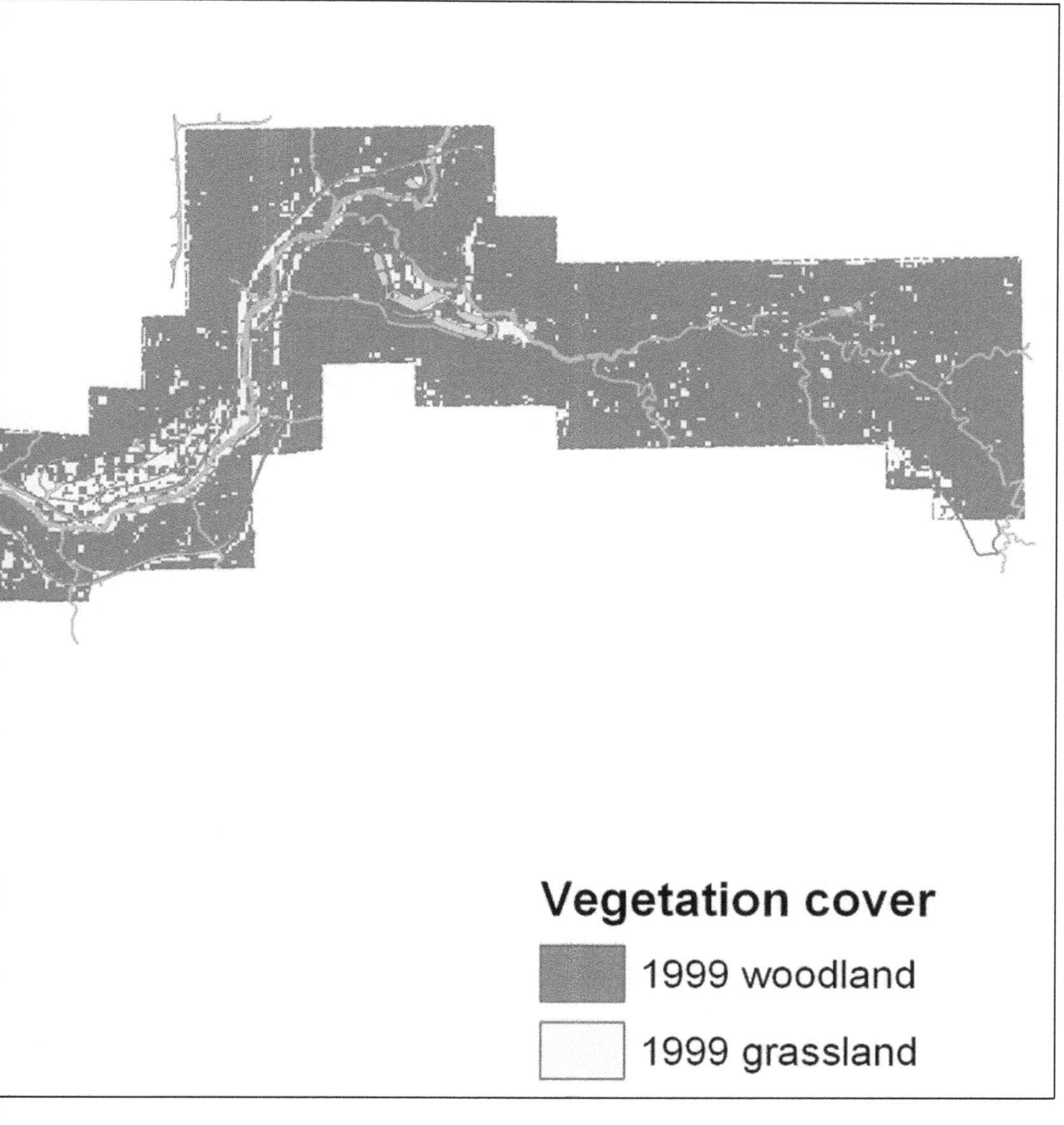

retain 2004 conditions and prevent additional cedar invasion. Such management would be cost- and labor-intensive and raises the question of whether the effort would be justified to retain a condition that is neither historically significant nor an improvement in the ecological status of the vegetation.

Alternatively, preservation may be interpreted as simply letting the existing conditions of vegetative release continue. While this would require minimal cost and effort, it would permit, if not promote, continuing enclosure and cedar invasion, again creating a situation where vegetation is neither historically appropriate nor ecologically functional. Thus, both interpretations of preservation are unsatisfactory, creating historically inaccurate appearances and dysfunctional ecological systems. In other words, preservation does not provide much benefit other than, possibly, ease of management. In fact, preservation, often seen as an "easy" or "low-impact" treatment, could encourage, from a systems standpoint, continued degradation.

Revising Rehabilitation to Accommodate Ecology

When restoration and preservation are inappropriate, rehabilitation is the next logical consideration. Perhaps because rehabilitation can become a "suspect" treatment of expediency—a label thrown on a project when historic fabric must be destroyed in favor of development—it has been the most restrictively defined treatment. A review of the guidelines indicates that four actions are acceptable for vegetation under rehabilitation: (1) identification and retention of historic vegetation (examples are mostly documentation and propagation of individuals for genetic diversity), (2) protection and maintenance of existing and historic vegetation (what we might call "repair," such as rejuvenating pruning), (3) altering vegetation for a new use (such as adding a vegetative screen), or (4) replacement of deteriorated or missing historic vegetation (it should be noted that removing vegetation and not replacing it is cited as a nonexemplary treatment).[18]

The limited nature of these actions is, I argue, derived from an emphasis in this treatment on human use. If rehabilitation means that change can be accommodated when human use is valued, this practice makes sense for architectural features, yet it overly confines our ways of treating and conceptualizing treatment of landscapes and living systems. If, in addition to acknowledging the importance of human values, landscape preservation acknowledged the importance of ecological values, then rehabilitation might become a different and more useful treatment. The field might, for example, take a page from the practice of ecological restoration, which indicates that if an "ideal" state cannot be restored, then it might be restored or managed for other aspects, such as biological diversity, ecosystem health, or ecosystem function.[19]

For the Platt District, an ecologically based rehabilitation of vegetation could be designed to create a self-sustainable and stable system (Figure 6.8). To accomplish this, former grasslands would be returned to their previous condition by mechanically removing red cedar from large parts of the park. A prescribed cyclical burn would be instituted to maintain these grasslands. Historic screening—ornamental and enclosure plantings—would be retained, but other planted and free-seeded cedars would be removed and not replanted to reduce, if not eliminate, propagation of this invasive plant. This rehabilitation would not strictly duplicate a historic condition related to significance or the period of significance. While it would create a condition close in appearance and aesthetics to 1940, it would be significantly different in terms of intent, since the original designers wished to reforest the area. In some respects this rehabilitation could be considered an anachronistic treatment in that it would "return" the area to something closer to a pre-park condition, one that never coexisted with the extant historical structures and that is not related to their significance. However, despite the historical "problems" with this treatment, gains in terms of the district's ecology would be great. Biodiversity in the landscape would be increased, an ecosystem native to the area would be returned, and the "restored" grassland would be more easily and less expensively maintained through periodic burning.

Incorporating Ecology into Landscape Preservation Treatment

Landscape preservation has yet to incorporate ecological principles substantively into practice. Despite many similarities, ecological restoration and landscape preservation have remained largely separate endeavors, with distinct literatures and methodologies. This separation may be due to the fact that the fields often work at different scales (e.g., garden vs. ecosystem), have different goals (re-creating "history" vs. re-creating "nature"), and have different origins (humanities vs. science; academia vs. government).

While I make no claims that the vegetative rehabilitation project for the Platt District is an "ecological restoration," it does show how much landscape preservation might learn from that process. Since the 1960s, ecologists have focused their restorations on technical performance—structural replication, species composition—and on functions, such as wetland filtration and their effectiveness, especially with respect to their benefit to current human needs. Ecologists have also considered economics.[20] They have, in a sense, developed multiple ways to design and evaluate their efforts. In contrast, landscape preservation has considered and defined only one yardstick of success, that of historic appearance. Has landscape preservation perhaps overemphasized historical appearance and human use over other concerns? Should historical restorations of landscapes only look and feel historic? Should they also function historically? Should they function sustainably? How do we make trade-offs between historical accuracy and biodiversity? By beginning to incorporate ecological ideas and principles in a more rigorous way, we may begin to solve some of our conceptual, technical, and methodological roadblocks, or at least bring some light to the dark corners of our practice.

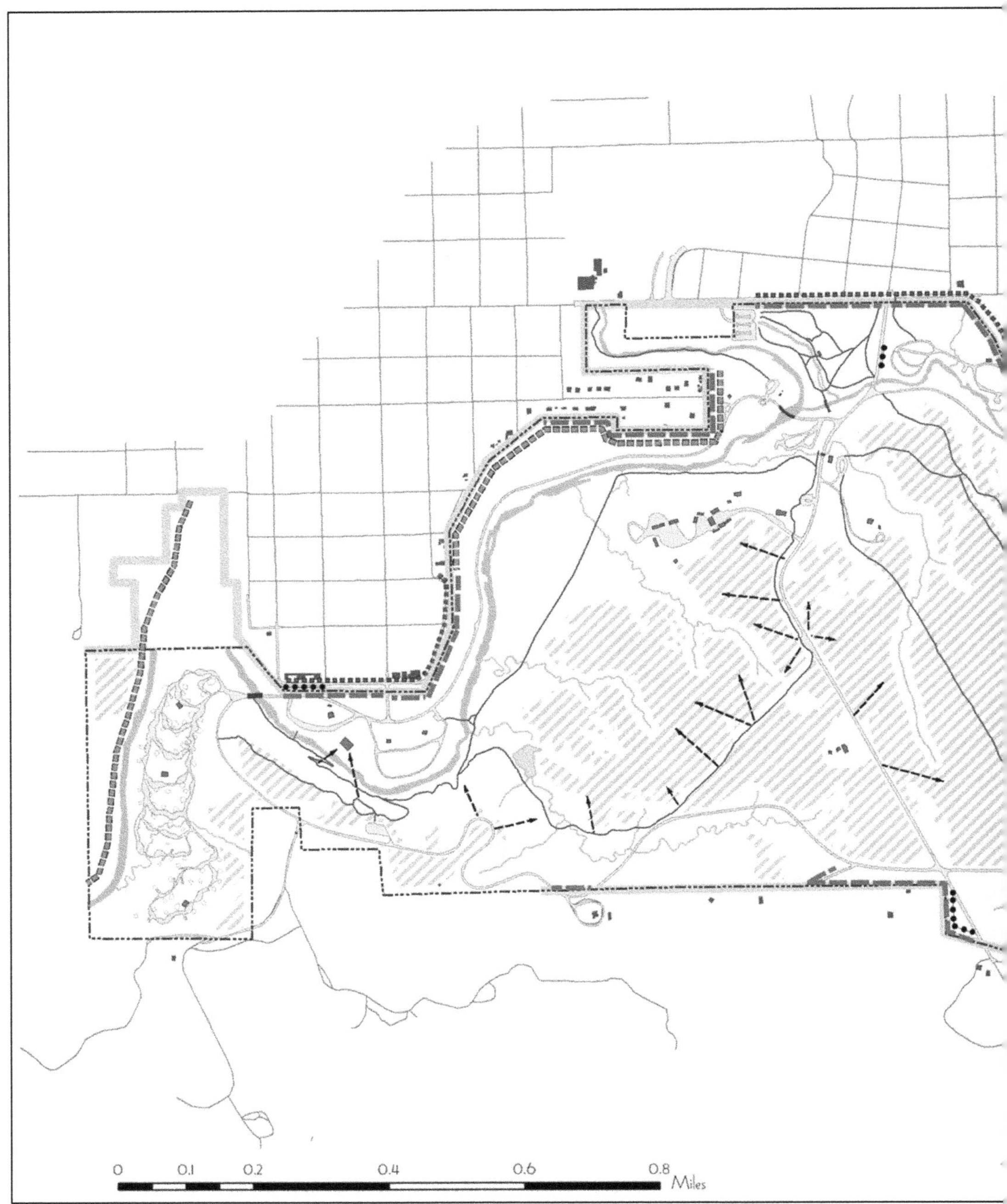

Figure 6.8. Plan for an "ecological rehabilitation" of Platt Historic District, with proposed grassland rehabilitation areas hatched. Image by author.

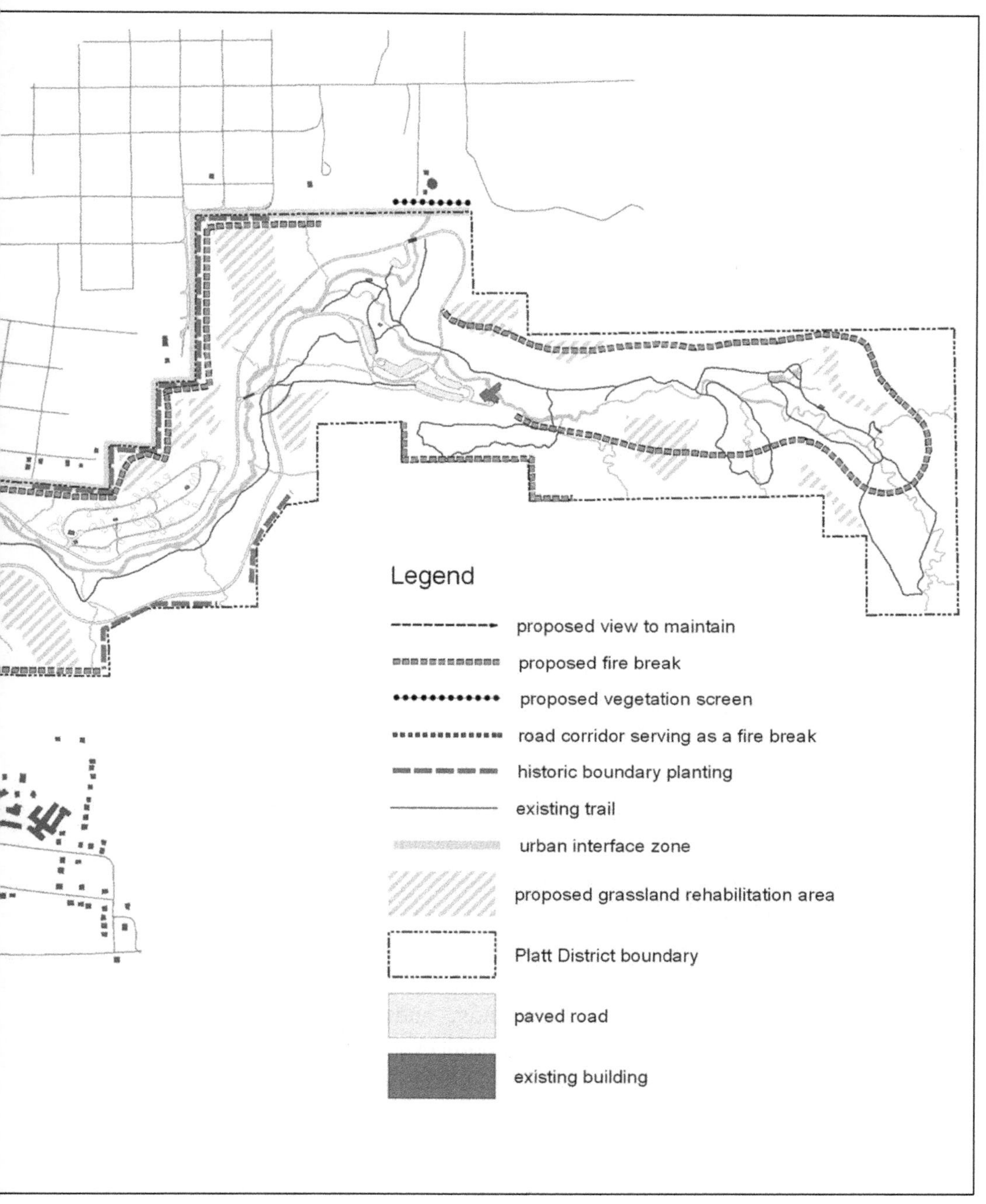

Legend
proposed view to maintain
proposed fire break
proposed vegetation screen
road corridor serving as a fire break
historic boundary planting
existing trail
urban interface zone
proposed grassland rehabilitation area
Platt District boundary
paved road
existing building

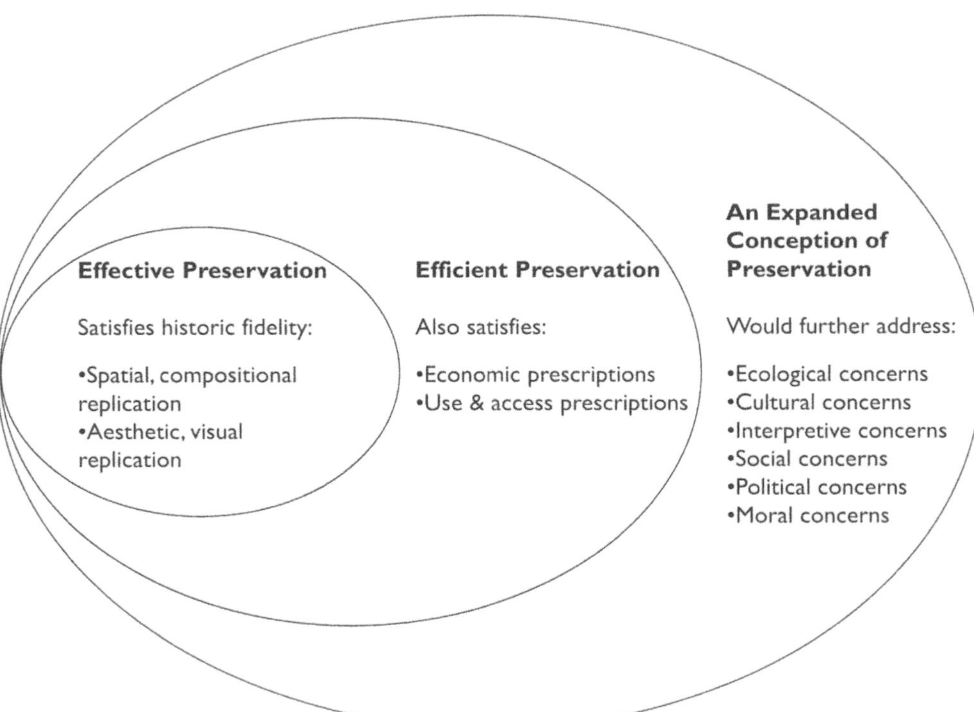

Figure 6.9. Model for an expanded conception of good historic landscape preservation, based on Higgs's model, to address values and needs, such as ecological issues, not addressed in current guidelines.

At the same time, ecological restoration has its own blind spots. Historically this practice has had a bias toward restoring "nature" as presettlement or prehuman conditions. Such a bias does not acknowledge the role that human interaction has had on the landscape.[21] Yet as the field has recognized this bias, realizing that "nature" is actually a cultural term, a strong internal critique of the field has developed.[22] Ecological restoration has begun to discuss conflicting values in restoration, including social, political, moral, and aesthetic values.[23] In fact, there has been a call for an "expanded conception of good ecological restoration" that addresses ecological fidelity (structure, function, durability), efficiency (economic prescriptions), and values (historical, cultural, social, political, moral, aesthetic).[24]

No such strong internal critique exists in landscape preservation. Yet it seems that historic landscape preservation might benefit from an "expanded conception of good historic preservation treatment," one that begins to address in an explicit manner some of the other values we address when treating cultural landscapes (Figure 6.9). While we have focused on the primacy of historical values in treatment to great effect in the past twenty years of practice, we have downplayed the impacts other issues—including economics, universal access, ecology, and class—can have on the realities of treatment decisions. This essay begins to expand our conception of the role of ecological values in preservation; it is now perhaps time to begin examining, and acknowledging, the others.

Notes

1. Charles A. Birnbaum, ed., with Christine Capella Peters, *The Secretary of the Interior's Standards for the Treatment of Historic Properties with Guidelines for the Treatment of Cultural Landscapes* (Washington, D.C.: National Park Service, 1996).

2. Joan Iverson Nassauer, "Cultural Sustainability: Aligning Aesthetics with Ecology," in *Placing Nature: Culture and Landscape Ecology*, ed. Joan Iverson Nassauer (Washington, D.C.: Island Press, 1997), 76.

3. Ian Firth, *Biotic Cultural Resources: Management Considerations for Historic Districts in the National Park System, Southeast Region/Research/Resources/Management Report SER-82* (Atlanta: National Park Service, 1985). The second edition, with an addendum, was issued ca. 1999. The integrity discussion (p. 10) also focuses on making biotic resources "fit" the seven aspects of integrity. As revised, these aspects are location, setting, material (species composition), design (community organization), workmanship (management techniques), feeling, and association. Nowhere is function or health incorporated into this definition of integrity. There is an assumption that a system works if its composition and organization are present. But is this actually the case?

4. W. E. Bruner, "The Vegetation of Oklahoma," *Ecological Monographs* 1 (1931): 142.

5. A. R. Greene correspondence, included in "Superintendents' Monthly Reports, Platt National Park, 1907–1909," typescript, 146, Chickasaw National Recreation Area Archives, Sulphur, Okla. (hereafter CNRA).

6. Greene correspondence, 260–62.

7. Edmund B. Walkowiak, "Yearly Report: Conservation Work, First and Second Periods, May 27, 1933–March 31, 1934. Report to the Park Superintendent through the Resident Landscape Architect," typescript, 1934, n.p., CNRA.

8. Charles A. Richey and Walter D. Popham, "Report to the Chief Architect through the Superintendent of Platt National Park: Construction Report: Conservation Work, CCC Camp No. 808, May 16, 1933–April 1, 1934," typescript, 1934, 5, CNRA.

9. Richey and Popham, "Report to the Chief Architect," 5, 8.

10. Charles A. Richey and Jerome Miller, "Report to the Chief Architect through the Superintendent of Platt National Park: Construction Report: Conservation Work, CCC Camp No. 808, October 1, 1934–March 31, 1935," typescript, 1935, 4; Richey and Miller, "Report to the Chief Architect through the Superintendent of Platt National Park: Construction Report: Conservation Work, CCC Camp No. 808 (NPI), April 1–September 30, 1934," typescript, 1934, 4; N. E. Dole Jr., "The Vegetation Type Survey of Platt National Park," typescript, 1937, 16, all CNRA.

11. Katarzyna Grala, "Spatial Analysis for the Vegetation Management of the Platt District, Chickasaw National Recreation Area" (M.L.A. thesis, Iowa State University, draft, 2004), n.p.

12. Dole, "Vegetation Type Survey," 2.

13. E. E. Dale Jr., "Final Report on Vegetation and Microenvironments of Platt National Park," manuscript, 1965, 9, CNRA.

14. Heidi Hohmann and Katarzyna Grala, "Cultural Landscape Report for the Platt Historic District," 2004, 297, CNRA.

15. The "Cultural Landscape Report for the Platt Historic District" was conducted under the auspices of the National Park Service in 2003–04. This essay addresses one aspect of the cultural landscape report's recommendations.

16. The Park Service recognizes four treatments for historic properties: preservation, rehabilitation, restoration, and reconstruction. Preservation perpetuates "the existing form, integrity, and materials" of a landscape. Rehabilitation allows repairs, alterations, and additions to provide for a new, but compatible, use. Restoration accurately depicts "the form, features, and character" of a landscape at a specific historic period. Reconstruction re-creates a nonsurviving landscape; see Birnbaum, ed., *Guidelines*, 18, 48, 90.

17. Robert Cook, "Is Landscape Preservation an Oxymoron?" *George Wright Forum* 13: 1 (1996): 42–53.

18. Birnbaum, ed., *Guidelines*, 63–67.

19. Eric Higgs, "What Is Good Ecological Restoration?" *Conservation Biology* 11 (April 1997): 340.

20. Ibid., 338.

21. Ecologists have also tended to beg the question of whether what presettlement or prehuman conditions can actually be documented or known.

22. For one take on this subject, see Nassauer, "Cultural Sustainability," 65–83, as well as other essays in that anthology.

23. There are many writings on ecologists' struggles with these ideas. For a sampling, see Paul Gobster, "Visions of Nature: Conflict and Compatibility in Urban Park Restoration," *Landscape and Urban Planning* 56 (2001): 35–51; Nassauer, ed., *Placing Nature*; William R. Jordan III, *The Sunflower Forest: Ecological Restoration and the New Communion with Nature* (Berkeley: University of California Press, 2003); and Matthias Gross, *Inventing Nature: Ecological Restoration by Public Experiments* (Lanham, Md.: Lexington Books, 2003).

24. Higgs, "What Is Good Ecological Restoration?" 338–48.

7. A Continuum and Process Framework for Rural Historic Landscape Preservation

Revisiting Ebey's Landing on Whidby Island, Washington

NANCY D. ROTTLE

EBEY'S Landing National Historical Reserve on Whidbey Island, Washington, was established in 1978 to "preserve and protect a rural community which provides an unbroken historical record from nineteenth century exploration and settlement in Puget Sound to the present time." The fertile landscape of this 17,400-acre reserve—a National Park Service unit wherein the land remains primarily in private ownership—has supported farming and forestry since the 1850s. This legacy is evident in the spatial patterning of the landscape, an impressive collection of historic farmsteads and unbroken vistas across active agricultural fields (Figure 7.1). Because lands are still privately held, they are only partially protected through their reserve status and their listing on the National Register of Historic Places.

One of the first designated cultural landscapes, Ebey's Landing served as a testing ground for the development of landscape architect Robert Melnick's seminal work *Cultural Landscapes: Rural Historic Districts in the National Park System.*[1] The report proposed a set of criteria for documenting rural landscapes to conserve their signature elements more effectively. In 1983 the buildings and landscape of Ebey's Landing were inventoried according to this new method, which then existed in draft form. Equipped with this detailed record, an updated National Register nomination, and over twenty years of experience managing the reserve, in 2000 the Park Service commissioned a new study to reassess the condition of the landscape and to provide strategies for its future.[2] The study's underlying purpose was to reveal the impact of the Park Service's twenty-year general management plan and to augment the reserve's 1995 National Register nomination with evaluation of the historic agricultural landscape. The results told a clear story of the landscape's evolution under the loose protective measures that existed. While key questions were answered, larger framework issues arose. First, how can the integrity of the reserve—and similar privately owned lands in rural historic districts—best be preserved while allowing life in the private sector to continue as part of contemporary social and economic contexts? Equally important, what guiding framework for "significance" and "integrity"—two key determinants to qualify properties for historic status designation—would best protect the historic agricultural landscape?

Figure 7.1. Ebey's Landing National Historical Reserve, Whidbey Island, Washington. General view, showing farmstead, fields, woodland, and Puget Sound. Photograph by author, 2000. Courtesy of National Park Service.

As expressions of vernacular histories and local evidence of national historical trends, our nation's farmsteads are precious heritage. But many of our nation's agricultural lands that are the richest in cultural stories, soil fertility, and scenic value are situated near enough to metropolitan areas to be subjected to intense pressures of urbanization.[3] The historical importance of these landscapes aggregates with their value as productive farmland and begs for their protection. However, while National Register listing brings recognition and may aid protecting these tracts, National Register criteria are based on preserving set forms on or in the land rather than on dynamic landscapes. Beyond delineating the results of the Ebey's Landing study, this chapter examines potential implications of current National Register criteria applied to agricultural landscapes. It also proposes an alternate framework based on precepts of *continuum* and *process* that may better protect these continually evolving places.

The Ebey's Landing Study

In the new Ebey's Landing study, the planning team asked three basic questions. First, how has the reserve's landscape changed, and what are the pressures and patterns that, if left unchecked, will continue to degrade its scenic and cultural significance? These matters were addressed by evaluating the changes to the landscape features that were inventoried in 1983. We reinventoried the landscape using then current aerial photographs and visual inventories, created Geographic Information System (GIS) databases and maps, and compared them with the GIS maps prepared from the 1983 inventory. The GIS software gave numerical percentages of change in landscape features such as land use, vegetation, roads, buildings, farmstead clusters, and boundaries. We supplemented this analytic methodology with photographs of key views and interviews with reserve managers (Figure 7.2).

The second question was, do the defining cultural landscape characteristics—using current Park Service definitions—retain their historical integrity? To

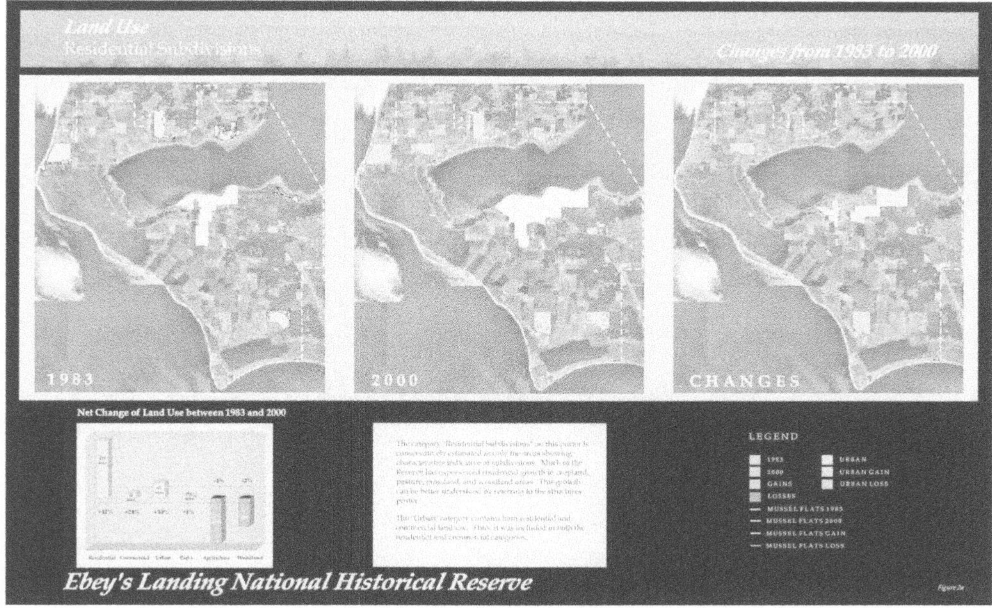

Figure 7.2. Ebey's Landing, "Land Use" poster, showing increase of 233 acres in residential subdivisions and decrease of 158 acres in agricultural land between 1983 and 2000. Image by Jones & Jones. Courtesy of National Park Service.

develop an answer, we researched historic conditions, primarily using pre-1950s USGS maps and aerials, historic photographs, original Government Land Office surveys, and written histories. From these we developed comparative maps, again using GIS to map the information, but primarily relying upon visual interpretation to assess integrity of the landscape characteristics of buildings and structures, land use, vegetation, circulation, cluster arrangements, spatial organization, natural systems and features, and views and vistas. Following the National Register standard that requires historic resources be at least fifty years old unless they are of exceptional significance, the operational period of significance spanned from 1850 to 1950. Landscape characteristics were judged to maintain integrity if at least half of the historic elements originating from this time period were still remaining (Figure 7.3).

The third question was, what can be learned from innovative agricultural preservation strategies implemented by federal, state, local, and nonprofit entities in other parts of the country? We developed case studies and recommendations to improve the viability and sustainability of farms on the reserve. These case studies and strategies were presented in two linked Web documents to make them easily accessible to the public (Figure 7.4).[4]

The results of the study were both encouraging and foreboding. The positive findings were that all cultural landscape characteristics investigated—such as

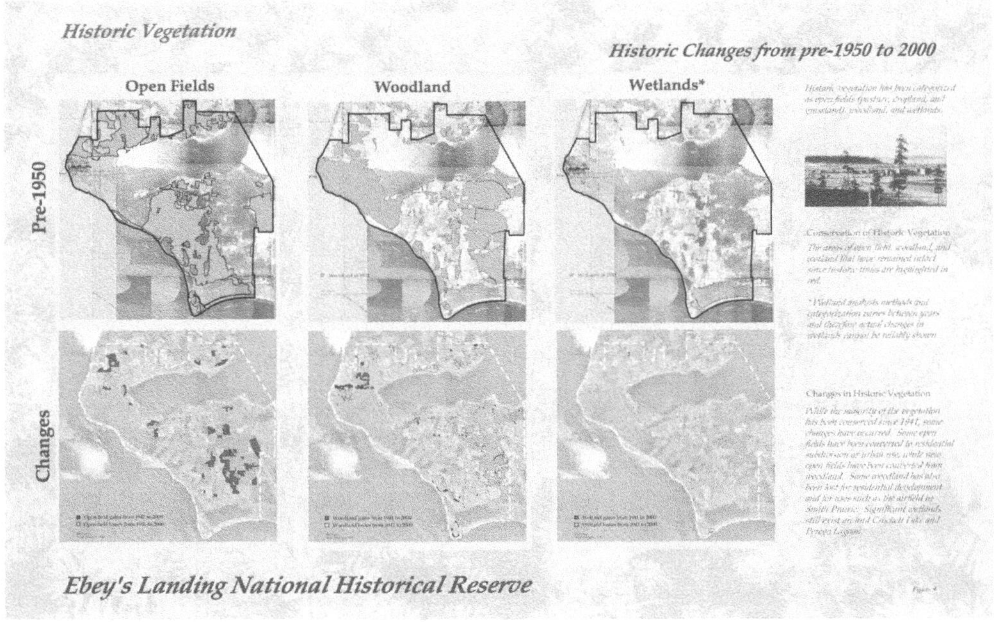

Figure 7.3. Ebey's Landing, "Historic Vegetation" poster, showing spatial changes in open fields, wetlands, and woodland (mostly conversion of woodland to open fields) between 1941 and 2000. Images by Jones & Jones. Courtesy of National Park Service.

historic land use, spatial organization, and building clusters—retained historical integrity from fifty years previous. Some characteristics showed losses but retained at least half of the historic qualities or features in each category. The stunning historic views and vistas across the prairies remained open and unimpaired, testament to the effectiveness of existing easements, the commitment of local farmers, and the efforts by the reserve staff to work with landowners. The Park Service has acquired more than two thousand acres of scenic easements since 1980. The majority of historic buildings and structures remain; 14 of the 358 identified in 1983 have been lost. Spatial patterning of the cultural landscape clearly follows the organizational divisions established by the 1850 Donation Land Claim (DLC) Act, which, to provide an impetus to land settlement in the Pacific Northwest, entitled citizens to claim 360 acres each. Hundreds of acres of woodlands and shoreline have been acquired by Washington State Parks and nonprofit land preservation organizations. The amount of active cropland actually grew 1 percent since 1983, and most farms are still in operation, partly aided by the income generated from selling their development rights in scenic easements to the Park Service.

On the dark side are the pressures of suburbanization. The most striking results from the analysis of contemporary changes were the dramatic growth in the

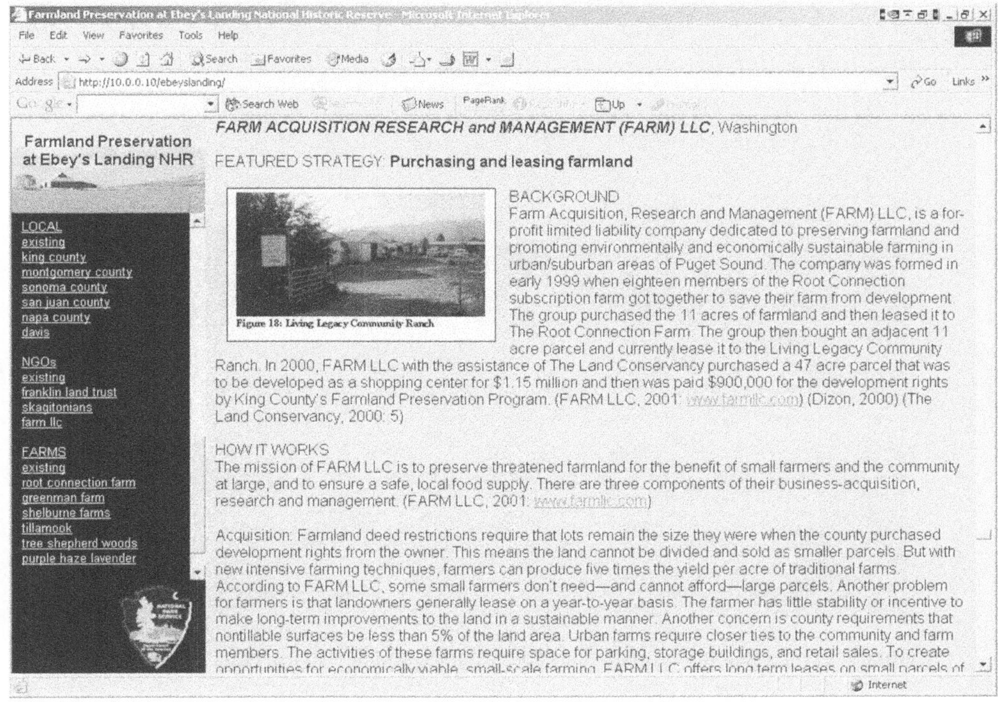

Figure 7.4. Screen capture of a farmland preserve case study, one of a set that illustrates a range of strategies. Image by Jones & Jones. Courtesy of National Park Service.

numbers of new structures—more than 1,000, a 44 percent increase in the past twenty years—and a concomitant proliferation of roads—more than 24 miles spread out over the landscape. In addition, a clear pattern of agricultural entropy emerged: active use of pasture lands declined, while fallow grasslands increased, with a common pattern of residential subdivisions and rural residential housing subsuming former grassland. While the overall decline of agricultural land use was small (4 percent), it signals a direction of change; indeed, often the most dramatic landscape transformations are incremental. Visually, the studding of the landscape's fabric with large houses was just beginning. While the scenic impact of this substantial growth has been partly mitigated by the design review process, the shift from agricultural to suburban land uses is dramatically evident in places—in the subdivision pockets of nontraditional housing and in suburban spatial arrangements as well as in relatively dense, rural tracts scattered within the historic grid (Figure 7.5). The effect of these changes is an overall finer division and dissection of the landscape—an alteration of its character and, perhaps most critical, to its functionality for agriculture.

To compound matters, local zoning, always subject to the winds of political change, has recently become less restrictive, and the list of properties for which

Figure 7.5. Large new houses on five-acre lots at Ebey's Landing National Reserve, showing substantial change to the character as well as the use of former farmland. Photograph by Amy Cragg, 2004. Courtesy of National Park Service.

protection by scenic easements is needed is still long. How should new growth, clearly on its way, be directed in order to least threaten the historic agricultural tenor of the "unbroken historical record"? Should residential development follow the historical, orthogonal, DLC spatial division patterning, further dissecting the prairies and farm fields but preserving the rural atmosphere, or should new housing be clustered in subdivisions?

Less visible but most ominous at Ebey's Landing, a farming family owning two farms filed Chapter 11 bankruptcy, requiring purchase by the Park Service to prevent their sale to developers. This shift is a common one in urbanizing rural areas (the reserve is a two-hour drive and ferry ride from Seattle), rapidly triggering a downward spiral for agricultural enterprises and landscapes. Typically, residential uses cause land values to rise, especially in scenic areas with grand views, which increase economic pressure and motivation to convert land. Loss of available acreage and active farms reduces flexibility in crop management, eliminates social and economic partners for cooperative operations, and undermines suppliers and support services needed for efficient, profitable operations.[5]

Our research of agricultural support strategies underscored the need for both controls and incentives to counteract suburbanization pressures, with three pri-

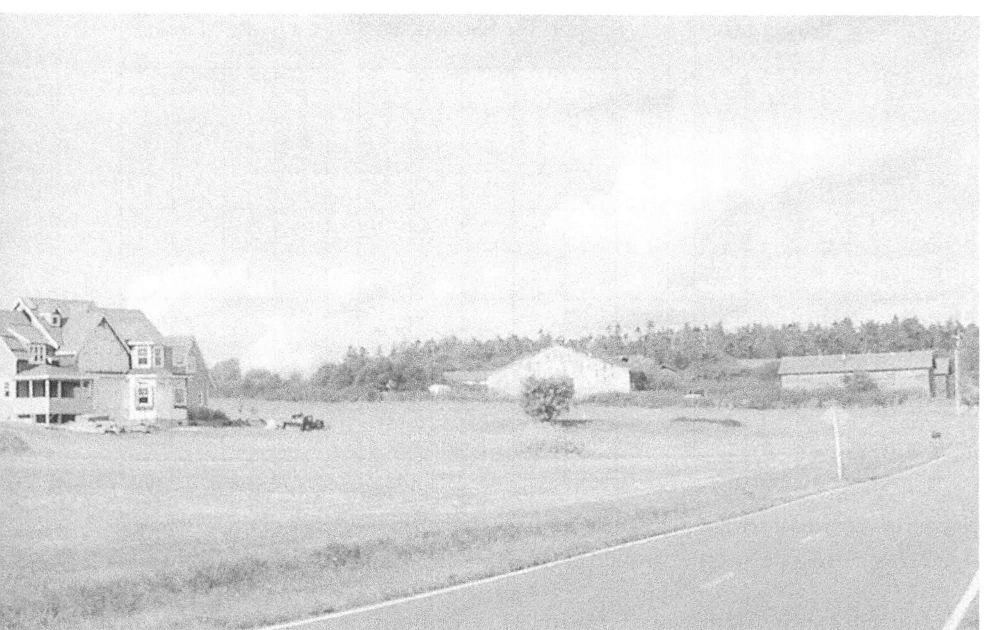

mary goals: protect the farmland, support the farmers, and cultivate new markets (Figure 7.6). The scope of effective protections we proposed included easements, zoning, and development right transfers, while support for farmers encompassed the actions of business and economic assistance, linking farms and prospective farmers, relieving challenges of intergenerational farm transfer, advocacy and education, and manufacture of value-added products. Cultivation of new markets would include local farmers' outlets, agricultural tourism, and a special label to promote local products. We recommended formation of a new nonprofit organization to support agricultural preservation, such as an "Ebey's Farmland Trust," and the formation of a farmer's cooperative to cultivate new markets.[6]

Analysis of the topic made it clear that for farms to survive at all, their size, operations, crops, and the necessary physical structures and land patterns might need to change. How would such changes affect the reserve's historical integrity? What impact, for instance, would the addition of such agricultural elements as greenhouses, new processing buildings, farm stands, vineyards, or orchards have? Would not any agricultural use extend the essential continuity of the landscape, retaining the historical human relationship to the landscape, whereas capitulation

		Protect the Farmland			Support the Farmers						Cultivate Markets			
		Overlay District	Conservation Easements	Development Credit Bank	Advocacy & Education	Washington FarmLink	Farmland Leasing	Tax Relief	Farm Business Incubator	Value-Added Practices	Ebey's Reserve Label	CSA	Farmers' Markets	Ag-Tourism
N	Island County	X		X				X						
P +	Ebey's Farmland Trust		X	X	X	X	X	X	X					
S	Ebey's Farmers Coop				X				X	X	X	X	X	X

Figure 7.6. Diagram of suggested mechanisms for implementing agricultural preservation strategies through partnerships with the National Park Service. Graphic by Jones & Jones. Courtesy of National Park Service.

to suburban subdivisions would destroy it? Is relationship more important than appearance?

Continuum: A Framework for Significance

Devising a sound strategy that balanced continuity of use and retention of historical integrity raised a larger issue related to the National Register criteria for evaluation. For a historic resource to qualify for the National Register, it must contain two essential qualities: significance and integrity. Integrity is defined as the ability of a property to convey its significance. For vernacular landscapes, significance is often based on association with historical trends or themes, and a period or periods of significance are identified for their associated historical context.[7] The National Register criteria require a discrete period of historical significance generally terminating at least fifty years ago.[8] However, a deeper examination of cultural landscapes argues for a period of significance that allows for a continuum inclusive of the present. The concept that rural historic landscapes belong to a continuum of use over time has been integral to the cultural landscape preservation discussion from its beginning. Melnick and his associates proposed the following in 1984:

> Recognizing that places may represent more than one historical period is vital to understanding rural landscapes and to any discussion of the significance and integrity of a rural historic district. The continuum of land-use and landscape modification will, by definition, reflect changes in human beliefs, available technologies, and forces external to the cultural group(s) primarily responsible for the landscape.[9]

Landscape historian Melody Webb expanded this perspective three years later, noting the conflict between the then prevailing static view of historic places representing a single period of significance and the dynamic nature of cultural landscapes: "Because continuum recognized function more than age, rules requiring that historic places be fifty years of age or be of overriding significance were inappropriate criteria for cultural landscapes."[10] Park Service guidelines for evaluating and documenting rural historic landscapes have been modified to allow for the idea that there can be multiple and long periods of significance. For these landscape types, the period of significance "more often . . . extends many years, covering a series of events, continuum of activities, or evolution of physical characteristics."[11]

Catherine Howett, another distinguished landscape historian, outlined the "shift to the evolutionary nature of the historic landscape" in definitions of historical integrity. She pointed out the shortcomings of the National Register requirements for a fifty-year break between the protected past and present, which fails to recognize the continuity of land use and character extending to the present day.[12] She noted Webb's recommendation that "[t]raditional concepts in historic preservation must be reshaped to address cultural landscapes. The criteria for the National Register should be revised to reflect current thinking and philosophy."[13] While the concept of continuum is now referred to in numerous excellent guidance materials the Park Service has produced for documenting, evaluating, and treating rural historic landscapes, the overriding National Register framework criteria for evaluation of significance and integrity have not been correspondingly adjusted.[14] Particularly for historic landscapes whose integrity is based on both past and contemporary agricultural use, the fifty-year requirement misses the importance of including the present time within the period of significance.

Within the existing criteria, if a property changes substantially from its period of significance—for instance, a farming district sprouts a substantial number of shiny metal barns, vineyards cover the area where a large field grew hay, or greenhouses become a dominant new production system—the district could be vulnerable to losing its integrity based on the loss of the historical character, "design," or "feeling," since it no longer appears as it did in the historic period.[15] But consider this scene if the period of significance extends to the present—where the historic structures and spatial organization of the historic period are intact—and farming continues. Would not this landscape convey the continuum of time and therefore retain integrity? The period of significance in this case is a living time frame in which we are still participants, rather than a clip of the past from which we are separate. French historian Pierre Nora made this distinction in distinguishing memory from history: "Memory is a perpetually actual phenomenon, a bond tying us to the eternal present; history is a representation of the past." Along the same lines, Howett has convincingly argued that if integrity is the ability of a landscape to tell its story, it is not only physical evidence that is important but also the richness of the story to be told. A continuum of significance, while potentially messy, encompasses the complexity and temporal interactions—within and between periods—that are reflective of an authentic, layered history inclusive of the present. More than three decades ago, planner Kevin Lynch termed this rich physical manifestation of overlapping time "temporal collage."[16]

The paradox of preserving the historical integrity of agricultural landscapes is that in order to preserve the character of a historic period, the landscape must in most cases continue to evolve in agricultural use. Indeed, it seems inevitable that in most rural historic landscapes the period of significance must continue to the present in order to be preserved. Cultural landscapes are, by definition, natural landscapes modified by human actions, and without the characteristic actions of agricultural practices, these landscapes will, by default, change. Not only will the fallow landscape exhibit the dynamic characteristics of vegetation maturation and succession, but without active husbandry, the cultural markers of the landscape will disappear. In the best cases, fields become weedy or forested, fences disappear, and farmsteads fall into disrepair—as happened at Boxley Valley in Buffalo River National Park (Arkansas) and at Cuyahoga Valley National Park (Ohio), where a program of leasing rehabilitated farmsteads to qualified farmers is now being implemented.[17] More commonly, in metropolitan areas not receiving substantial protection and agricultural support, the pressures of suburbanization and the challenges of farming become too great for the farmer to bear, and land capitulates from agricultural to residential functions, erasing the artifacts of the past and interrupting the continuity of use. Preserving these agricultural landscapes requires management protocols that prioritize processes of living, working landscapes.

Time and Change

Continuation of agricultural land use provides the best method of protection for rural landscapes; however, it is likely that contemporary agricultural practices will alter the appearance of the historic "scene." This perspective is acknowledged in the Park Service's *Guide to Cultural Landscape Reports* (1998), which states that "[t]he appropriate level of change in a cultural landscape is closely related to its significance. . . . In a landscape significant for the pattern of use that has evolved, physical change may be essential to the continuation of use."[18] The results of using the existing static evaluation framework may disqualify the eligibility of the property or district for the National Register. However, it is also arguable that such changes may actually help to convey the significance of a landscape over time, highlighting the evolutionary arc set up by the interplay of human activity and regional geographical resources.

Change over time is indeed a dominant quality of all agricultural landscapes as they respond to markets, technology, weather, blight, fashion, and local and global economies. The history of Whidbey Island provides a prime example, where between 1850 and 1900 there were "discernible shifts in . . . farming." Cultivation of potatoes, oats, and wheat and the raising of hogs and cattle in the 1850s and early 1860s gave way to sheep farming in the late 1860s and early 1870s. By the beginning of the twentieth century, sheep farming had declined, and field crops as well as fruit orchards dominated agricultural production. Environmental historian Richard White characterized these patterns: "Island County agriculture swung from plantings of a regular annual crop to rapid shifts from one crop to another. The extremes dominated. There was rarely any middle ground."[19] Between 1900 and 1940 "small fruits" played a significant role in the county; dairy and poultry products were produced in significant quantities. Today, seed crops are grown, in addition to the remaining dairy industry. To freeze a landscape of substantial size in one of these short periods is not only impractical and possibly inauthentic, but runs counter to a rich, historical evolution.

The essence of time is that it continues. We are constantly creating new history through the ways we choose to manipulate the present. Historian and geographer David Lowenthal "insists . . . that preservation is itself a form of history making and hence inescapably an expression of contemporary culture."[20] We mold history through our actions whether they are ones of preservation, protection, exploitation, or apathy. Lowenthal sees this layering of tangible history positively: "surviving heritage ever accreted new substances and accrues new meanings, its look and relevance altering for each successive inheritor. . . . Lamentable as heritage losses often seem, they are in the long run more than compensated by heritage gains." As participants in the "stream of time," what we shape in the present in addition to what we preserve from the past can tell a full, cohesive, and authentic story only if we maintain a reasonable sense of continuity. J. B. Jackson repeatedly stressed the interaction of past and present in the landscape. He proposed that "the ideal landscape [be] defined not as a static utopia . . . but as an environment where permanence and change have struck a balance."[21]

Allowing change in landscape elements within the rubric of preservation standards and practices acknowledges this essential quality of time and landscape change and can honestly highlight the role of contemporary preservationists in influencing an evolving landscape. Officially incorporating the concept of "continuum to the present" in our definitions of significance for these landscapes could actually help to preserve their narrative capacities, with new additions to the landscape consequently contributing to integrity.

Figure 7.7. Ebey's prairie, comparative views taken in 1901 *(top)* and 2001 *(bottom)*, showing the continuity in agricultural use and development patterns achieved through concerted efforts of local residents, the National Park Service, and Ebey's Landing Trust Board. Bottom spliced photograph by Jones & Jones, 2000. Both photographs courtesy of National Park Service.

A Hierarchy of Landscape Characteristics

In the alternate scenarios of farm disuse or conversion of land to large-lot residential development—where the characteristic of *land use* has changed—the landscape's character and ability to tell the story of a discrete period of significance, and therefore its integrity, are highly compromised. Thus, the most critical component is continuity in the *process of using the land*, such that the human relationship to the landscape remains one of cultivating it to produce living commodities.

The Park Service system of documenting and assessing the integrity of historic landscapes according to their "landscape characteristics" is a useful one, developed through several iterations over the past twenty years. National Register guidelines group the characteristics typical of rural historic landscapes into *processes*—land uses and activities, patterns of spatial organization, response to the natural environment, and cultural traditions—and *components*—which include circulation networks; boundary demarcations; topography; vegetation

related to land use; buildings, structures, and objects; clusters; archeological sites and small-scale elements.[22] The guidance bulletin states that certain characteristics are more critical to integrity than others for certain types of landscapes. Robert Melnick and Arnold Alanen make the distinction between process and component, observing: "Foremost among the factors that differentiate cultural landscape preservation from its associated fields is the recognition that the landscape is both artifact and system; in other words, it is a product and a process."[23] To take this distinction further, a hierarchy of these characteristics would be useful to guide treatment. For true preservation and protection of agricultural historical landscapes, *processes* are the most critical. It is, after all, the processes that produce the artifact components. Conversely, the importance of the components lies in their signification of landscape meanings associated with processes such as farming, settlement, resource use, and social traditions. A parallel could be drawn to restoration and rehabilitation of ecological landscapes, where management aims to act on a part of the system through natural processes: fire is used to arrest succession to maintain prairies, and shade-tolerant cedars and firs are planted in the understory to accelerate succession in conifer forests. Similarly, in living agricultural landscapes, it is the continuity of human processes interacting with the natural landscape—farming versus (sub)urbanization—that will best ensure protection of the cultural resource. In this hierarchy, human relationship to the landscape ranks higher than the physical substance or appearance of the landscape. To be sure, the physical components of the past should still be safeguarded to the highest degree possible; indeed, the maintenance of hedgerows, barns, sheds, fences, and other features of past agricultural eras is paramount. But maintenance of specific "scenes" should not take precedence over insertion of new agricultural elements or crops if they respond to contemporary farming exigencies. After all, such elements will become additional chapters in the landscape's history as physical manifestations of then-to-be historical processes.

A Systems Approach to Treatment

With this framework in mind, treatment options could be expanded. The first standard for treatment under the rubric of rehabilitation, as defined by the Park Service, is, "A property will be used as it was historically or be given a new use that requires minimal change to its distinctive materials, features, spaces, and spatial relationships."[24] In addition to the recommended treatment actions of *preserve, protect and maintain, repair, replace, design for missing features* and *compatible alterations and additions,* we might add a category called *intervene* that would include such activities as counsel, economic stimulation, and influencing the system of use.[25] For example, for agriculture to continue, farmers may need processing facilities to increase the value of their products, advisement on a business plan, low-interest loans, a local label under which to sell produce, or assistance with forming cooperatives or organizations that can influence local economic or regulatory conditions. While as "treatment" these operations do not act directly on the material culture that conveys the significance of the particular landscape, they do act on parts of the *system* that creates and maintains the cultural landscape, interacting with the *process* as well as the product. Ecologist Robert Cook suggested that a process-system approach used in ecosystem management be applicable to cultural landscapes, recognizing that "cultural relics surviving from the past are just one part of a dynamic, living, present."[26] Employing the framework of a period of significance that begins with a historical period and continues to the present (and will become part of the future), a process-systems approach would work within the standards for historic preservation, removing the paradox of preserving agricultural districts within the stream of time and honestly recognizing preservationists' roles in not only protecting but also contributing to the continuum of history.

Proactive intervention to support farming is an approach currently used at Cuyahoga Valley National Park near Cleveland, Ohio. With the assistance of a nonprofit organization, the Cuyahoga Valley Countryside Conservancy, the Park Service is restoring and leasing formerly defunct farms to qualified farmers committed to sustainable agriculture. Three farms began operation in 2001, with three more to be leased in 2005 and every two years thereafter, for a total of thirty-five. These heritage properties are cultivated as small family farms using traditional methods, but with attention to environmental values such as wetlands and woodlands. One of the initial group, a winery, aroused local concerns about nontraditional use until the region's nineteenth-century history as a wine-producing center was revealed. An interdisciplinary team and staff from the state historic preservation office reviewed the proposed new buildings and landscape elements to ensure compatibility with the protected cultural landscape. The conservancy has also initiated a farmers' market, facilitated direct sales of produce to restaurants, and assisted with food processing and product branding.[27]

Intervention in the systems and processes that shape the cultural landscape is a strategy that has been used to manage the cultural landscapes of Ebey's Landing. During its first two decades, the primary preservation tool was the purchase of conservation easements. While easements generally do not require continued active farming, they do help to stabilize the farming operation, allow for expansion of operations, or provide for secure retirement and intergenerational land transfers, thereby assisting with the continuity of active agriculture. At Ebey's Landing, the Park Service initially purchased farms vulnerable to housing development and then sold the lands back to local farmers while retaining the development rights. Reserve staff actively continue to seek funding and negotiate with willing sellers to purchase conservation easements when funds allow.

Now more direct measures to promote agricultural health are being implemented. The Park Service has again purchased a large farm in bankruptcy to forestall sale for residential development and is leasing the land back to the original farming family. The reserve manager is actively working to facilitate formation of partnerships between local dairies and value-added product manufacturers to promote new processing and production facilities. Reserve staff members advocate for, support, and educate farmers about resources and markets available to them. Local farms are diversifying into specialty products and truck gardens, using parcels as small as ten acres and converting edges of large hay and dairy operations, yielding extra income that provides them greater financial stability. The Coupeville farmers' market, now with an expanded range of products, has outgrown its space and may relocate onto Park Service land. A label for local products will feature the reserve's logo, further raising awareness and consumer demand.[28]

Concurrently, reserve staff members are working more actively with local government officials on regulatory approaches. While zoning remains permissive, the Park Service's draft general management plan recommends that the county government adopt a special zoning overlay area, limiting small-lot (five acres or less) zoning and retaining large agricultural parcels.[29] The county's Historical Review Committee for Ebey's Historic District, formerly just an advisory body, has been given greater authority to shape new building and land development through the design review process. It is crucial that this body prioritize continuation of agricultural land-use processes within the context of the evolving historic landscape, while ensuring that additions to the landscape, especially those of a residential nature, are compatible with its scenic and historic character.

The emphasis on continuum in the reserve's enabling legislation brings a keen awareness that the landscape being made today is not only protecting the past but is creating the history of tomorrow. Stewards of the reserve are "managing change," working to protect the material and process legacies of the past, integrating new components so that the overarching appearance of these heritage lands remains intact, and facilitating new approaches to support the continuation of farming.[30] A treatment protocol of proactive intervention in the community and economy of local agriculture is beginning to be tested.

Applying the Proposed Framework

Applying continuum and process constructs to Ebey's Landing, we return to questions raised by the results of our assessment of the reserve. Should new agricultural practices be encouraged, even if they alter the historic scene? Yes, to preserve the continuity of use, active farming advocacy is essential, but compatibility with the character of the historic landscape remains a goal as well. Small-scale farms can maintain that character where they relate to the natural topography. The addition of new barns and other working structures can compatibly express our own era while following the spatial patterning of clustering if they are sited to maintain field flexibility and scaled to fit their contexts. Change in crops, responding to natural soil and water conditions, is part of the cyclical pattern—vineyards would be an iteration of bygone berry fields. Small-plot farming and the addition of fences that create smaller enclosures would actually restore aspects of the scene to the appearance of former eras. Llama husbandry—the thought of which may be initially jarring—could offer a reminder of the historic global cross-pollination of agricultural products, stimulate storytelling about nineteenth-century hog and sheep farming on the island, and interpret the changing nature of the agricultural livelihood. This approach is more honest about history than an unfarmed field or even a weedy prairie. Judgments about how actions from new agricultural trends will impact historic features will need to be carefully considered, with preserving historic components always critical to the equation.

The issue of appropriate allowance for housing is less clear, but the proposed framework provides direction. A living community needs to be able to grow; however, this residential pressure is a driving force of whole landscape change. Should planning allow the grain of the landscape to continue to be dissected, following the historical orthogonal spatial pattern but allowing smaller lots, or should housing be congregated in subdivisions? Using the framework that gives priority to continuity of land use, the answer is perhaps a bit of both. Traditional farming would demand that parcels be large (on the order of forty acres) to maintain the critical mass of farms, farmers, and contiguity of lands needed for dairy and seed crops. However, smaller parcels (ten acres) in more topographically confined areas, with buildings aligned with historic roads and clustered with contiguous open space, would allow intensive, small-scale berry and truck farming and still follow historic patterns. The existing five-acre parcel zoning creates a scale that both is inconsistent with the historical character and limits capability for farming. Rather, most new housing should be encouraged to locate in the existing subdivisions, within the growth boundaries of the town of Coupeville, and in compact housing developments to form new villages that follow a grid patterning instead of adopting suburban layouts. This solution not only preserves the most land for farming but also best follows the historic settlement pattern of large open spaces with centers of activity. To effect this outcome, stronger zoning controls and protective easements must intervene against the land value–driven economic system and manage growth so that farming capability and the structure of the cultural landscape are preserved. Such measures would help retain the historic integrity aspects of "design" and "feeling."[31]

Conclusion

Agricultural regions across the country are experiencing relentless pressure from urbanization and suburban sprawl. Not only are these farmlands important as resources for sustainable food production and local food security, they are most often the repositories of precious vernacular landscape histories. The significance of these histories, especially when recognized through national designation, adds important layers of value that can help to safeguard farms, an agricultural way of life, and the material culture that conveys the landscape's past. If National Register criteria were to recognize the inevitable dynamic nature of agricultural landscapes, historic designation could provide a critical preservation impetus for scores of additional farms and rural districts that are vulnerable to development, thereby enabling the significance and stories of these cultural legacies to be studied and told. By adopting a more fluid framework of continuum and process for the designation criteria, we would recognize that living farms and ranches should not be locked into a static condition that disables viability and eventually leads to wholesale erasure of the historic resource. Incorporating the concept of an ongoing continuum of significance and a process-systems priority for treatment into the guiding framework would clarify the policies that are needed to preserve historic agricultural landscapes and would initiate a dynamic preservation ethic to further a property's continual evolution along its historical trajectory.

Notes

The author wishes to thank those who provided guidance during the study and subsequently provided insights for this essay: Gretchen Luxenberg, Susan Dolan, Cheryl Teague, Keith Dunbar, and Dianne Croal of the National Park Service, and Rob Harbor and Pat Cozine of Ebey's Landing National Historical Reserve. Thanks also go to the staff at Jones & Jones Architects and Landscape Architects, who assisted in the research, supplied technical expertise, produced report components, and gave moral support in the original study: Keith Larson, Nate Cormier, April Mills, Rene Senos, and Chris Overdorf. My appreciation is also extended to Robert Melnick, who introduced me to the concept of cultural landscape more than twenty years ago and who continues to provoke critical thinking about how we can best preserve these dynamic treasures.

1. Robert Z. Melnick, with Daniel Sponn and Emma Jane Saxe, *Cultural Landscapes: Rural Historic Districts in the National Park System* (Washington, D.C.: National Park Service, 1984).

2. Nancy D. Rottle and Jones & Jones, "An Analysis of Land Use Change and Cultural Landscape Integrity for Ebey's Landing National Historic Reserve," in "Ebey's Landing National Historic Reserve Draft General Management Plan and Environmental Impact Statement, Vol. II, Technical Supplement," National Park Service, 2005 (hereafter "Ebey's Landing Management Plan").

3. Valuable studies of the subject include Samuel N. Stokes, *Savings America's Countryside* (Baltimore: Johns Hopkins University Press, 1989); Stokes, "America's Rural Heritage," in *Past Meets Future: Saving America's Historic Environments,* ed. Antoinette J. Lee (Washington, D.C.: Preservation Press, 1992), 196–203, 248–49; Michael Woods, *Rural Geography* (London: Sage, 1995); John Fraser Hart, *The Rural Landscape* (Baltimore: Johns Hopkins University Press, 1998); and Mark B. Lapping and Owen J. Furuseth, eds., *Contested Countryside: The Rural-Urban Fringe in North America* (Brookfield, Vt.: Ashgate, 1999).

4. Jones & Jones, "Farmland Preservation Case Study for Ebey's Landing National

Historical Reserve," and Jones & Jones, "Farmland Preservation Recommendations for Ebey's Landing National Historical Reserve," in "Ebey's Landing Management Plan."

5. Geographer John Fraser Hart described this common pattern: "[Farmers] can sell their land to developers at whopping prices, but each departing farmer reduces the number of customers available to support dealers in machinery, fertilizers, feed, and other necessary farm supplies for those who remain" (*Rural Landscape*, 330).

6. See Jones & Jones, "Farmland Preservation Case Studies," and "Farmland Preservation Recommendations." Other valuable studies of rural land protection include Stokes, *Saving America's Countryside;* Stokes, "America's Rural Heritage"; Randall Arendt, *Rural by Design* (Chicago: Planners Press, American Planning Association, 1994); Arnold R. Alanen, "Considering the Ordinary: Vernacular Landscapes in Small Towns and Rural Areas," in *Preserving Cultural Landscapes in America,* ed. Arnold R. Alanen and Robert Z. Melnick (Baltimore: Johns Hopkins University Press, 2000), 112–42; and William H. Whyte, *The Last Landscape,* reprint ed. (1968; Philadelphia: University of Pennsylvania Press, 2002). Useful organizations and Web sites include American Farmland Trust (http://www.farmland.org), Community Food Security Coalition (http://www.foodsecurity.org), Farmland Information Center (http://www.farmlandinfo.org), and Glynwood Center (http://www.glynwood.org). The National Heritage Areas program has been successfully used as a nonregulatory preservation strategy for agricultural areas; see Alanen, "Considering the Ordinary"; http://cr.nps.gov/heritageareas; and http://www.silosandsmokestacks.org.

7. "How to Apply the National Register Criteria for Evaluation," *National Register Bulletin* 15 (1997): 12; Linda Flint McClelland, J. Timothy Kelley, Genevieve P. Kelley, and Robert Z. Melnick, "Guidelines for Evaluating and Documenting Rural Historic Landscapes," *National Register Bulletin* 30 (1999): 2.

8. McClelland et al., "Guidelines for Evaluating and Documenting Historic Landscapes," advise: "Continuous land use, association, or function does not by itself justify continuing the period of significance.... Fifty years ago may be used as the closing date for the period of significance if a more specific date cannot be identified" (21). "How to Apply the National Register Criteria" states, "The National Register Criteria for Evaluation exclude properties that achieved significance within the last fifty years unless they are of exceptional importance. Fifty years is a general estimate of the time needed to develop historical perspective and to evaluate significance" (41).

9. Melnick et al., *Cultural Landscapes,* 2.

10. Melody Webb, "Cultural Landscapes in the National Park Service," *Public Historian* 9 (spring 1987): 84. Other scholars have also called for modification to criteria for a period of significance. Architectural historian Richard Longstreth illuminates the value of the recent past and proposes that we eliminate a period of significance requirement for historic districts; see Longstreth, "When the Present Becomes the Past," in *Past Meets Future,* ed. Lee, 218, 222. Ecologist Robert E. Cook questions the concept of period of significance, proposing that the "object of preservation ... [become] less the material constituents and more the whole system in its present day operation." See Robert E. Cook, "Is Landscape Preservation an Oxymoron?" *George Wright Forum* 13: 1 (1996): 42–53. It is noteworthy that the World Heritage Convention's definition of cultural landscape includes the "continuing landscape ... one which retains an active social role in contemporary society closely associated with the traditional way of life, and in which the evolutionary process is still in

progress. At the same time, it exhibits material evidence of evolution over time"; http://whc.unesco.org/opgulist.htm (accessed October 2005).

11. McClelland et al., "Guidelines for Evaluating and Documenting Historic Landscapes," 6.

12. Catherine Howett, "Integrity as a Value in Cultural Landscape Preservation," in Alanen and Melnick, eds., *Preserving Cultural Landscapes,* 191.

13. Webb, "Cultural Landscapes," 89.

14. The Cultural Resource Management Guideline NPS-28 states, "In a landscape significant for the pattern of use that has evolved, physical change may be essential to the continuation of the use. In the latter case, the focus should be on perpetuating the use while maintaining the general character and feeling of the historic period(s), rather than on preserving a specific appearance"; *NPS-28, Cultural Resource Management Guideline No. 5* (Washington, D.C.: National Park Service, 1997), chapter 7, 1. *A Guide to Cultural Landscape Reports: Contents, Processes, Techniques* restates this policy, adding, "When land use is a primary reason for significance of a landscape, the objective of treatment is to balance perpetuation of use with retention of the tangible evidence that represents its history"; Robert Page, Cathy A. Gilbert, and Susan A. Dolan, *A Guide to Cultural Landscape Reports: Content, Process and Techniques* (Washington, D.C.: National Park Service, 1998), 110.

15. The secretary of the interior's criteria for evaluation state: "For a district to retain integrity as a whole, the majority of the components that make up the district's historic character must possess integrity even if they are individually undistinguished.... A district is not eligible if it contains so many alterations or new intrusions that it no longer conveys the sense of a historic environment"; "How to Apply the National Register Criteria," 44–46.

16. Pierre Nora, *Realms of Memory,* vol. 1, *Conflicts and Divisions* (New York: Columbia University Press, 1996), 8; Howett, "Integrity as a Value," 205–7; Kevin Lynch, *What Times Is this Place?* (Cambridge, Mass.: MIT Press, 1972), 168–73.

17. Webb, "Cultural Landscapes,"84–88; Alanen, "Considering the Ordinary," 132–33. The Cuyahoga Valley National Park Countryside Initiative states that "preserving and protecting the park's rural countryside for public use and enjoyment has turned out to be an extremely complex and elusive goal.... Without a viable community of working farms, the countryside... quickly disappears... most park farms have continued their long slide into disuse and disrepair and quickly became overgrown with weeds and brush"; Cuyahoga Valley National Park, "Countryside Initiative Request for Proposals," National Park Service, Cuyahoga Valley, Ohio, 2001. The environmental impact statement for this initiative sets the goal of "revitalizing a sense of place in the Cuyahoga Valley versus 'scene setting.' Cultural landscapes at CVNP are preserved to maintain their character and feeling rather than a specific appearance or time period"; "Draft Rural Landscape Management Program Environmental Impact Statement," National Park Service, Cuyahoga Valley, Ohio, 2002. The park is discussed further in the text below.

18. Page et al., *Guide to Cultural Landscape Reports,* 99.

19. Richard White, *Land Use, Environment and Social Change: The Shaping of Island County, Washington* (Seattle: University of Washington Press, 1992), 62, 69.

20. As summarized by Howett in "Integrity as a Value," 200.

21. David Lowenthal, "Pioneering Stewardship: New Challenges for CRM," *CRM: The Journal of Heritage Stewardship* 1 (fall 2003): 11; John Brinckerhoff Jackson, "Sterile Restorations Cannot Replace a Sense of the Stream of Time," *Landscape Architecture* 66 (May

1976): 194, quoted in Alanen and Melnick, eds., *Preserving Cultural Landscapes,* 16; John Brinckerhoff Jackson, *Discovering the Vernacular Landscape* (New Haven, Conn.: Yale University Press, 1984), 148.

22. McClelland et al., "Guidelines for Evaluating and Documenting Historic Landscapes." Alternately, the component landscape characteristics recommended in Page et al., *Guide to Cultural Landscape Reports,* are circulation, topography, vegetation, buildings and structures, views and vistas, constructed water features, small-scale features, and archeological sites. The process characteristics are identical to those given by McClelland and her associates, although the distinction between process and components is not made in this publication.

23. Alanen and Melnick, eds., *Preserving Cultural Landscapes,* 16.

24. *The Secretary of the Interior's Standards for the Treatment of Historic Properties* (Washington, D.C.: National Park Service, 1995), quoted in Page et al., *Guide to Cultural Landscape Reports,* 88.

25. Page et al., *Guide to Cultural Landscape Reports,* 90.

26. Cook, "Is Landscape Preservation an Oxymoron?" 49.

27. Personal communications with Dave Humphrey, cultural resource manager, Cuyahoga Valley National Park, and with Darwin Kelsey, executive director, Cuyahoga Valley Countryside Conservancy.

28. Personal communication with Rob Harbour, reserve manager, Ebey's Landing National Historic Reserve.

29. "Ebey's Landing Management Plan."

30. Personal communication with Gretchen Luxenberg, historian, National Park Service liaison to the Ebey's Landing Historical Reserve Trust Board. Cultural geographer Lesley Head underscored the need for managing for change in order to preserve cultural and natural sites, particularly in light of continuing climate modification: "the ideal [of preservationist rhetoric to] somehow . . . freeze time, does not help us think about managing for change"; Lesley Head, *Cultural Landscapes and Environmental Change* (New York: Oxford University Press, 2000), 98.

31. *Secretary of the Interior's Standards,* 44–45.

8. Natural and Cultural Resources

The Protection of Vernacular Landscapes

SUSAN CALAFATE BOYLE

A vernacular landscape illustrates people's attitudes and values toward the land and reflects patterns of settlement, use, and development over time.

—NATIONAL PARK SERVICE, *CULTURAL RESOURCE MANAGEMENT GUIDELINES*, 1998

Unless we reconsider our attitude towards landscape resources, the way we describe those resources, and our professional and intellectual boundaries, we will continue to be limited in land management and protection potentials.

—ROBERT Z. MELNICK, 1996

An ecological perspective should be an essential part of analyzing vernacular landscapes—those that evolve through use by people—and of their protection and management. Classifying and treating all landscapes as "traditional" cultural resources in the currently conventional manner have meant that a major segment of our nation's cultural landscapes has been ignored. The methodology developed for the study of cultural landscapes needs to be modified so that it can be successfully applied to resources that have strong natural components, are dynamic in complexion, and are not easily defined.[1]

The need for action is nowhere more critical than in the western United States, an area dramatically impacted by growth in the past forty years. Urbanization and increasing oil and gas exploration pose substantial threats to some of the country's most dramatic and pristine vernacular landscapes, that is, those that retain their historical character and integrity. Given today's political and economic climate, it is imperative to develop realistic management strategies for their protection before they are lost.[2] The challenge is formidable. Most western cultural landscapes can be classified as vernacular, with the characteristics of both natural and cultural resources. These places thus require management practices that are dynamic, innovative, and sensitive to their special nature. Nobody questions the visible nature of landscapes; however, other sensory elements, such as the feel of the wind, scents, humidity, the sound of rivers and creeks, and the absence of industrial and urban noise, are essential characteristics that should be considered in planning for their protection. The presence of wildlife may be an important landscape component and likewise factor in the development of protection strategies.

Cultural landscapes are now an attractive topic in preservation, and their study is becoming an important consideration for those employed in the field. International organizations such as UNESCO and ICOMOS strongly support the cultural landscape approach; however, scholarship so far tends to be descriptive and does not provide the analytical tools needed to facilitate landscape evaluation and protection.[3]

The study of landscapes is intricate and involves numerous disciplines, including ecology, landscape architecture, history, and cultural geography. Controversy is basic to the concept of landscape and abounds in its study. Cultural geographer D. W. Meinig remarked that the term *landscape* is appealing, important, and ambiguous—that it is at once an old and pleasant word in common speech and a technical term in special professions. The central problem in examining landscapes, he argues, is that they are composed not only of what lies before our eyes but also what lies within our heads, concluding that we should be concerned less with the elements than with the organizing ideas we use to make sense of what we see.[4] The continual controversy over the term's definition, usage, and contribution to various disciplines was explored in detail by landscape architect Eugene J. Palka. After a systematic examination of eighty years of literature on landscapes, he identified four common qualities: (1) emphasis on that which is visible, (2) understanding that landscapes evolve through a process of human-land interaction, (3) recognition of a time dimension, as it pertains to landscape evolution, and (4) vagueness surrounding the spatial dimension or aerial extent of the landscape.[5]

In assessing key issues and research priorities today, landscape ecologists share most of Palka's conclusions. They agree that landscapes are composed of physical, ecological, socioeconomic, and cultural patterns and processes and that landscapes are spatially extended, dynamic, and complex systems in which heterogeneity, nonlinearity, and contingency are the norm. These ecologists emphasize as well the interdisciplinary and holistic nature of the study of landscape, acknowledging that their field cannot explain all processes but can help in the understanding of the complexity of landscapes. J. A. Wiens, a leading landscape ecologist, concluded that "it would be naïve to conduct basic scientific investigations of landscapes without considering the anthropogenic forces that have shaped them."[6]

Ecologists often use the term *landscape* interchangeably with *ecosystem.* They tend to focus on large, heterogeneous areas to explore how the landscape has changed over time and how it might change in the future. The boundaries of an ecosystem or landscape may be small—a lake and its tangent land mass—

or large—an entire region. In all instances, however, ecologists recognize that energy, water, nutrients, and organisms move back and forth across whatever boundaries are established. For these reasons, ecosystems and landscapes are viewed as open systems that are neither static nor easily defined, in marked contrast with the approach used for historic properties.[7]

Landscapes that are heterogeneous, dynamic, nonlinear, and unpredictable may seem unsuited subjects for historic preservation philosophy and methods. The National Park Service, however, has played a key role in seeking to bridge the two spheres. Working with specialists in the private sector, Park Service personnel have developed an analytical process that can be used by communities, institutions, and individuals to nominate cultural landscapes to the National Register of Historic Places. Among federal agencies, cultural landscapes are considered cultural resources and are thus the responsibility of the secretary of the interior, whose duty is to establish professional standards and to provide advice on the preservation of cultural resources listed or eligible for listing on the National Register. These standards include four treatments—preservation, rehabilitation, restoration, and reconstruction—which can be applied to all historic resource types encompassed by National Register criteria: buildings, structures, sites, objects, districts, and landscapes.[8]

Cultural resource management guidelines developed by the Park Service identify four types of historic landscapes: historic sites, designed, vernacular, and ethnographic (traditional cultural properties). Historic sites are significant for their associations with important events, activities, and persons. Designed landscapes are deliberate, artistic creations reflecting recognized artistic patterns of expression. Vernacular landscapes illustrate peoples' values and attitudes toward the land and reflect patterns of settlement, use, and development. Most of the methodology for their analysis has focused on agricultural properties. Ethnographic landscapes are those used or valued in traditional ways by contemporary ethnic groups.[9]

The methodology developed by the Park Service for the systematic analysis of landscapes is composed of three basic steps. First is the identification of landscape characteristics, four of which are processes instrumental in shaping the land: land uses and activities, patterns of spatial organization, response to the natural environment, and cultural traditions. The remaining seven are physical components: circulation networks; boundary demarcations; vegetation related to land use; buildings, structures, and objects; clusters; archeological sites; and such small-scale elements as footbridges, paths, gravestones, fence posts, and road markers. This classification system is a tool for gathering and organizing information: it allows the development of historical context, it evaluates the significant properties of a rural area, and it facilitates the determination of the significance and integrity of any property.[10]

The second step is an evaluation of significance according to the four categories of the National Register criteria. Here, conventional assessments of historic integrity are not applicable to most vernacular landscapes. This methodology was crafted principally for designed landscapes and can be most successfully applied to them.[11] Designed landscapes tend to be more akin to the buildings and structures whose preservation was the primary concern of those framing the National Historic Preservation Act of 1966 and, with it, the National Register. The legal boundaries of such properties are clearly defined. They are often of modest size. Sufficient historical evidence frequently exists to allow for their thorough study and evaluation. There is a tendency to manage them so that they remain much as they were during their period of significance. All treatment standards—preservation, rehabilitation, restoration, and reconstruction—are potentially applicable.

Vernacular landscapes, however, have strong natural resource components, as can be found at agricultural properties; industrial sites involving mining, lumbering, fishing, and shipbuilding; hunting or fishing camps; transportation systems; migration trails; and ceremonial sites. The Park Service's *Guidelines for the Treatment of Cultural Landscapes* acknowledges that preservation planning for cultural landscapes involves a broad array of dynamic variables, including the landscape's ever-changing nature, and also admit that for some cultural landscapes, "especially those considered ethnographic or heritage," the guidelines may not apply.[12]

This major gap needs to be addressed. Transportation networks—historic trails, highways, rivers, canals, excavated irrigation systems, railroad lines, and the like—are good examples of vernacular landscapes because of their importance and scale. They include numerous nationally significant linear resources closely tied to this country's heritage. Some are national historic landmarks, such as South Pass in Wyoming, the most widely used crossing of the Rocky Mountains during the nineteenth century (Figure 8.1). Their length is considerable. At the moment there are more than 24,000 miles of designated national historic trails. Among them are the Lewis and Clark, Oregon, California, Mormon Pioneer, Pony Express, Trail of Tears, Santa Fe, and El Camino Real de Tierra Adentro (Figures 8.2, 8.3). Other well-known transportation networks include Route 66 and the Lincoln Highway, both of which traverse a considerable portion of the United States. Most of the twenty-three national heritage areas also contain extensive linear landscapes.[13] For example, the Cache la Poudre National Heritage Area in north-central Colorado comprises more than two hundred miles of irrigation systems, which date from the mid-nineteenth century (Figure 8.4).

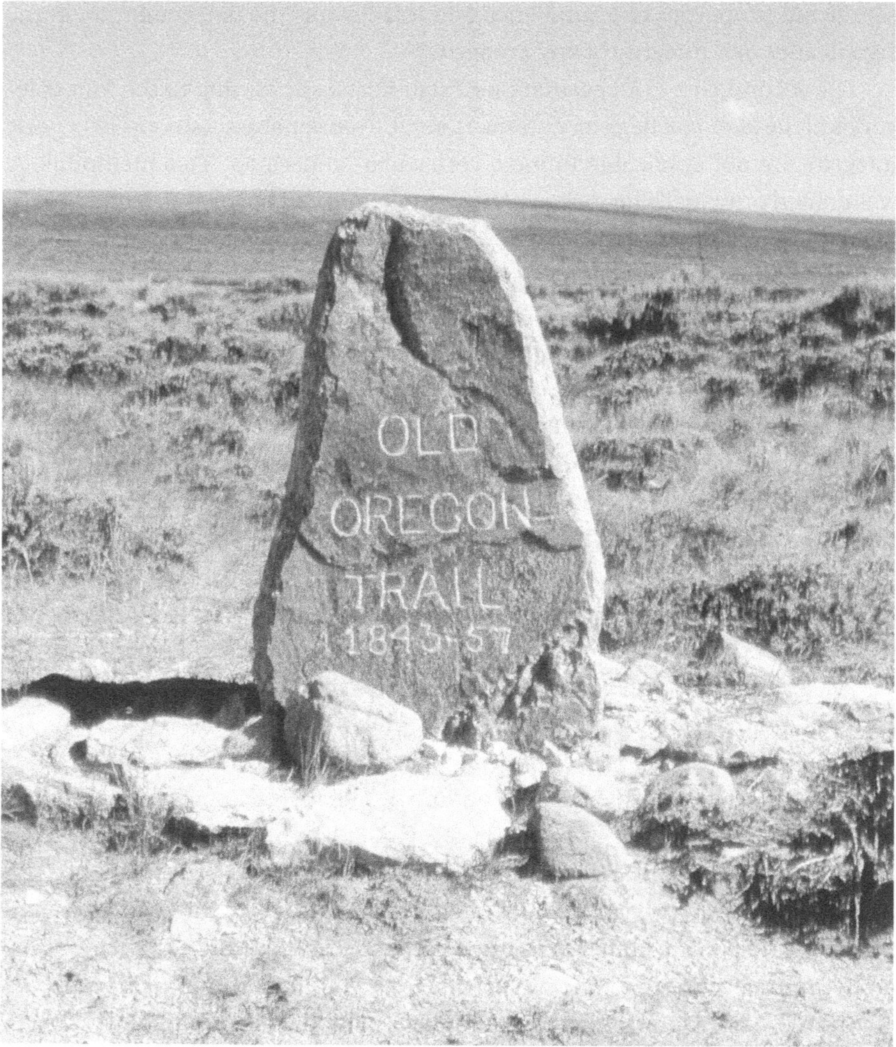

Figure 8.1. Oregon Trail, Ezra Meeker marker stone, South Pass, Wyoming. Photograph by author, 1998.

Interest in landscapes and transportation corridors is not limited to the United States. El Camino de Santiago, a pilgrimage route to Santiago de Compostela, which crosses both France and Spain, is a designated UNESCO World Heritage Site. Currently six Latin American countries—Colombia, Ecuador, Peru, Bolivia, Chile, and Argentina—are working cooperatively to nominate the Inka Road to the list of UNESCO world heritage sites. With more than twenty thousand miles of pathway to protect and very limited resources, the need to develop sensible strategies for the identification and protection of these Andean landscapes is a challenging one indeed.

Figure 8.2. Swales, Fandango Valley National Historic Trail, California. Photograph by author, 1995.

Figure 8.3. La Jornada de Muerto, New Mexico, a segment of El Camino Real de Tierra Adentro, blazed by Juan de Onate in 1598. Photograph by author, 1996.

Since they are primarily corridors, transportation networks are excellent examples of vernacular landscapes where natural components are ubiquitous and where the application of traditional historic preservation standards is difficult, if not impossible (Figure 8.5; see also Figures 8.1–8.4). These resources pose major challenges to managers. They have been used for centuries, often have several periods of significance, represent multiple uses and cultural values, are part of ethnographic landscapes, and are subject to the priorities of numerous owners

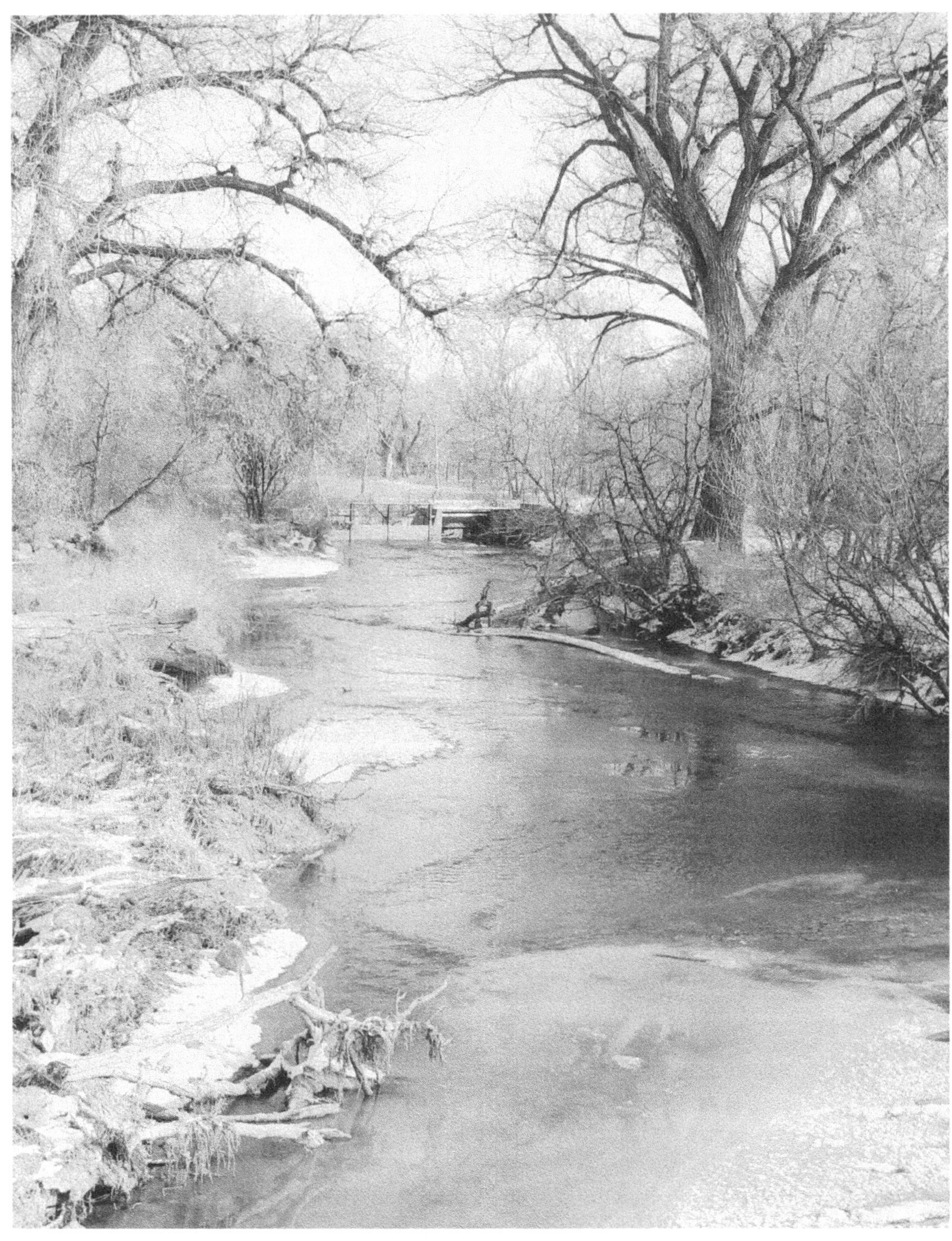

Figure 8.4. William R. Jones ditch, Cache de la Poudre National Heritage Area, Colorado. Photograph by author, 2004.

Figure 8.5. Lander Road, crossing central Wyoming. Photograph by author, 2003.

and jurisdictions. Legal property lines seldom match the limits of such a landscape. Moreover, it is difficult to demark where one landscape "ends" and the next one "begins." The horizon, which can be more than thirty miles away in any direction, is often the only clear visual boundary, and it changes with the movement of the observer. Historical documentation for specific segments of these landscapes is hard to find. Several landscape characteristics used in preservation—including patterns of spatial organization; boundary demarcations; vegetation related to land use; buildings, structures, and objects; and clusters—are irrelevant or very difficult to apply.

The major landscape characteristics that exist in transportation corridors are a function of environmental factors such as vegetation, climate, topography, and soils. Variations among these sometimes can help to identify boundaries. The width of the corridor fluctuates as it incorporates variations in routes and alignments (also the result of environmental factors) and is dependent on landforms. The corridor thus may include narrow canyons or extensive viewsheds. It may traverse a variety of ecoregions that create a multitude of landscapes of varying length and width. It is not possible to "freeze" or restore them as they were during their period of significance or to keep them from changing in unique and unpredictable ways.

Given their multifaceted complexion, transportation corridors can serve as a model for integrating natural and cultural resources into an effective preservation management plan. The Lander Road near Pinedale in west-central Wyoming provides a good example, stretching across an extensive area of sagebrush with few, if any, visual intrusions. Established in 1858, it was an important route for immigrants during the 1860s to reach both Oregon and the Montana minefields. Natural resources are essential components of this cultural landscape (see Figure 8.5). Yet there is little agreement on just what constitutes the resource that needs to be protected. Traditionally the ruts, or swales, have been considered *the* resource, but they have little meaning without the landscape of which they are a part—historically, visually, and ecologically. No strategy exists to provide the managers or owners of such resources with effective tools for their protection. One can even argue that the application of current preservation methodology to such landscapes may be neither desirable nor realistic given their size and complexity.

How can the results of research conducted by landscape ecologists assist in developing protection practices that are feasible and sensitive to the special nature of such landscapes? To make this connection, it is important to explore the relationship between ecologists' perspectives on landscapes and the evaluation process recommended by the National Register. Of the three steps in the evaluation process—identification of landscape characteristics, evaluation of their historical significance, and assessment of their historical integrity—only the second is not generally affected by the ecological perspective. That perspective can do much to assist in the other two, closely related steps, which must overcome the challenges of logical boundary demarcation.

Landscape ecologists also struggle in establishing boundaries. They view landscapes as open systems that are not static and cannot be easily defined. Understanding the fundamental mechanisms, spatial dynamics, and variability of ecological flow of materials, energy, and information across landscape boundaries is central to their research.[14] Given these circumstances, what approaches can be used to afford vernacular landscapes a level of protection? One possibility is the use of Geographic Information System technology to map and design protected viewsheds where visual intrusions are prohibited, as occurred at the Rock Springs District in Wyoming, a jurisdictional division of the Bureau of Land Management, in the late 1990s. This project, which aimed to protect the cultural landscape of South Pass, established a six-mile buffer zone (three miles on each side of the trail) where oil and gas exploration would be limited to those areas not visible from the trail.[15] The three-mile criterion was selected as a management compromise since some development would be visible beyond that limit. The solution was not ideal, but it affords some level of protection to a national historic landmark and attempts to address the issue of landscape boundaries in an effective way. However, even though the strategy proved practical and should prevent visual intrusions, it does not appear that it will be adopted in other Bureau of Land Management districts, due to that agency's current emphasis on mineral exploration.[16]

Identifying other landscape characteristics is not as challenging as determining boundaries but should also be carried out keeping in mind the perspective of landscape ecology—that patterns of change in any landscape will be unique, highly variable, and unpredictable. It is questionable to assume that the character-defining features of any landscape will remain unchanged or will follow expected patterns of evolution—a basic tenet of current preservation policies.

Assessing the historical integrity of vernacular landscapes is another task for which one should consider the research of landscape ecologists. Their studies conclude that landscapes are the product of a continually changing, dynamic configuration of natural elements that emphasizes disturbance as a constant agent of change within the system. Natural disturbances—for example, droughts, floods, and fires—and those caused by humans—including the introduction of exotic plants—are integral to any system and central to our cultural heritage. In this view, the specific dynamics of a given system are contingent on its history, on the accidents of arrivals as species disperse into the site, and on the nature of the system's interaction with surrounding landscapes.[17]

These conclusions challenge the value of the restoration of any landscape of large size since its long-term effectiveness cannot be guaranteed. Landscape restoration is a very costly management practice that may be neither feasible nor desirable. A current development provides a good example of the impact of unpredictable disturbances on landscapes. At this moment drought has caused a widespread beetle infestation of pinyon trees *(Pinus edulis)* throughout the Southwest, particularly in New Mexico, where in some areas more than 90 percent of the trees are dying. These trees are not only an important visual component of the southwestern landscape, but they have provided the timber used in building the early pit houses of Mesa Verde (AD 400–900), the pitch to caulk native baskets, and the pine nuts that have been a major food source for Native Americans, in some cases providing most or all of their winter diet.[18] It is a serious loss, but not one that can be corrected through landscape restoration.

Reaching an agreement on landscape integrity issues can be easier than establishing logical boundaries for extensive transportation corridors. Simple solutions might be possible and more cost-effective, although they will still require substantial political support. For example, the photographs of William Henry Jackson provide extensive evidence of what the landscape of southern Wyoming was like during the 1870s. In some areas changes have been dramatic. In others the landscape retains a remarkable level of integrity.[19] Can we realistically restore the landscapes that lost their integrity to their condition in the nineteenth century? It seems that where change has been dramatic and integrity is mostly lost, restoration is not a viable option given the size of the area and the unpredictable nature of landscape processes. It might be prudent to direct new development to those areas where integrity has already been compromised. Protection efforts should be concentrated on those relatively unchanged areas, where exclusion of development should be a primary goal.

How can we design and adopt practical, sensible, and scientifically based guidelines to assist with the protection of such an important component of our heritage? Because of the complexity and the size of the resources, it would be presumptuous to present a single, definitive answer at present. However, the first step should be to agree that the protection of these landscapes is important and needs to be addressed systematically to reach some degree of consensus, even if it means agreement that there will not be a single protection strategy for all these landscapes. There should also be some general guidelines that would keep in mind and complement existing historic preservation strategies. This latter objective could be done in a series of multidisciplinary workshops sponsored by those federal agencies that manage most of these vernacular landscapes. Landscape ecologists and other scientists, cultural geographers, landscape architects, historians, managers, landowners, and representatives of other pertinent groups should all participate.

The complexity and fluidity of the processes that influence the nature of landscapes are likely to preclude the development of rigid, easily applied guidelines. Continuous dialogue with land management agencies can assist in making decisions that take into consideration costs, political reality, and the nature of the resources in need of protection. Recently developed scientific approaches may be helpful. Since historic evidence of integrity is not always available, for instance, it might be possible to use the ecoregion concept as a preliminary basis for identifying landscape characteristics and degree of integrity. Various federal agencies, such as the Environmental Protection Agency and the USDA Forest Service, are conducting systematic work on this topic, and the information is widely available. Ecoregions are developed by delineating and classifying ecologically distinctive areas of the earth's surface. Each area is viewed as a discrete system, the result from the interplay of geology, landforms, soils, vegetation, climate, wildlife, water, and humans. The dominance of any one or a number of these factors varies with the given ecological land unit. This holistic approach to land classification can be applied incrementally on a scale-related basis from very site-specific ecosystems to very broad ones. Each ecological land unit has certain characteristics that reflect how processes have been instrumental in changing the land.[20]

Using already designed ecoregions can potentially assist in making rough estimates of the historical integrity of vernacular landscapes. Determining the ecological characteristics of these landscapes and their degree of integrity is a site-specific activity that requires intimate knowledge of both the historical and ecological context of the area. At the same time, since transportation networks extend for hundreds of miles and across various ecoregions, it is not likely that a single prescription for one such network in its entirety will be adequate. Flexibility is necessary to address the distinctive issues and problems associated with each component landscape.

Protection strategies should also consider that while the visual characteristics of a landscape are important, other sensory components make valuable contributions to its historical significance and help us make sense of and value what we see. The feel of the wind, the scent of vegetation, the presence of wildlife, and the sound of creeks, rivers, and birds are all key historic elements that are an integral part of the exceptional nature of some of these resources. We should also remember that protecting the visual does not necessarily prevent resource damage. Mining activities in Nevada, which have taken place outside the viewshed of historic trails, have dropped the water table to such a degree that all the springs used during the nineteenth century to sustain the immigrant population have dried out. This is another example of the need to consider the highly complex nature of landscapes while planning for their protection.

Finally, there is a great need for an integrated planning process to address cultural landscapes instead of just focusing on traditional historic preservation tools. Ample opportunities exist to use some of the strategies from natural resources management to assist in developing strategies that can successfully complement and enrich the current preservation models.

Arguments for widespread economic development throughout the country continue and are becoming increasingly hard to ignore. Vernacular landscapes are seriously threatened by both population growth and by rapidly increasing oil and gas exploration. We need to argue effectively for their protection before they are lost. Those arguments must be practical and based on scientific data reflecting what we have learned about landscapes during the past several decades. Guidelines for their protection need to be developed and made part of our federal protection before it is too late.

Notes

1. National Park Service guidelines recognize the need to preserve the biotic systems of designed landscapes, but their methodology so far has not addressed how to deal with them within the context of vernacular landscapes; NPS-28: *Cultural Resource Management Guidelines* (Washington, D.C.: National Park Service, 1998), 103–5.

2. The terms *preservation* and *conservation* tend to be used interchangeably with *protection*. However, they imply a greater level of intervention that may not be possible or

desirable in the case of vernacular landscapes. Throughout this chapter *protection* has been used because it suggests a more "natural" method of ensuring that these landscapes will not be destroyed.

3. Elias Mujica Barreda, ed., *Paisajes culturales en los Andes: Memoria narrativa, casos de estudio, conclusiones y recomendaciones de la reunion de expertos* (San Borja, Perú: UNESCO & CERVESUR, 2002).

4. D. W. Meinig, *The Interpretation of Ordinary Landscapes* (New York: Oxford University Press, 1979), 1–2; Meinig, "The Beholding Eye: Ten Versions of the Same Scene," *Landscape Architecture* 66 (January 1976): 47–54. Meinig discusses the multiple ways of examining landscapes, such as landscape as nature, as habitat, as artifact, as system, as problem, as wealth, as ideology, as history, and as place.

5. Eugene J. Palka, "Coming to Grips with the Concept of Landscape," *Landscape Journal* 14 (spring 1995): 63–73. Palka's analysis explores the evolution of the concept of landscape across time and cultures.

6. Olaf Bastian, "Landscape Ecology—Towards a Unified Discipline?" *Landscape Ecology* 16 (2001): 757–66; Jianguo Wu and Richard Hobbs, "Issues and Research Priorities in Landscape Ecology: An Idiosyncratic Synthesis," *Landscape Ecology* 17 (2002): 355–65; J. A. Wiens, "Toward a Unified Landscape Ecology," in *Issues in Landscape Ecology*, ed. J. A. Wiens and M. R. Moss (Guelph, Ont.: The Association, University Guelph, 1999), 148–51, quote on p. 149.

7. Dennis H. Knight, *Mountains and Plains: The Ecology of the Wyoming Landscapes* (New Haven, Conn.: Yale University Press, 1994).

8. According to Charles A. Birnbaum, ed., with Christine Capella Peters, *The Secretary of the Interior's Standards for the Treatment of Historic Properties with Guidelines for the Treatment of Cultural Landscapes* (Washington, D.C.: National Park Service, 1996), "preservation" standards require retention of the greatest amount of historic fabric, including the landscape's historic form, features, and details as they have evolved over time; "rehabilitation" standards acknowledge the need to alter or add to a cultural landscape to meet continuing or new uses while retaining the landscape's historic character; "restoration" standards allow for the depiction of a landscape at a particular time in U.S. history by preserving materials from the period of significance and removing materials from other periods; "reconstruction" standards establish a framework for re-creating a vanished or nonsurviving landscape with new materials, primarily for interpretive purposes.

9. A "designed historic landscape" is one that has significance as a design or work of art; was consciously designed and laid out by a master gardener, landscape architect, architect, or horticulturalist to a design principle, or by an owner or another amateur using a recognized style or tradition in response or reaction to a recognized style or tradition; has a historical association with a significant person, trend, or event in landscape gardening or landscape architecture; or has a significant relationship to the theory or practice of landscape architecture. J. Timothy Keller and Genevieve P. Keller, "How to Evaluate and Nominate Designed Historic Landscapes," *National Register Bulletin* 18 (1992): 1–2. A "rural historic landscape" is a geographical area that historically has been used by people; that has been shaped or modified by human activity, occupancy, or intervention; and that possesses a significant concentration, linkage, or continuity of areas of land use, vegetation, buildings and structures, roads, and waterways, and natural features. Linda Flint McClelland, J. Timothy Kelley, Genevieve P. Kelley, and Robert Z. Melnick, "Guidelines for Evalu-

ating and Documenting Rural Historic Landscapes," *National Register Bulletin* 30 (1992): 1–2. An "ethnographic landscape" is one containing a variety of natural and cultural resources that associated people define as heritage resources, and/or a landscape used or valued in traditional ways by contemporary ethnic groups. Robert R. Page, "Cultural Landscapes Inventory Professional Procedures Guide" (Washington, D.C.: National Park Service, 1998), 56–57.

10. McClelland et al., "Guidelines for Evaluating and Documenting Rural Historic Landscapes," 15–18.

11. National Register regulations contain four criteria to establish national significance: (a) association with events that have made a significant contribution to the broad patterns of our history; (b) association with the lives of persons significant in our past; (c) embodiment of the distinctive characteristics of a type, period, or method of construction; representation of the work of a master; possession of high artistic values; representation of a significant or distinguishable entity whose components may lack individual distinction; and (d) ability to yield, or may be likely to yield, information important in prehistory or history. "Guidelines for Applying the National Register Criteria for Evaluation," *National Register Bulletin* 15 (1990): 3–4. The Park Service continues to refine its methodology to facilitate the identification and evaluation of landscapes by both its staff and those interested in nominating a property to the National Register. The level of detail is quite exhaustive and demonstrates a serious commitment to the topic. See Page, "Cultural Landscapes Inventory Professional Procedures Guide."

12. Birnbaum, ed., *Guidelines,* 10.

13. South Pass is south of Lander in west-central Wyoming. Fondago is a portion of the California Trail at the northeastern corner of California. La Jornada del Muerto is a sixty-mile stretch of trail Juan de Onate used in 1598 to settle what is now New Mexico; this segment is near Paraje Robledo in south-central New Mexico.

14. Knight, *Mountains and Plains,* 5–9.

15. South Pass was designated a national historic landmark in 1981. At that time, boundary demarcation was not a requirement for the nomination process. Today, no agreement exists as to the legal boundaries of the site.

16. Letter to author from Russ Tanner, archeologist, Rock Springs District, Bureau of Land Management, Rock Springs, Wyoming, 1998.

17. Robert E. Cook, "Is Landscape Preservation an Oxymoron?" *George Wright Forum* 13 (1996): 42–53.

18. Michael T. Friggens, "Drought Induced Pinyon Mortality in the Los Pinos Mountains, Socorro County, New Mexico, 1998–2003," http://sevilleta.unm.edu/~friggens/final; "Ips Bark Beetles: Silvicultural Handbook," http://www.fs.fed.us/r2/fhm/bugcrud/silvips.html; Stuart Wier, "The Pinyon Pine of the Southern Rocky Mountains," http://homeartlink.net/~swier/PinyonPine.html.

19. Kendall Jonson, *Rangeland through Time: A Photographic Study of Vegetation Change in Wyoming, 1870–1986* (Laramie: University of Wyoming Agricultural Experiment Station, Miscellaneous Publication 50, 1987).

20. J. M. Omernik, "Ecoregions: A Framework for Managing Ecosystems," *George Weight Forum* 12 (1995): 35–51; Robert G. Bailey, *Descriptions of the Ecoregions of the United States* (Washington, D.C.: U.S. Department of Agriculture, Forest Service, Miscellaneous Publication 1391, 1995).

9. Cultural Landscapes

Venues for Community-based Conservation

SUSAN BUGGEY AND NORA MITCHELL

Over the past two decades, recognition of the heritage value of cultural landscapes has contributed to an expanded vision for the field of historic preservation in the United States, Canada, and other countries.[1] Considering cultural landscapes led to the inclusion of diverse worldviews, cultural traditions, and natural resources as determinants of heritage values and management objectives. This broadened perspective has transformed ideas of what is significant and authentic and has fostered integration with other cultural interests and community goals alike. Contributions from interdisciplinary partnerships and innovations in community-based approaches to landscape management have also added new insights and methodologies. Perhaps most importantly, application of the concept of cultural landscape has demonstrated the value of engaging people who live and work in these places and whose commitment is critical to their preservation.

The heritage of large-scale vernacular and associative cultural landscapes is usually linked to traditional ownership and management practices. Community involvement is thus not only key to the conservation process, but success depends on applying locally based collaborative strategies that respect cultural, religious, and historical traditions along with ecological systems. Case studies from First Nations in northern Canada and ranching landscapes of the American West illustrate how community-based conservation can enable people to cooperate in both identifying and retaining the values and the essential character of places by planning for the future and managing change. The process has reached new constituencies for historic preservation and has laid the foundation for sustaining important cultural landscapes.

Interdisciplinary Contributions to the Concept of Cultural Landscape

Recognition of cultural landscapes within the field of historic preservation has broadened the meaning and interpretation of human interaction with the land. In the past twenty years, the historic preservation movement has actively expanded its purview to encompass landscapes that are defined by broader human

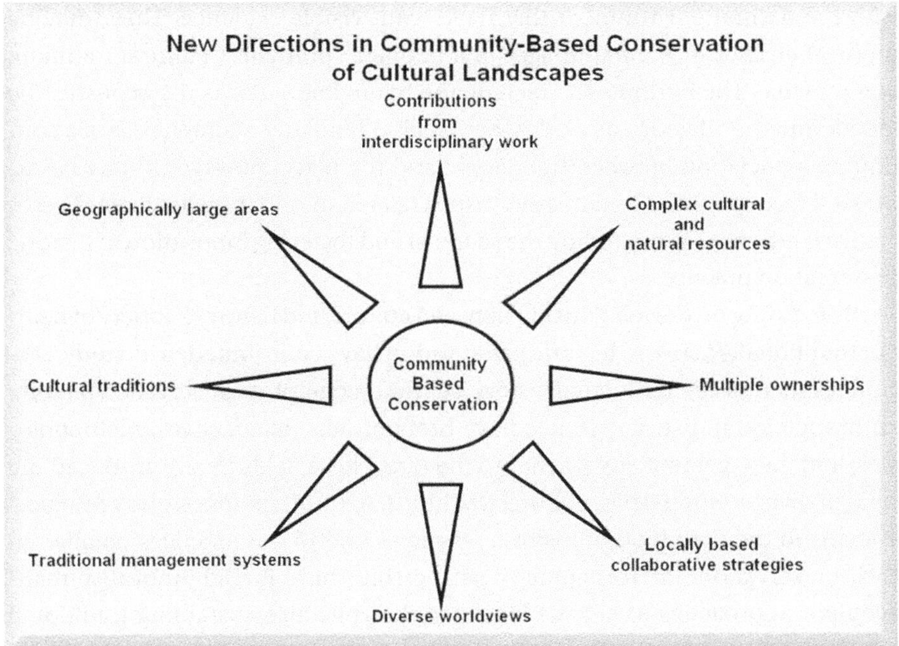

Figure 9.1. Conceptual diagram of components of community-based preservation of cultural landscapes. Image designed by Leslie Shahi.

relationships to place. This new perspective gives value to the material evidence of how people have adapted to and shaped the land on which they live (Figure 9.1). Cultural landscapes reflect processes and activities related to land and sea in such basic ways as settlement, agriculture, fishing, mining, forestry, and sustainable harvesting. Cultural landscapes can be characterized by patterns and interactions as much as by physical features. The concept of cultural landscape thus recognizes that many human relationships to the land and sea—religious, artistic, spiritual, and cultural—are not primarily reflected in material evidences.

In both the United States and Canada, most of the early work on cultural landscapes focused primarily on historic designed landscapes such as gardens, estates, and parkways. Increasingly over the past few years, attention has extended to vernacular and associative cultural landscapes. Vernacular landscapes are defined by the continuation of cultural traditions and land management activities in association with the natural environment. These landscapes are accumulative; they include material evidence from previous generations as well as ongoing cultural activity. As a result, they continue to evolve as the people occupying them respond to changes of many kinds. Associative cultural landscapes mark a significant departure from conventional heritage concepts rooted in physical resources. Associative landscapes have strong religious, artistic, or cultural links with the natural environment that have scant visible evidence. They "may be physical entities or mental images in a people's spirituality, cultural tradition, and practice. The attributes . . . include the intangible, such as the acoustic, the kinetic and the olfactory, as well as the visual . . . [and] the maintenance of a continuing association between the people and the place, however it may be expressed through time."[2] Addressing issues related to both vernacular and associative landscapes is expanding the scope of and fostering innovation in historic preservation practice.

By focusing on the relationship between culture and nature, a variety of fields not traditionally active in historic preservation have contributed to its study. Disciplines such as environmental history, cultural geography, conservation biology, anthropology, and social science have brought new perspectives, methodologies, and management approaches to the fore. These fields have introduced the roles of diverse worldviews, cultural traditions, natural resources, and ecological systems to the definition of historic resources and to the practices entailed in their preservation. Interdisciplinary partnerships have forged innovative management approaches to engage local people while also sustaining traditional land uses that shaped the region, strengthening nature conservation and retaining cultural traditions, landscape character, and economic viability.

New interfaces with environmental history and historical ecology have opened different ways of looking at the values of a place. With strong public interest in the environment, the interpretive perspective has focused management attention on the impact of past human actions on the natural world. Methodologies used by historical ecologists offer further opportunities to understand the cultural and natural history of landscapes and to develop management approaches that respect their values. Ecologist Emily Russell, for example, links ecology and history to explore the causes of past changes to ecosystems and the effects of past activities on present ecosystems, such as lakes, woodlands, and agricultural areas.[3]

Traditional methodologies of cultural geography and of natural resource management have contributed to looking at cultural landscapes as interconnected systems, which ecologist Robert Cook illustrated in exploring the oxymoron of landscape preservation.[4] Recognizing the role of not only specific natural resources but also natural systems in shaping the character of a place has contributed to redefining values in cultural landscapes. A new emphasis on patterns and processes of the landscape—both often shaped by an area's natural systems—has recently helped to move decision-making analysis from a focus primarily on the historic features and materials to spatial organization, land patterns, and landforms themselves (Figure 9.2).[5]

Common ground is increasingly recognized between cultural landscapes and protected landscapes and seascapes, one of the World Conservation Union's

Figure 9.2. Marsh-Billings-Rockefeller National Historical Park, Woodstock, Vermont, view of watershed, showing the complexity of vernacular cultural landscapes where culture and nature have shaped the character and where the future will be shaped by partnerships of residents, business, and local, state, and federal governments. Photograph by Barbara Slaiby. Courtesy of Conservation Study Institute.

(IUCN's) six categories of protected areas.[6] Protected landscapes and seascapes attribute value to the role people play in sustaining biological and cultural diversity. Much of the comprehensive management approach in IUCN's recent *Management Guidelines* can be readily adapted to vernacular and associative cultural landscapes, where management studies and guidelines are still notably missing.[7]

Recognizing the role of natural systems as an integral part of heritage values has substantially changed perspectives toward cultural landscapes. For example, the Rideau Canal—the central feature of a 202-kilometer cultural landscape in eastern Ontario—utilizes a series of excavated channels, masonry locks, dams, weirs, and embankments to join the watersheds of two major river systems. Traditionally, the nationally significant, early-nineteenth-century defensive waterway has been recognized and managed primarily for its engineering achievement, for the high level of integrity of its cultural resources, and for its recreational role. However, in its construction, the slack water system that engineers used to raise shallow waters to navigable levels and to regulate water flow resulted in extensive drowned lands. These activities significantly altered the regional ecosystem but also created new wetlands, including new or substantially enlarged lakes. As a result of the addition of this environmental history to the traditional military and settlement history, the canal's historical significance now embraces the alteration of the natural environment. Today the natural ecosystem of the canal corridor is managed as an integral component of the historic site.[8]

Cultural anthropologists such as Setha Low have developed techniques for assessing sociocultural values related to cultural heritage sites, using cognitive, observational, and constituency analysis methodologies that are applicable to cultural landscapes as well. "Rapid Ethnographic Assessment Procedures," used at National Park Service historical parks, for example, can provide insight into social dynamics that elude traditional preservation analyses.[9] In Ontario, landscape architect Nancy Pollock-Ellwand has outlined strategies for bridging the gap between government policy makers and community residents in understanding and conserving landscapes through land-use planning. These approaches recognize the power of human dynamics in understanding and protecting landscapes.[10]

The exploration of landscapes as cultural processes focuses on people's relation to place. Intangible traditions related to place preserve cultural memory through social structure, economic activity, language, and spiritual beliefs. Participatory action research, such as the Traditional Environmental Knowledge Pilot Project of the Dene Cultural Institute, exemplifies how the involvement of aboriginal peoples, particularly elders, has refocused research from analysis of physical resources to recognition of the holistic, essentially spiritual relationship of people and land.[11] In this project, First Nation peoples in Canada's north played a key role in directing the research design and implementation for studies that served their needs. Among Western societies, Australia in particular has integrated social values into the assessment of its historic places. A recent discussion paper on social significance published in New South Wales advocates "putting archaeological, architectural and historical significance within a broader context, such that rather than being the primary determinants of significance, they become tools to support and better understand the attachment of communities to heritage places and items."[12]

Highlighting Community Values

The preservation movement has traditionally not done well in recognizing and protecting historic resources associated with the immense cultural diversity of North America outside the dominant culture. The integration of cultural landscapes into that movement during the past decade, however, has opened opportunities for recognition of the ties between place and identity in communities. The concept of cultural landscape has fostered pride and recognition of historic places in ethnocultural communities and has been especially important in addressing the long history of aboriginal peoples in North America. From their perspective, connectedness has always framed perceptions of landscape. Landscapes are defined not by natural resources, not by economic uses, not by social values, not by psychological values, but by the relatedness of all these and other considerations as well. Winona LaDuke, an Anishinaabeg of Minnesota, explained: "The struggle to preserve the trees of White Earth is not solely about forest preservation and biodiversity. It is also about cultural transformation, for the Anishinaabeg forest culture cannot exist without the forest."[13] Indigenous peoples in many parts of the world who conceive landscape fundamentally in spiritual rather than material terms identify traditional knowledge closely tied to place at the heart of their cultural identity.

While Western science has long viewed culture and nature as separate spheres, aboriginal worldviews see a holistic universe in which the cosmological, geographic, ecological, cultural, and spiritual are intimately connected. Because this worldview is so different from traditional Western perspective, cultural landscapes often embody conflicting values, as architect and educator Rina Swentzell explained in examining her native Santa Clara Pueblo in New Mexico and the adjacent Bureau of Indian Affairs day school. The respective relationships to land, she emphasizes,

> reflect the divergent world views of two cultures, as well as their differing methods and content of education. . . . [In the Pueblo] humans exist within the cosmos and are an integral part of the functioning of the earth community. . . . There are no outdoor areas that attest to human control over nature, no areas where nature is domesticated.[14]

Aboriginal peoples' intimate knowledge of the natural resources and ecosystems of the territories they traditionally occupied and the respect they have for the spirits that inhabit these areas molded life on the land. Through shapes, names, spirits, and related behavior, places act as mnemonic devices for recalling the narratives that instruct the people from generation to generation in knowing and living with these landscapes. As Yukon anthropologist Julie Cruikshank expressed it, "Oral tradition is mapped on the landscape . . . events are anchored to place and people use locations in space to speak about events in time."[15] Protection of these places is key to long-term survival of First Nation cultures. Identity is encoded not only in place-names and narratives but also more broadly in language. Threats to the survival of traditional languages are intimately associated with threats to biodiversity, cultural identity, and place. Speaking in 1999 on the occasion of the political creation of Canada's new northern territory, Nunavut, where 85 percent of the population are Inuit, Peter Irniq, then deputy minister of the Department of Culture, Language, Elders, and Youth, captured the relationship of language, identity, and place in stating that "the landscape speaks Inuktitut."[16]

The 1990s witnessed a significant shift in the recognition of values in places associated with aboriginal peoples from a focus on archaeological resources and material culture analysis, to ethno-archaeology, and then to cultural landscapes. The new direction underlines the involvement of local people, particularly elders, and their long and intimate connection with the land. A core principle accords respect and weight in decision making to traditional knowledge related to the land, including traditional ecological knowledge, that incorporates aboriginal worldviews, oral narrative traditions, and the inseparability of cultural and natural values.[17]

The Kazan River Fall Caribou Crossing in Nunavut is one of a number of aboriginal cultural landscapes lying within the traditional territories of several First Nation groups in Canada that have been designated as national historic sites since 1992 (Figure 9.3). Based on community identification and management of places that aboriginal peoples consider important, these landscapes incorporate community engagement and a values-based management approach.

The designated area of the Kazan River Fall Caribou Crossing—stretching from the spectacular twenty-five-meter-high Kazan Falls (Qurluqtuq) to the east end of Thirty Mile Lake (Quukitlruq)—lies on Inuit-owned lands in the traditional territory of the Harvaqtuurmiut people in Nunavut. The Harvaqtuurmiut identified the Fall Caribou Crossing site as historically significant because here the 320,000-strong Kaminuriak caribou herd, whose calving grounds are nearby, crosses the river in spring and fall migrations. These annual movements shaped the seasonal routine of the inland Inuit in the tundra barrenlands for centuries. The crossing embodies the view held by many indigenous peoples that they are part of a living landscape, where they are one with the animals, plants, and ancestors whose spirits inhabit the land. Intimate knowledge of and respect for the land and the annual fall caribou hunt molded Inuit life and was indeed crucial to surviving the long, dark, and viciously cold winter. Inuksuit—structures made of stone to direct caribou and guide travelers—mark the landscape, as do archaeological remains such as hearths, food caches, and hunting blinds. Place-names for landscape features serve as mnemonic devices for events, resources, and dangers that guide the Inuit in reading the land; songs composed primarily of series of place-names tell their journeys.[18]

Since national heritage designation provides no legal protection, preserving such a landscape requires development of management objectives and their integration with local planning, economic development, and tourism initiatives. The Nunavut Land Claims Agreement (1993) and the subsequent Inuit Impact and Benefits Agreements provide the legislative framework for protection of

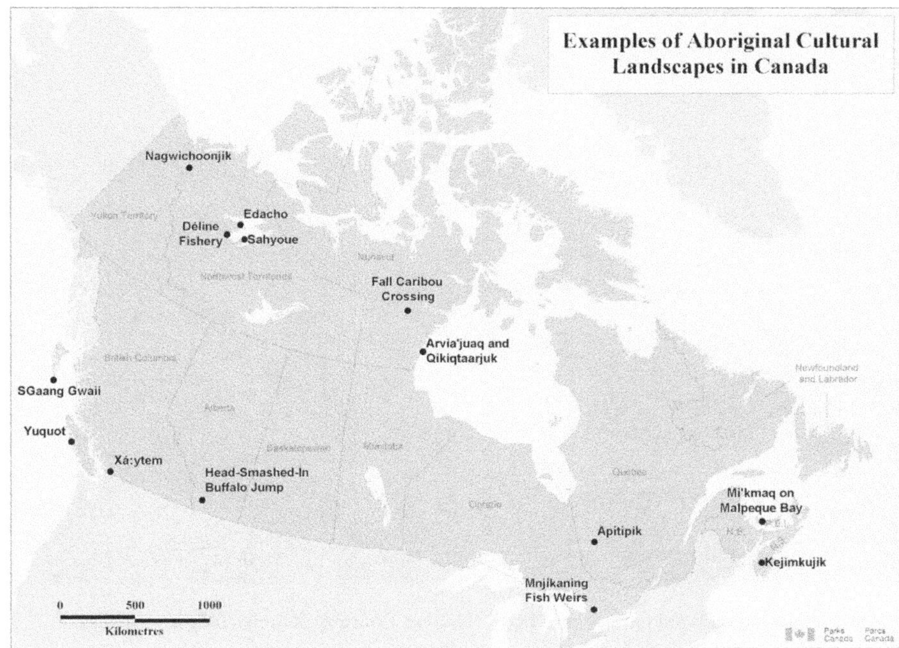

Figure 9.3. Map of Canada, showing some cultural landscapes of First Nation groups designated national historic sites since 1992. Image by Dan Pagé. Courtesy of Archaeological Services Branch, Parks Canada.

Inuit heritage. They ensure integration of the regional economy and Inuit culture in all planning and development in the territory.

For the Fall Caribou Crossing, the Harvaqtuuq Historic Site Committee, the Harvaqtuurmiut Elders, and Parks Canada developed a document that delineates the objectives for ensuring the site's protection The key components were respect for traditional Inuit beliefs and practices and for the wishes of the elders, recording and interpreting traditions through oral histories and other means so that they can be transmitted to future generations, leaving archaeological remains undisturbed unless related to research, retaining low-impact land-use practices, and monitoring the health of the Kaminuriak caribou herd and of the Kazan River.[19]

The Harvaqtuurmiut elaborated these objectives as a strategy, with a set of goals and actions for protecting the cultural landscape in a conservation report. They submitted this report to the Nunavut Planning Commission and the Nunavut Water Board, and they gained commitment from the planning commission to maintain the GIS database for the site. They also used the regional land-use plan to provide protection against development in the cultural landscape by specifying low-impact land use and by prohibiting new permanent structures, thereby avoiding damaging archaeological resources and disturbing movement of the

Figure 9.4. Caribou trails at Piqqiq, Kazan River, Nunavut. Courtesy of Archaeological Services Branch, Parks Canada.

caribou (Figure 9.4).[20] The approach illustrates the potential for linking historical and cultural significance with protection to influence land-use planning and other decisions that affect aboriginal cultural landscapes.

In addition to these planning initiatives, the community carries out a guardian-monitoring program through which members report observations of significant changes, threats, or looting during periodic site visits. Proper conduct in visitation, operation, protection, and interpretation at the crossing is guided by traditional Inuit values and beliefs. Conservation planning and presentation—site-oriented activities that relate to visitor services and communication of values—undertaken for the cultural landscape have thus been designed to safeguard the integrity of the traditional relationship of the Harvaqtuurmiut people to the crossing. Values-based management and community-based conservation predicated on the traditions of the Harvaqtuurmiut provide the opportunity for protecting and sustaining this cultural landscape; however, it will take time to assess its effectiveness.

Protecting Traditional Cultures

Conservation of cultural landscapes presents many challenges, in particular, sustaining the traditional functions that shaped the landscape in the context of changing social and economic conditions. Successful conservation of such living places accommodates change while retaining landscape character, cultural traditions, and economic viability. These landscapes often involve many landowners and stakeholders over multiple jurisdictions, so conservation requires partnerships and flexibility. The importance of developing some type of community-based governance for decision making is also a key ingredient for the success and sustainability of conservation. Examples from ranches in the western United States illustrate innovative entrepreneurial approaches that capitalize on regional cultural traditions to revitalize economies through collaboration, integrate natural resources protection, and experiment with place-based products.

The Malpai Borderlands is a million-acre region lying just north of the U.S.-Mexican boundary in both Arizona and New Mexico. Today, thirty-five ranching families and various state and federal agencies own and manage the land. They also share a long history of conflicting interests and antagonistic relationships. Ranching, the socioeconomic life of the region since the late nineteenth century, has become increasingly threatened by escalating land values and fragmentation of the open landscape by housing development. The centuries-old native desert grasslands, with a rich diversity of plant and animal species, were ecologically fragile and fire-dependent systems that had been transformed through overgrazing and fire suppression into less desirable range dominated by woody plants. In the early 1990s, a group of neighboring ranchers began to discuss their mutual problems; three years later they formed the Malpai Borderlands Group, now a nonprofit organization. This management initiative illustrates how a focus on what is right for the resources of the region provides common ground for multiple stakeholders with divergent interests to cooperate on the long-term sustainability of both ranching life and biological diversity.[21]

The collaborative approach of the Malpai Borderlands Group represented a dramatic departure from the previous strategies of lobbying and fighting. The ranchers sought a more positive, proactive way to address their problems, one that would create more effective, lasting solutions. Through discussions with representatives from the Nature Conservancy—an international organization that protects land for biological diversity—and federal and state agencies, the ranchers found that unfragmented, open grassland represented common ground. One rancher explained, "it's the lifestyle that the ranchers are fighting for as well. We have to take care of the land so we can stay here. We want to be ranchers. We want the open space lifestyle."[22] This identification of shared interests and the building of trust over time became the basis for new cooperative strategies between private landowners and public land managers.

The group began with fire management and evolved a more comprehensive natural resource management and rural development agenda, including ecosystem planning and associated scientific research. One of the most successful efforts was the creation of "grass banks" in cooperation with the Nature Conservancy. Many ranchers use rangeland in degraded condition because they do not have the option of removing their cattle to allow its rehabilitation. With grass banking, ranchers are able to exchange access to other locations (the "grass bank") for specific ecological protection on their own lands. Ranchers also have the opportunity to work with range managers to develop a sustainable grazing plan for their land. The program is entirely voluntary, gives ranchers flexibility, allows renovation of public and private lands, and has enabled many ranchers to make their business profitable again. The grass banks of the 322,000-acre Gray Ranch, approximately one-third of the Borderlands region, possess exceptional grassland and riparian significance, including distinct soils and landforms and high species diversity (Figure 9.5). A major boost to the grass bank initiative occurred in 1990 when the Nature Conservancy purchased this ranch. The tract is now owned, with conservation restrictions, by the local, nonprofit Animas Foundation. A member of the Malpai Borderlands Group, the foundation is dedicated to protecting the ranch's ecological values as well as the cultural and economic heritage of the region.[23] The Malpai Borderlands Group is one of the best examples of ranching collaboration in the West and has fostered a significant new trend.[24]

An initiative from the Yampa River valley in northwestern Colorado illustrates an entrepreneurial approach to preserving the ranching way of life in the face of rapidly increasing land values. A variety of strategies have been developed to conserve the natural and agricultural heritage of the valley, including testing innovative ranching and grazing practices, purchasing through conservation easements a rancher's right to develop property, and establishing the Yampa Valley Beef program.[25] In 1998, an alliance of ranchers, conservationists, business owners, and government officials explored ways to counter the enticement of selling ranch land for development. Through the creation of a niche market, they provided the means by which ranchers could get premium prices for beef raised on conserved land. Attracted by this concept, the Nature Conservancy became a partner in the effort. In 2000–01, more than twenty ranchers sold over thirty thousand pounds of beef, about 50 percent of which had been nurtured on land protected by conservation easements. A local Economic Development Committee also supported this initiative. Area restaurants and grocery stores became the primary market, but sales on the Internet were also explored. Some corporate profits are donated to a local land trust for preservation of open space, but sustaining the ranching lifestyle is the primary motivation for the participants.

A similar market-based landscape conservation program has been initiated in Montana's Madison Valley, also in cooperation with the Nature Conservancy.[26] The strategy is based on informed consumer choice in support of protecting

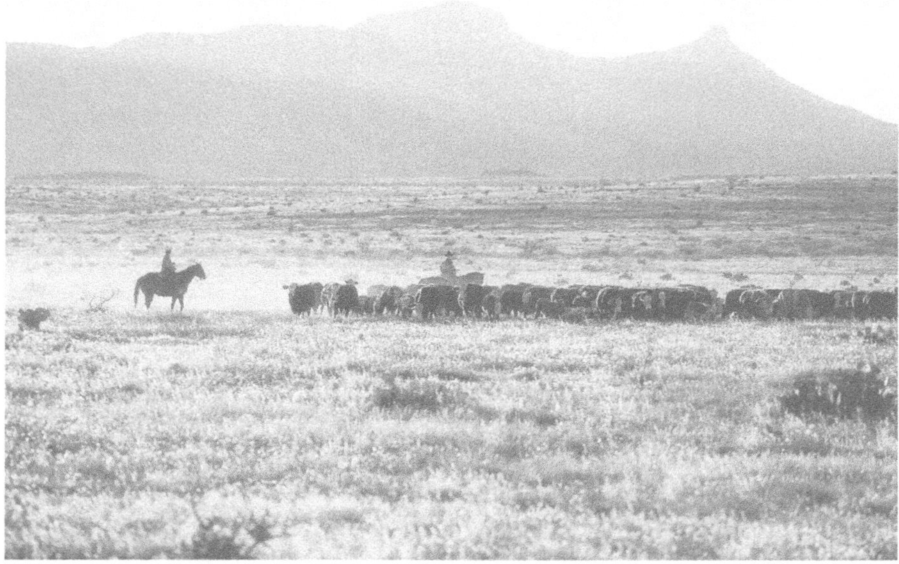

Figure 9.5. Gray Ranch, Malpai Borderlands, New Mexico. Photograph copyright Will Van Overbeek.

ranches as well as biological diversity. Producing mature, grass-fed, free-range beef requires relearning older ranching traditions and then combining them with landscape conservation on ecologically significant lands.[27] Permanent conservation easements are encouraged on the most significant and fragile habitats. By 2004, three ranches in the Madison Valley were participating in the program, and two others in California were in negotiations. Recently, the owners of one of the largest ranches in southwest Montana, the 18,000-acre Sun Ranch, donated an easement to the Nature Conservancy of Montana, protecting the significant wildlife habitat and an environment conducive to raising top-grade beef.[28] There has been good response to the program by consumers, chefs, and the ranching community. Two challenges remain: to reach large-volume markets and to create year-round supplies, which will require raising beef in a variety of places with different climates.

Over the past several years, the National Cattlemen's Beef Association and the Nature Conservancy have worked closely together on national legislation through the Farm Bill to authorize funding over six years to purchase easements on two million acres of prairie and native grasslands.[29] This collaboration on the Grassland Reserve Program was possible only after years of cooperating on the ground to keep ranches—and the cultural tradition they represent—intact and viable, while protecting their natural resources.

All of these examples are relatively recent and have yet to be tested by time and circumstance; however, they offer promise for long-term management of

Figure 9.6. Ranchers, Malpai Borderlands. Photograph courtesy of Kelly Cash/Nature Conservancy.

working cultural landscapes and may provide models that can be applied elsewhere. In light of the intense land development pressures in the West, this type of private-public cooperation and a community-based approach, designed and driven by key stakeholders, will continue to be essential to sustain ranching as a cultural tradition as well as to conserve the landscapes' rich biodiversity (Figure 9.6).

Conclusion

Experiences such as those in the Canadian North and the American West have created greater awareness and understanding of the opportunities in large, multistakeholder, multijurisdictional cultural landscapes. Each of these initiatives encompassed the interaction of culture and the natural environment, the socioeconomic needs of communities, and the culture of the people who live there (Figure 9.7).[30] Intangible heritage often plays a crucial role in decision making about these cultural landscapes in concert with conservation of the area's physical resources and sense of place. The meanings that people attach to the landscapes and their active involvement in the process have become core elements in retaining the essential character of these places while accommodating change.[31]

In his work for the Getty Conservation Institute, economist David Throsby defines a "sustainable solution to a problem [as one] ... that is not a quick fix but is likely to provide a more permanent or lasting remedy...," adding, "principles of long-term decision-making [and] concern for future generations ... are im-

Figure 9.7. Conceptual diagram of factors entailed in community-based cultural landscape preservation. Image designed by Leslie Shahi.

portant for the disciplines of both conservation and economics in their respective analyses of cultural heritage."[32] Sustainability thus includes the recognition of multiple ecological, economic, social, and cultural values that are integral to the character of the cultural landscape and that are integrated into community-based decision making and governance structures. This substantial broadening of the concept of cultural landscapes demands preservation leadership that is respectful, collaborative, and flexible. While this development represents tremendous progress, the need remains to integrate cultural landscapes and their values more effectively within North American society. Through a more inclusive approach, cultural landscape conservation can touch the lives of many citizens and engage them in caring for the special landscapes of their communities.

Notes

1. Bernd von Droste, Harald Plachter, and Mechtild Rössler, eds., *Cultural Landscapes of Universal Value: Components of a Global Strategy* (Jenna, Germany: Gustav Fischer in cooperation with UNESCO, 1995); Rolf Diamant et al., *Stewardship Begins with People: An Atlas of Places, People and Handmade Products* (Woodstock, Vt.: Conservation Study Institute, 2007). In Canada and many other nations *conservation* is used in more or less the same way as *preservation* and *historic preservation* are used in the United States. In this

chapter, *conservation* is used as a term that includes the U.S. concept of historic preservation but extends this concept to include natural resources and community engagement.

2. "The Asia-Pacific Regional Workshop on Associative Cultural Landscapes, A Report to the World Heritage Committee," Australia ICOMOS, 1995, sects. 1, 4, http://whc.unesco.org/archive/cullan95.htm (accessed 24 June 2004). The landscape categories outlined here were codified by UNESCO in 1992; UNESCO World Heritage Convention, *Operational Guidelines for the Implementation of the World Heritage Convention* (Paris: UNESCO, 1994), clauses 35–42.

3. Emily W. B. Russell, *People and the Land through Time: Linking Ecology and History* (New Haven, Conn.: Yale University Press, 1997).

4. Robert E. Cook, "Is Landscape Preservation an Oxymoron?" *George Wright Forum* 13: 1 (1996): 42–53, http://www.icls.harvard.edu/ecology/cook2.html (accessed 24 June 2004).

5. Charles A. Birnbaum, ed., with Christine Capella Peters, *The Secretary of the Interior's Standards with Guidelines for the Treatment of Cultural Landscapes* (Washington, D.C.: National Park Service, 1996); "Landscapes," in *Parks Canada—Standards and Guidelines for the Conservation of Historic Places in Canada* (Gatineau, Que.: Parks Canada, 2004), http://www.pc.gc.ca/doc/pc/guide/hldclp-sgchpc/sec3/page3e_e.asp (accessed 14 September 2004).

6. Nora Mitchell and Susan Buggey, "Protected Landscapes and Cultural Landscapes: Taking Advantage of Diverse Approaches," *George Wright Forum* 17: 1 (2000): 35–46.

7. Adrian Phillips, *Management Guidelines for IUCN Category V Protected Areas, Protected Landscapes/Seascapes* (Gland, Switzerland: IUCN, World Conservation Union, 2002); http://www.iucn.org/themes/wcpa/pubs/guidelines.htm (accessed 24 June 2004).

8. "Rideau Canal National Historic Site of Canada. Draft Management Plan," Parks Canada, Smiths Falls, Ont., 2000.

9. Setha M. Low, "Anthropological-Ethnographic Methods for the Assessment of Cultural Values in Heritage Conservation," in *Assessing the Values of Cultural Heritage*, ed. Marta de la Torre (Los Angeles: Getty Conservation Institute, 2002), 31–49.

10. Nancy Pollock-Ellwand, "Landscape Policy and Planning Practice: The Gap in Understanding, Ontario, Canada," *Landscape Research* 26 (April 2001): 99–118.

11. Martha Johnson, "Documenting Traditional Environmental Knowledge: The Dene, Canada," in *Listening for a Change: Oral Testimony and Community Development*, ed. Hugo Slim et al. (Philadelphia: New Society Publishers, 1995), 116–25.

12. Jason Ardler, foreword to *Social Significance: A Discussion Paper*, ed. Denis Byrne et al. (Sydney: New South Wales National Parks and Wildlife Service, 2003), iii. See also Randall Mason, "Management for Cultural Landscape Preservation: Insights from Australia," chapter 10, this volume.

13. Winona LaDuke, *All Our Relations: Native Struggles for Land and Life* (Minneapolis: South End Press 1999), 127.

14. Rina Swentzell, "Conflicting Landscape Values: The Santa Clara Pueblo and Day School," in *Understanding Ordinary Landscapes*, ed. Paul Groth and Todd W. Bressi (New Haven, Conn.: Yale University Press, 1997), 56.

15. Julie Cruikshank, "Oral Traditions and Oral History: Reviewing Some Issues," *Canadian Historical Review* 75 (September 1994): 409.

16. Peter Irniq, speaking on "The World at Six," CBC Radio, 1 April 1999.

17. Susan Buggey, *An Approach to Aboriginal Cultural Landscapes* (Ottawa: Parks Canada, 1999), http://www.pc.gc.ca/docs/r/pca-acl/index_e.asp (accessed 24 June 2004).

18. Darren Keith, "The Fall Caribou Crossing Hunt, Kazan River, Northwest Territories," Parks Canada, Historic Sites and Monuments Board of Canada, 1995–28.

19. "Fall Caribou Crossing National Historic Site, Conservation and Presentation Report, including Commemorative Integrity Statement," Harvaqtuuq Historic Site Committee and Parks Canada, 1997.

20. Ibid.

21. Ted Bernard and Jora Young, "Finding the Radical Center," in *The Ecology of Hope* (Gabriola Island, B.C.: New Society Publishers, 1997); R. Randall Schumann, comp., "The Malpai Borderlands Project: A Stewardship Approach to Rangeland Management," in *Impact of Climate Change and Land Use in the Southwestern United States,* http://geochange.er.usgs.gov/sw/responses/malpai/ (accessed 24 June 2004); Julia M. Wondolleck and Steven L. Yaffee, *Making Collaboration Work, Lessons from Innovation in Natural Resource Management* (Washington, D.C.: Island Press, 2000).

22. Bernard and Young, "Finding the Radical Center," 124.

23. Ibid.; Schumann, "The Malpai Borderlands Project."

24. Jamie Williams (Montana state director, the Nature Conservancy), telephone interview by Nora Mitchell, 27 January 2003.

25. Concerning the Nature Conservancy, see http://www.nature.org/wherewework/northamerica/states/colorado/work/art383.html (accessed 6 July 2004). Concerning the University of California Cooperative Extension's project, Sierra Nevada Beef, with information on Yampa Valley Beef, see http://www.ucece,ucdavis.edu/filelibrary/1808/3690.pdf. See also 3689, 3692, 3693. Concerning the Yampa Valley Land Trust, see http://www.yvlt.org/index.html (accessed 24 June 2004).

26. See www.conservationbeef.org (accessed 6 July 2004).

27. Brian Kahn, telephone interview by Nora Mitchell, 7 January 2003.

28. See http://www.conservationbeef.org/SunRanchPress.pdf (accessed 6 July 2004).

29. See http://nature.org/pressroom/press/press645.html (accessed 6 July 2004).

30. Jessica Brown, Nora Mitchell, and Michael Beresford, eds., *The Protected Landscape Approach: Linking Nature, Culture, and Community* (Gland, Switzerland and Cambridge, U.K.: IUCN, 2005); Marta de la Torre and Randall Mason, introduction to *Assessing the Values of Cultural Heritage,* ed. de la Torre, 3–4; Nora Mitchell, Barbara Slaiby, and Mark Benedict, "Local Community Leadership: Building Partnerships for Conservation in North America," *Parks* 12: 2 (2002): 55–66; Jacquelyn L. Tuxill and Nora J. Mitchell, eds., *Collaboration and Conservation: Lessons Learned in Areas Managed through National Park Service Partnerships* (Woodstock, Vt.: Conservation Study Institute, 2001); Jacquelyn L. Tuxill, *The Landscape of Conservation Stewardship: The Report of the Stewardship Initiative Feasibility Study* (Woodstock, Vt.: Marsh-Billings-Rockefeller National Historical Park, Conservation Study Institute, and Woodstock Foundation, 2000).

31. de la Torre and Mason, introduction; Randall Mason, "Assessing Values in Conservation Planning: Methodological Issues and Choices," in *Assessing the Values of Cultural Heritage,* ed. de la Torre, 5–30.

32. David Throsby, "Cultural Capital and Sustainability Concepts in the Economics of Cultural Heritage," in *Assessing the Values of Cultural Heritage,* ed. de la Torre, 102.

10. Management for Cultural Landscape Preservation

Insights from Australia

RANDALL MASON

By their changeful nature, cultural landscapes present many obstacles to preservation. Standard models and methods used in historic preservation—based on "arresting decay," narrow conceptions of cultural significance, or other specialist concerns—fall short of the target of allowing landscapes to change while ensuring the core aspects of their significance are preserved. Cultural landscape scholarship, led by geographers, has advanced the understanding of significant places immensely but rarely makes the leap to questions of managing landscapes and implementing preservation measures.[1] The pragmatic question for those interested in landscape preservation, therefore, is how one can take advantage of the holistic, dynamic perspective offered by cultural landscape studies and use it to manage and interpret change on the ground.

This essay examines how complex, changeful landscapes can be managed for preservation, focusing on Port Arthur, a nineteenth-century penal colony in the Australian state of Tasmania. At Port Arthur, management and planning measures are reacting positively to the challenges posed by landscape preservation; a dynamic, adaptive management system reconciles the often competing demands of retaining historical patterns and fabric while accommodating contemporary uses and changes.[2] As a cultural landscape, Port Arthur is typically complex. Rich in historical layering and nationally recognized as a "heritage place," a number of competing contemporary uses are evident, especially tourism. Port Arthur is a particularly interesting case because it has been a heritage site for about a hundred years, much longer than the forty-seven years it was operated as a prison, and Australia's approaches to heritage management regimes have changed markedly over time (Figure 10.1). The current national regime mandates protection of cultural values centered on convictism; meanwhile, the institution responsible for management has a mandate to seek economic self-sufficiency. The total management of the site—encompassing protection, conservation, research, interpretation, promotion, visitor service, new construction, and more—is achieved through flexible management practices, by support of creativity within the overall conservation-focused management policy, and by good partnership building externally as well as internally. Management practices adopted for Port Arthur in recent years are distinguished by reliance on values-

Figure 10.1. Tourists on a visit to Port Arthur, late nineteenth century. Courtesy of Allport Library and Museum of Fine Arts, State Library of Tasmania.

centered preservation theory, less-hierarchical management arrangements, and an emphasis on inclusive planning processes. The Port Arthur management approach, I argue, is congruent with the epistemology of the cultural landscape notion. Both accept the changeability of places through space and time, as well as the multivalence of attitudes toward place.

Issues

Understanding cultural landscapes is a passionate pursuit for many of us; it is the way we see the world. "Reading the landscape," as geographer Peirce Lewis implored, means constantly turning pages, reading between the lines, knowing the languages and grammars of nature and culture, and devouring the veritable libraries of information available to us. Identification is a first step toward preserving cultural landscapes, and many of us have been engaged in this as scholars or as advocates. But beyond recognizing and understanding landscapes, there is the messy, politicized, and necessary work of trying to preserve them. As landscape architects Arnold Alanen and Robert Melnick have noted, "there is a creative tension between *thinking about* and *doing* cultural landscape preservation."[3] It is a sizable leap from understanding landscapes to preserving and managing them. But it is a critically important leap, for which Port Arthur represents a model.

The changeful nature of cultural landscapes presents substantial obstacles to preserving them.[4] Land, buildings, flora and fauna, people, and the relations between all of them are constantly reshaping one another. Interpretations of history and memory, intimately tied to landscape, change even more frequently. Historic preservation, by contrast, has canonically focused far more on achieving stasis and arresting decay than on allowing change, though the pendulum is shifting. Museological and other curatorial theories of preservation fail us when it comes to preserving landscapes since the ideas are geared toward codifying meaning and enforcing an ideal, constant state. Preservation of landscapes will not, therefore, flow simply from greater understanding of them or from more sophisticated documentation methods, or from application of traditional architectural conservation principles.

So how does one preserve something so fluid by its nature as a cultural landscape? More to the point, how can the character and pace of landscape change be managed? By whom? And how do the decisions get made? On the basis of what kinds of research? What kind of planning responds best to the unique qualities of cultural landscapes as objects of preservation? Answers to these questions rest in taking a fresh approach to the management of *all* aspects of the landscape: economic development strategies and decisions, land management practices, real estate markets, recreational habits, commemorative places and events, building culture, stewardship of the natural environment, and responses to social justice or equity conflicts. All these activities have to be knitted together and cohere in a framework conceived to sustain the *whole* character and significance of the landscape, not just its individual parts.

Landscape preservation is best when it is adaptive and continual—a long-term process, not a one-shot project. The sustenance or disappearance of a landscape flows from myriad decisions made about preserving, changing, using, buying, or selling its various components. Understanding these decisions—and knowing how, when, and why to shape, change, and inform them—is the key to managing change. Once a full knowledge of the resources at hand has been achieved, preserving cultural landscapes consists largely of tasks of *management, decision making,* and *setting policy.*

Recent developments in preservation theory indeed point toward more flexible and decision-focused models for practice. Termed "values-centered" or "values-based" theory, this eclectic body of work has emanated from grassroots and practitioner concerns in many parts of the world for preservation methods that more directly respond to social needs as expressed through heritage.[5] Values theory begins with the assumption that there are *many* kinds of value ascribed to heritage in any given place and time instead of just historical and aesthetic values.[6] A particular old building, for example, may have artistic values as a design, historical value for association with some past event or person, urbanistic value as part of an ensemble, social value as a meeting place for a community group or religious congregation, and monetary value as real estate. These values all have legitimacy, and it is fully expected that some of them may be in conflict—or rather, the stakeholders asserting the different values will conflict.[7] Furthermore, the heritage values of a place are not always the most important. In some instances, creating a new school or a hospital might serve greater social good than preserving an existing building's historical layers. How values-centered theory differs from traditional fabric-centered theory is its frame of reference and its "client." Values theory acknowledges the full range of values ascribed to a place, whereas fabric-centered theory frames the objective of preservation as the study and protection of things more as specimens of cultural process itself.[8] Such holistic understanding of contemporary places and their evolution is an important contribution of cultural landscape studies to preservation thinking.

Another distinction of cultural landscape preservation stems from its radically holistic epistemology and the more fragmented, sometimes overspecialized knowledge of many preservation practitioners. Every field, discipline, and profession as well as every kind of government agency has its own, partial view of what constitutes a cultural landscape. The preservation field has fought long and hard for its legitimacy as a profession and its domains of specialty. But professionalization and specialization have worked against holistic understanding of landscapes, focusing the field on buildings as objects of concern, and preservationists as arbiters of their value.

One of the reasons why management is different from understanding is that while the latter can be done more or less independently—in our minds and on paper—management requires coordinated action among a number of different people and institutions. These people are trained in different disciplines, work in different sectors with their correspondingly different motives, have different politics, and affiliate with different cultures. The cast of characters that has to be organized to preserve a landscape is a priori eclectic and fragmented. To get them all to see and act in the holistic way that the cultural landscape perspective requires is no mean feat.

But there is cause for hope. The revelatory potential of cultural landscape studies—seeing the world with new eyes, connecting the world of political ideas and social conflicts with the material world we literally inhabit and make—contains the promise of transcending the narrow professional thinking that can haunt preservation and other fields.

Values-Based Management

Heritage site management may be defined simply as "the way that those responsible [for the site] choose to use it, exploit it, or conserve it."[9] Authorities, however, seldom make these choices solely on their own. As the interest in heritage and heritage sites has grown in recent decades, people have come to anticipate benefits from these resources, and authorities must take these expectations into consideration. Although heritage practitioners generally agree that the principal goals of cultural management are the protection and conservation of cultural resources and their presentation to the public, in reality cultural sites almost always have multiple management objectives. The result is that the various activities that necessarily take place at these sites—such as conservation interventions, visitor management, infrastructure development, and interpretation—are often handled separately, without a unifying process that focuses all decisions on the common goals.

Values-based site management addresses the need for coherence. It is defined as the coordinated and structured operation of a heritage site with the primary purpose of protecting its heritage significance as defined by designation criteria, government authorities or owners, experts of various kinds, and other citizens with legitimate interests in that place. In its strictest definition, values-based management does not assume the primacy of traditional heritage values over others that have gained recognition more recently. Historical and cultural significance are sometimes at odds with other, contemporary kinds of value. Once all the values of a site have been identified and weighed in relation to one another to establish its significance, a critical step—and one of the most challenging aspects of this approach—is determining where the values *reside*. In the most literal sense this process can mean mapping the values on the features of the site and answering questions such as which features capture the essence of a given value. What about these features must be guarded to retain that value? If a view is seen to be important to the value of the place, what are its essential elements? What amount of change is possible without compromising the value? Clear understanding of where values reside allows a site manager to protect what makes a site significant, and this understanding is a critical precedent to the inevitable trade-offs and other tough decisions faced by managers.

For all of its demands, an integrated approach to site management and planning derived from values-based theory provides clearer, more balanced, and better integrated guidance to decisions than traditional methods, which often focus on resolving specific problems and issues in isolation or without adequate consideration of their impact on the site and all its values. Values-based management is characterized by its ability to accommodate many heritage types, the wide range of threats to which they may be exposed, the diversity of interest groups with a stake in their protection, the consideration of the many types of benefits flowing from preservation, and a long-term view of management.

Values-based management taps many sources of information about the site. Historical records, assessment of physical conditions, and previous research findings have been the most used in the past and generally are consulted first. Great importance is placed on consulting stakeholders, that is, individuals and groups who have some interest in a site and who can provide information about the contemporary and historical values attributed to the place. Traditional stakeholders of cultural sites have been professionals in various disciplines—including history, archaeology, architecture, ecology, and biology—whose values are expressed through their research or expert opinions. More recently other groups who value heritage sites for different reasons have been recognized as stakeholders too: nearby residents, groups with traditional associations or ancestral ties, or people with specific avocational interests in a place, such as those with an interest in sites related to World War II. With their wide-ranging and sometimes conflicting interests, stakeholders may perceive a landscape's values quite differently. This broadened sense of who the stakeholders are presents both difficulties and opportunities. On one hand, having so many partners asserting their interests in a site makes the process of collaboration and negotiation potentially very complicated and time-consuming; on the other hand, understanding and acknowledging the different stakeholder interests expand the universe of audiences and partners that can be enlisted to implement preservation strategies.

Values-based management of heritage sites has been most thoroughly formalized in Australia, where the Burra Charter guides practice.[10] Faced with the technical and philosophical challenges posed by aboriginal places, nonarchitectural sites, and vernacular heritage, Australian heritage professionals found that the existing guidance in the field was inadequate. Building on the basic ethics and principles of the Venice Charter, they devised guidelines for heritage management: a site-specific approach that calls for an examination of the values ascribed to the place by all its stakeholders and the precise articulation of the site's significance. While it is officially endorsed only in Australia, the Burra Charter has become an adaptable model for culturally tailored approaches to site management in other parts of the world.

Port Arthur

Port Arthur, on the southeast margin of Australia's island state of Tasmania, was first built as a prison in the 1830s and continues to serve an important function in Australia's national memory by vividly representing the theme of convictism.

As a cultural landscape, Port Arthur must be seen as typical: terrains characterized by long-standing and complex relationships between natural and cultural processes; rich historical layering of built and natural traces; high levels of social complexity; and contemporary functions, including those related to heritage conservation and tourism. Unlike designed landscapes, the edges and boundaries of these places are unclear—both in space and in time—and their authors are many. Port Arthur has long been considered "historic" in the popular mind and among the scholarly community and thus has been the subject of decades of deliberate documentation, preservation, tourism development, museum curatorship and interpretation, and heritage management. The Tasmanian government's recent management and planning regime has been creative, successful, and sustainable—readily seen as state-of-the-art. Port Arthur's stewards use a values-centered approach, relying on partnerships between institutions from the public, private, and nonprofit sectors.

England's eighteenth- and nineteenth-century system of "transportation" of convicts was a foundational experience for the Australian nation. A series of prisons, colonies, and economic enterprises was created to house, employ, and punish the convicts. This system was formative of Australia's history, geography, and identity. Dating from 1830, Port Arthur was perhaps the most well-known and notorious site in the convict system; it is valued highly and frequently visited by Australians, particularly Tasmanians (Figure 10.2). Today, Port Arthur is a complex and rich heritage site; its significance is anchored in convictism but touches on a number of other themes as well. Dozens of buildings occupy a bowl-shaped valley around Mason Cove, which opens into Carnarvon Bay and the sea (Figure 10.3). Some buildings remain as ruins, and others are restored as museums or are adaptively used in a variety of ways. Some structures date from the convict period (1830–77), while many others represent later eras. The site is also rich in archeological resources. One of the most striking aspects of Port Arthur is the juxtaposition of the dreadful historical narratives rooted and remembered there with the spectacular natural setting (Figures 10.4, 10.5). Some observers believe this paradox enhances the overall value and impact of the site; others believe it unduly muddies the messages conveyed to visitors.

Aboriginal peoples are believed to have inhabited Tasmania for at least thirty-six thousand years prior to the arrival of the first Europeans in the mid-seventeenth century. The aboriginal peoples were exterminated or forced out by the English, and most of their traces were erased shortly thereafter. In 1803, the New South Wales government established the first British settlement in Van Dieman's Land (later Tasmania) near the present capital of Hobart. In 1830, the first convicts were sent to Port Arthur to cut timber—eucalypts and Huon pine, in great demand for shipbuilding. Soon, the island's third penal station was con-

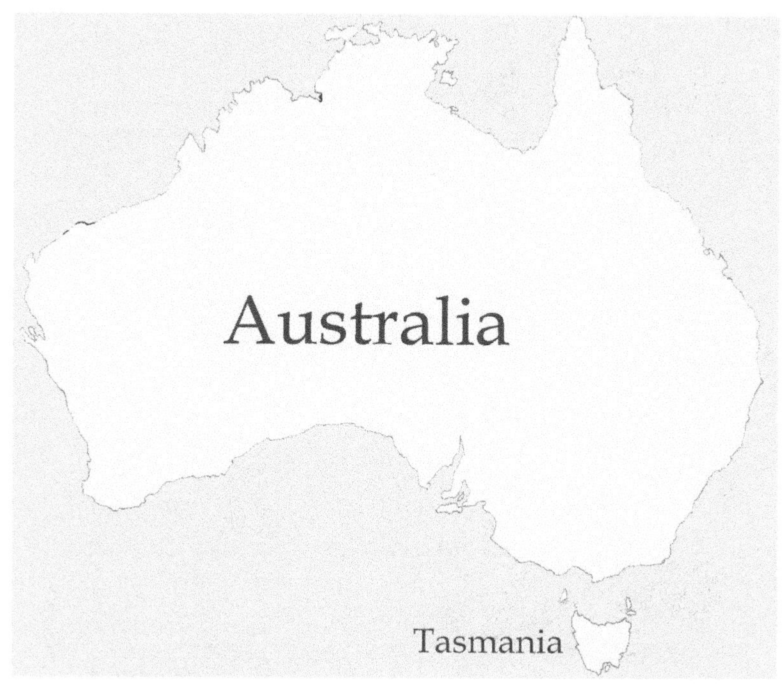

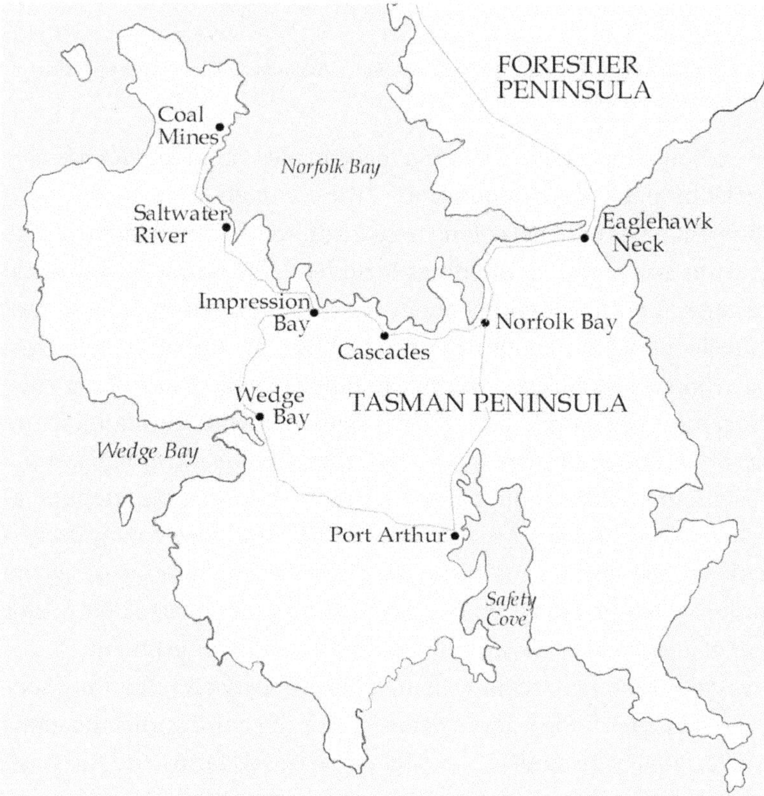

Figure 10.2. Maps of Australia, showing relation of Tasmania to mainland and location of Port Arthur on Tasman Peninsula. Courtesy of Getty Conservation Institute; copyright 2005 J. Paul Getty Trust.

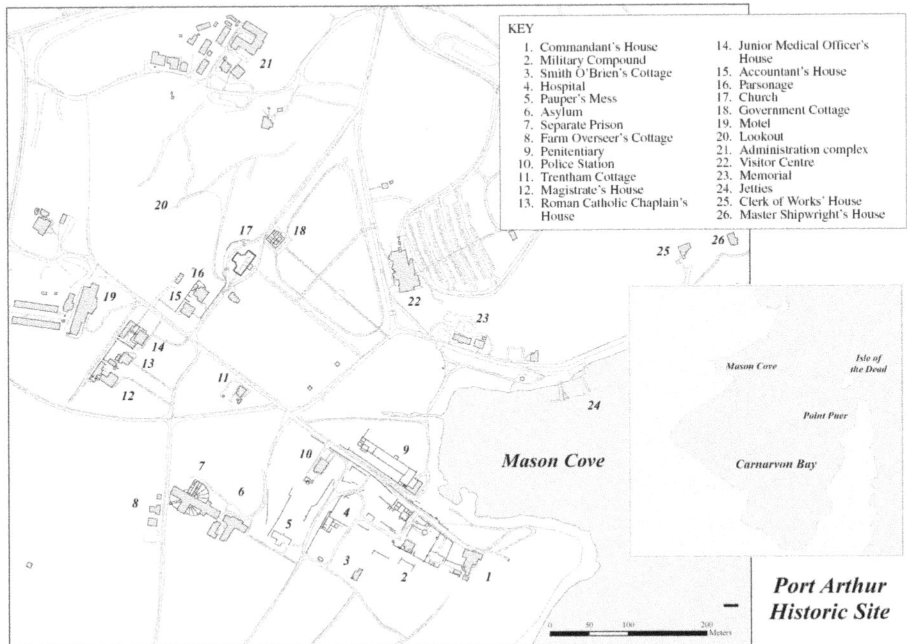

Figure 10.3. Map of Port Arthur in its current state, showing location of major facilities. Courtesy of Port Arthur Historic Site Management Authority.

structed there to house repeat offenders and incorrigibles, often sent for life sentences at hard labor in this most remote part of the continent.

Several different types of penal colony were instituted at Port Arthur over the half century it was in operation. Buildings included large barracks, industrial structures, cottages for officers, churches, and the Separate Prison, built in 1848 on the Pentonville model of panopticon prisons.[11] By 1836, the settlement contained almost a thousand convicts, plus three hundred boys in nearby Point Puer. Port Arthur became an economic center of consequence, with the manufacture of shoes, lime, brick, and pottery, as well as with shipbuilding, sawmilling, stone quarrying, coal mining, leather tanning, and farming. Following the adoption of a "probation system"—putting convicts to work outside the penal colony itself—in Tasmania in 1841, the Tasman Peninsula was chosen as the location of several probation stations administered from Port Arthur. This move turned Port Arthur into the center of a regional landscape of incarceration and punishment.

Port Arthur closed as a penal colony in 1877. More than twelve thousand sentences were served there in forty-seven years.[12] After the closing, the area drew free settlers, who, along with some ex-convicts, established farms and the small town of Carnarvon. Some Australians thought the heritage of the place repugnant. Talk of "the convict stain" was widespread, referring to the shame and violence of

Figure 10.4. Port Arthur, general view looking toward Carnarvon Bay, 1878. Courtesy of W. L. Crowther Library, State Library of Tasmania.

Figure 10.5. Port Arthur, general view taken from approximately the same vantage point as Figure 10.4. Photograph by author, 2002.

the punishments suffered in the prison system as well as undercurrents of homosexuality. From this perspective, it was only proper that bush fires and ecological succession erased many traces of the establishment. But virtually since the end of the penal colony, people were also *drawn* to visit Port Arthur by its dark history, picturesque ruins, and natural setting. Excursion boats sailed from Hobart for the day. Visitors enjoyed the forest preserve, established by the Tasmanian government in 1916, and frequented tours of abandoned prison buildings guided by former convicts. In 1913 Tasmanian government officials drafted the first set of recommendations for the site's management. The resulting Scenery Protection Board soon assumed management, making Port Arthur the first official preservation site in the country.[13] In 1946, the Tasmanian government purchased the whole town, which had earlier been renamed from Carnarvon to Port Arthur, to consolidate control over its future development and to assume responsibility for its protection. Preservation of individual buildings and work on building further tourist infrastructure began in the 1950s. In 1971, the state government dissolved the board, replacing it with the new National Parks and Wildlife Service, which assumed responsibility for management of Port Arthur.

The first substantial financial commitment to conservation at the site came eight years later when the Tasmanian government launched the Port Arthur Conservation and Development Project (PACDP) with AU$9 million from the commonwealth and the state. The task was enormous. With so many buildings, representing a number of different historical periods and narratives, Port Arthur presented a complicated set of decisions to make regarding which elements of the landscape to preserve and how much restoration and reconstruction was appropriate given the need for this remote place to attract visitors. Additional complexities included extreme climate and aggressive bush growth, the contrast between the remote, captivating natural setting and the legacy of punishment rooted there, and the controversial role of homosexuality in convictism. This intense, modern preservation project entailed extensive restoration of historic buildings, ruins stabilization, and the development of visitor-related facilities and infrastructure. The PACDP was very professional in terms of traditional, fabric-centered conservation practice. It was the largest heritage conservation and development project undertaken to that point in Australia and served as a significant training ground for the country's heritage professionals. At one point plans were formed to create a Williamsburg-like reconstruction of missing elements of the site. This training component produced a nationwide interest among the group that had worked with PACDP in the ongoing conservation and protection of the cultural resources at Port Arthur.

After the Tasmanian Minister of Arts, Heritage, and Environment halted funding for the project in 1986 due to a change in political priorities, the state parliament responded the following year by passing the Port Arthur Historic Site Management Authority Act. This legislation created and transferred authority over the site to the Port Arthur Historic Site Management Authority (PAHSMA), a government-business enterprise—known as a public development corporation in the United States—that would prove a crucial management change.

The story of the Port Arthur cultural landscape took a troubling turn in April 1996, when a modern tragedy was added to the legacy of convictism. A lone gunman went on a shooting spree, killing twenty people inside the Broad Arrow Café, a 1950s building otherwise of no heritage value. Most of the victims were visitors to the site, although a number of them both worked and lived at Port Arthur. The incident attracted international attention and swiftly catalyzed enactment of national gun control legislation. The event was traumatic for the site staff and the local community. That December, the Broad Arrow Café was partially demolished as a result. The Australian prime minister provided a special appropriation to construct a new visitor center to replace the café, as the wrenching process of managing the site through the tragedy began.[14] The shooting added a new significance to Port Arthur for all Australians.

Transformation

The tragedy also provoked an investigation into the management of Port Arthur. At issue were the PAHSMA board's handling of the development of plans for a new visitor center and parking area, its relations with employees in the aftermath of the tragedy, and the general handling of conservation and maintenance of historic resources at the site. The inquiry led to the board's reconstitution as well as amendments to the enabling legislation, making its financial performance goals less onerous and opening the door to looking at the site through the lens of values-centered conservation. In 2000, the Tasmanian premier announced that PAHSMA would receive AU$10 million for conservation over the ensuing five years, on condition of forming a new conservation plan. This decision set the stage for the new institutional arrangements and for a plan framed according to Burra Charter principles. A vigorous conservation program began, which has been a major benefit to, and rallying point among, the staff and external partners. The Australian national government simultaneously announced that state and commonwealth funding would be provided for creating a regional "Convict Trail" to connect historic sites across the peninsula. The same year, PAHSMA, the Tasman Council (the local government), and local businesses formed a partnership to market the whole region as a tourist destination.

The various plans completed for Port Arthur since the early twentieth century were designed not only to outline conservation strategies for historic fabric but to secure financing and resources either from the controlling agency or from the tourism market. The imperative to secure funding in an ever-changing political climate explains in large part the shifts in strategies over time—from the fabric conservation–centered, government-funded end of the spectrum to commercial-centered, market-oriented strategies. At present, PAHSMA holds the pendulum somewhere in the middle, balancing physical conservation and public interpretation of the site's histories with tourism access and other revenue-generation activities contributing to the long-term conservation of the site.

In its current configuration, Port Arthur affords an opportunity to see a deliberate and thoughtful conservation planning framework applied to a site with an extensive, complex set of physical resources and varied cultural heritage significance. The management framework acknowledges that the site's values are dynamic and that core cultural significance can be protected while responding to changing values and opportunities. The different values of Port Arthur are articulated exhaustively in the plans, though economic and cultural values are assessed differently and at very different levels of detail. The Burra Charter process generally excludes consideration of economic values, but PAHSMA's mandate of commercial viability has led it to integrate economic values of the site more fully. The current plan hinges on the principle that the conservation of cultural significance values has primacy. At the same time, it recognizes the essential role played by economic and social values, cultivating them through tourism, business development related to site operations, and emphasis on the site's positive impact on the Tasmanian economy. The experience of Port Arthur debunks the idea that commerce is the bane of conservation and that the separation of economic and cultural values is legitimate in site management.

Port Arthur has a clearly developed policy framework. The overarching frameworks of the "Conservation Plan" (2000) and supporting "Corporate Plans" (2002), plus the more detailed decisions worked out and recorded in supporting documents, give managers sufficient policy guidance, empirical information, and latitude to make decisions.[15] The institutional arrangements of the site represent an important emerging model in heritage management. PAHSMA enjoys the benefits of some government funding without all the strictures of operating as a governmental department in a large, hierarchical bureaucracy. PAHSMA also bears responsibility for generating some part of its revenue. Heading a small, independent entity, the organization's leaders can make decisions more quickly, more flexibly, and with a larger range of public- and private-sector partners.

While PAHSMA acts entrepreneurially within the bounds of retaining cultural significance—an approach that seems well suited to cultural landscape preservation—that independence and flexibility can be a double-edged sword. In its initial form, when annual profit was required, the government business enterprise institutional format was thought to be deeply flawed—it had strayed too far from its core conservation mandate. PAHSMA has evolved significantly in recent years, when, in response to the challenges and opportunities after the 1996 tragedy, its mandate was modified to replace profit making with the more reasonable goal of ensuring the conservation and presentation of the site while maintaining commercial viability.

Nevertheless, by relying on some mix of dedicated government funding and self-generated revenue, this kind of institutional structure exposes the site and its values to some risks. The site is vulnerable because if visitation drops off or government support is threatened, there would likely be pressure to become more commercial, undermining conservation measures and heritage values. The PAHSMA institutional framework enables the door to perpetually swing either way in favor of commercial or cultural values. Port Arthur has less of a "safety net" to guard against overdevelopment, though it has the same exposure to public sector disinvestment in conservation. In its commitment to the conservation plan, though, PAHSMA has accepted the primacy of its obligation to protect the cultural significance of Port Arthur over all other considerations. The institutional framework and its flexible style are also intended to help the organization respond to external crises—such as declines in the state's agricultural sector, fluctuations in the tourism economy, or natural disasters—by increasing, for instance, the capability of site managers to make alliances with regional tourism operators.

An important and somewhat controversial aspect of Port Arthur's management is *how* the different values are integrated. Dealing with the impact of the 1996 tragedy thus helped pave the way for a new planning process that turned the site's management around. The management philosophy shifted to include true collaboration across departments—conservation, archaeology, visitor services, interpretation, finance—horizontal management, and creating external partnerships, all of which seem to work well as long as everyone abides by the first principle of conserving and presenting the core cultural significance of the site.

At one level, the conservation plan's policies address values in a comprehensive way, acknowledging the trade-offs that sometimes occur between visitor access and conservation philosophy. In another sense, the management regime weighs and balances decisions about different values through the "Port Arthur way": the practice of routine consultation among senior staff in considering any decision. Flexible policies guide day-to-day management. Decisions are made not through hierarchical process according to codified rules but through avid consultation and full staff involvement. Irrespective of whether the decision is a major one, such as which material conservation projects to fund in a given year, or seemingly minor, such as approval of what items are offered in the gift shop, they are shared by staff leaders across all departments. The management style of the CEO has set an important tone: reaching consensus, building a management team, breaking down barriers among the different levels of staff, breaking down barriers between site personnel and local residents. All of these procedures contribute to a management strategy that does not get recorded or captured in documents, making them hard to convey but ever more important to the effective operation of the site. Establishment of the "Port Arthur way" is counted among the major accomplishments of the past few years. Perhaps a synonym for collaboration, collegiality, and teamwork, the "Port Arthur way" is a significant source of pride among the managing staff. It has also geared the organization to think opportunistically, respond to external conditions, and successfully preserve the historic landscape for which they are responsible.

Lessons

The management approaches and planning methods used at Port Arthur are successful in terms of cultural landscape preservation because they are congruent with fundamental insights of cultural landscape studies. The management scheme is encompassing and holistic regarding the different elements and values of the landscape: cultural and natural aspects of the place, heritage and contemporary values, cultural and economic uses. Just as important, the management of Port Arthur is flexible and adaptable, acknowledging the necessity of landscape change, the inevitability that sites evolve—physically and in the ways they are perceived—and the multiplicity of stakeholder values at play. Managing and planning the site are themselves valued as *ongoing* processes; adaptability of practices is embraced. The processes of understanding of the landscapes, of considering conservation and development options, and of making decisions on policies are indeed central to long-term preservation of the site. Excellence in heritage practices—conservation, interpretation, research, management—is one of the explicit goals of PAHSMA.

Deeply understanding the place, seeking multiple and diverse partners, pursuing clear and widely agreed-upon policies for conservation and development, having management that thrives on thoughtful, flexible collaboration within the organization and with external partners—all have gone a long way toward preserving the meaning, character, and usefulness of Port Arthur as a heritage landscape. For Port Arthur, it is the partnerships and management habits stemming from the planning *process,* rather than the plans themselves, that constitute successful landscape preservation. There is much to suggest that this approach can be adapted to the challenges of managing and preserving many types of cultural landscapes.

Notes

1. With my training as a geographer, the definition of *cultural landscape* I use begins with the tradition of Carl Sauer, J. B. Jackson, and Peirce Lewis; that is, a piece of territory

shaped by humans, integrating cultural and natural elements, and in a state of continual evolution. More recent scholarship, ranging beyond the geography field, challenges the empirical uses of cultural landscape and uses landscape as a way to criticize and reframe traditional takes on historic preservation. See Paul Groth and Todd Bressi, eds., *Understanding Ordinary Landscapes* (New Haven, Conn.: Yale University Press, 1997); Don Mitchell, "Cultural Landscapes: The Dialectical Landscape—Recent Landscape Research in Cultural Geography," *Progress in Human Geography* 26: 3 (2002): 381–89; Mitchell, "Cultural Landscape: Just Landscapes or Landscapes of Justice?" *Progress in Human Geography* 7: 6 (2003): 787–96; and Chris Wilson and Paul Groth, eds., *Everyday America: Cultural Landscape Studies after J. B. Jackson* (Berkeley: University of California Press, 2003).

2. Fieldwork for this paper was made possible through a research project funded by the Getty Conservation Institute and led by Marta de la Torre. My understanding of the issues discussed herein has greatly benefited by working with her, as well as with David Myers, others of the Getty research team examining site management cases, and those engaged in such managing. The result of this research is four case studies: Port Arthur, Hadrian's Wall in England, Chaco Canyon in New Mexico, and Grosse Ile in Quebec. See Marta de la Torre, ed., *Heritage Values in Site Management: Four Case Studies* (Los Angeles: Getty Conservation Institute, 2004). The individual cases can be viewed and downloaded at http://www.getty.edu/conservation/resources/reports.html.

3. Arnold R. Alanen and Robert Z. Melnick, eds., *Cultural Landscape Preservation in America* (Baltimore: Johns Hopkins University Press, 2000), 20, emphasis added. This distinction between "thinking about and doing cultural landscape preservation" and the value of jumping across the divide it represents defines an important shift in my own professional development. After bachelor's and master's degrees in geography, and working in preservation and architecture firms, I returned to school for a doctorate in urban planning. While sticking to my roots in cultural geography and landscape studies, I was looking for ways to implement what I had learned and help actually change the built environment and how people think and feel about it.

4. Robert Z. Melnick, "Changing Views, Missing Linkages: The Enduring Dynamic of Landscape, Environment, and Cultural Heritage," in *Durability and Change: The Science, Responsibility and Cost of Sustaining Cultural Heritage,* ed. Wolfgang E. Krumbein et al. (New York: John Wiley and Sons, 1994), 137–46.

5. Erica Avrami, Randall Mason, and Marta de la Torre, eds., *Values and Heritage Conservation* (Los Angeles: Getty Conservation Institute, 2000); Randall Mason and Erica Avrami, "Heritage Values and Challenges of Conservation Planning," in *Management Planning for Archaeological Sites,* ed. Jeanne Marie Teutonico and Gaetano Palumbo (Los Angeles: Getty Conservation Institute, 2002).

6. Alois Riegl, "The Modern Cult of Monuments: Its Character and Its Origin," 1903, trans. Kurt W. Forster and Diane Ghirardo, *Oppositions* 25 (fall 1982): 23.

7. This notion of the multiple values of heritage places parallels the theme of D. W. Meinig's essay "The Beholding Eye: Ten Versions of the Same Scene," well-known to devotees of cultural landscape studies; see D. W. Meinig, *The Interpretation of Ordinary Landscapes* (New York: Oxford University Press, 1979), 33–48.

8. Editor's note: This characteristic generally applies to sites preserved for museum purposes. On the other hand, in many historic districts the act of preservation is itself an agent of change and thus may be considered as contributing to the ongoing evolution of

cultural landscape. Indeed, the creation of local historic districts can be examined as a major force in urban development in the United States over the past half century.

9. Michael Pearson and Sharon Sullivan, *Looking after Heritage Places: The Basics of Heritage Planning for Managers, Landowners, and Administrators* (Carlton, Victoria: Melbourne University Press, 1995), 7. This section of the essay is adapted from Randall Mason et al., *Hadrian's Wall World Heritage Site, English Heritage: A Case Study* (Los Angeles: Getty Conservation Institute, 2003).

10. The Burra Charter is the popular name for the "Australia ICOMOS Charter for the Conservation of Places of Cultural Significance," which was adopted by Australia ICOMOS in 1979 at Burra, Australia. The charter has since been revised and updated, and the sole version now in force was approved in 1999. It is available online at http://www.icomos.org/australia/burra.html.

11. For background, see John Hirst, "The Australian Experience: The Convict Colony," in *The Oxford History of the Prison: The Practice of Punishment in Western Society*, ed. Norval Morris and David J. Rothman (New York: Oxford University Press, 1995), 262–95; and Norman Johnston, *Forms of Constraint: A History of Prison Architecture* (Urbana: University of Illinois Press, 2000), 89–95.

12. "Overview," http://www.portarthur.org.au/overview.pdf (accessed 28 March 2002).

13. David Young, *Making Crime Pay: The Evolution of Convict Tourism in Tasmania* (Hobart: Tasmanian Historical Research Association, 1996), is an informative, detailed source on the history of Port Arthur as a heritage landscape.

14. Jane Lennon and Associates, "Broad Arrow Café Conservation Study," May 1996, report in author's collection.

15. *Port Arthur Historic Site Conservation Plan, Volume 1: Overview Report* and *Port Arthur Historic Site Conservation Plan, Volume 2: Supporting Information* (Sydney: Godden Mackay, 2000); "Port Arthur Historic Site Management Authority Corporate Plan 2001/02," Port Arthur Historic Site Management Authority, 2002.

11. Are We There Yet?

Travels and Tribulations in the Cultural Landscape

ROBERT Z. MELNICK

My title is taken from that great vernacular expression of impatience that I suspect we have all uttered or have had spoken to us by our children: "Are we there yet?" To cut to the end, no, we are not there yet, but we have come far on this journey of discovery, recognition, and protection of the cultural landscape. This reflection on what has been accomplished—and not accomplished—in the past twenty-five years is a rather personal one, with a bit of nostalgia as well as hope for what we have yet to do. I am taking the opportunity to reflect rather than predict, to prod rather than boast, and to ruminate rather than catalog.

I cannot quite remember the first time I realized that landscape was important to me. I suppose I was quite young, perhaps eight or ten. Although I grew up in New York City, I spent each summer of my pre-adult life outside of the city, in a rural area of small summer cottages in Putnam County, up and down a long and winding gravel road dotted with weather-worn houses, dairy farms, apple orchards, and pigs—all surrounded by hills and trees. As a city boy I underwent a dramatic transformation each summer, as I left my friends and streets and hard-edged playgrounds the day after school ended in June, only to discover and rediscover the woods and stone walls and worn paths through the forest that I could traverse at night without a flashlight.[1] It was in many ways, I now know, a wonderfully rich climax deciduous forest, with oaks and maples and ferns, but also with bugs and worms and too many birds for me to ever name and fox and deer, of course. There was the occasional bear, but whether that was truth or rumor I am still not sure. Although I was always told it was the "country," it was, more importantly, a landscape rich in Native American history and where the non-native population settlements dated to the earliest times of the Dutch and English on this continent.

There were place-names from early European settlements but also place-names tied to landscape form and process. Putnam County itself is named for a general of the Revolutionary War, but there were also names like Peekskill Hollow Road, with its reference both to the Dutch and the landscape; Piano Mountain, named for the shape of its ridgeline against the sky; Bryant Pond Road; Roaring Brook Lake; Four Partners Road; Shrub Oak, a village so small and so personal; Wappinger Falls; Philipse Manor; and the list goes on. They are not terribly unusual, yet they fascinated me, with their references to both place and past. It was only later in our history, when towns were platted as speculative property, that we acquired the ubiquitous Elm and Maple streets, and even then there are precedents tied to street tree plantings.

For me, then and now, this landscape was a remarkable and joyous place. There were sounds I heard only in the summer, like the incessant hum of crickets until dawn.[2] There were smells and sights, like a summer rain that was not steamy or the flowers of honeysuckle and lilac and daylily and rose of Sharon that my mother grew beside our house. It was, of course, a domesticated family landscape, made comfortable in a 1950s mode, in the midst of a rural (now suburban) landscape that had at one time been wilderness. But it was not wilderness, even though the contrast with the wilds of the city could not have appeared to be greater. And there were wonders that awaited me, even though they were sometimes unpleasant.

I could get lost, without my familiar landmarks of street signs and shops and bakeries and bus stops and elevated subway sounds, or slip and fall, only to return crying to our house. I was not alone in this landscape. There were friends whose adult friendship I treasure to this day, all children of the postwar boom who, like so many others, sought and found another home in this landscape. They are friends forever linked, in my mind, to that place.

Our small and quite modest summer bungalow—as it was known—was near a lake, a small pond really. There I discovered other wonders, like leeches and snapping turtles that rumor held were two hundred years old. Could I possibly say that was wrong? But here, also, I learned to use a rowboat and a canoe and quietly explored the edges of this pond, with its grasses and lily pads. I understood that, for some reason, there were warm and cold spots of water when I swam. I learned to leave the pond's edge at dusk or risk being eaten alive, as we used to say, by the blackflies. There were red-winged blackbirds, which hovered near the water, and there were butterflies. The cool air coming off the pond made us glad that we were away from the unforgiving and unrelenting intensity of a New York summer.

In this rural landscape I learned to play baseball and hike and pick flowers and watch for shooting stars on late August nights. With friends I often slept outside, staring at the vast sky, feeling even then that it was a precious time. My grandmother, who lived all of her adult life in the city, would sometimes visit and inevitably remark that she could never sleep because of the ceaseless noise of the crickets and birds—this complaint, I might add, from someone whose New York bedroom window opened next to a bus stop. How could she not treasure my landscape as much as I did? Her own landscapes were hers, not mine, but I could not comprehend that. Any landscape is linked to identity, shared experience, and, ultimately, to an emotional sense of belonging. Landscapes help us mature; they participate in our upbringing and maturation.

In the city I also knew the landscape, but one of a different kind. There was Van Cortlandt Park in the Bronx, where I would ice-skate every winter with friends, and Inwood Park at the northern tip of Manhattan, where the notorious purchase of the island allegedly occurred and where I would play on rock outcroppings; and there were smaller green patches of neighborhood landscape; and there was Central Park. I was warned regularly to be extra careful in Central Park: never go there at night, and even during the day to stay on the edges, to always be able to see the street. It was this edge between "wilderness" and "civilization" that marked where I was safe and where I was not.[3] There were always news stories and neighbors' whispers about Central Park—stories of muggings, killings, or rapes. We all knew that Central Park was a place gone bad. It was only later, as a graduate student, when I left New York for good and could return to visit with fresh eyes, that I fully discovered the joys and intricacies and delight of Olmsted and Vaux's design.

What was it, then, that made these landscapes so special, so magical in my life? And what makes them still important today? What do we value about these landscapes that makes us want to ensure their life for the future, that makes us want to know that years and decades from now others will come to treasure them as much as we do, although perhaps in different ways?

Every one of us has our own magical landscapes, those places that evoke memory, passion, joy, and even melancholy. Our world is often marked by our personal and communal association with place, by our remembrances of events both joyous and sad and the places where they occurred. It is this very personal connection to landscape that intrigues and frustrates at the same time.[4]

We cannot all be connected to every landscape we see, yet our common goal is to recognize, understand, and protect those landscapes that in some way are special, important, and significant. We have, as a community of scholars, practitioners, advocates, and critics, spoken for years of the need to recognize the importance of the American landscape, both generalized and detailed, in our history. We have fought for surveys, listings, and the acceptance of our vision that landscape is tangible and not merely ephemeral or unknowable. We have argued that designed landscape protection, cultural landscape protection, and historic preservation more broadly are essential to safeguard our cultural heritage.[5]

In spite of our many collective successes, we have a long road ahead. I am personally troubled, yet professionally gratified, when we codify our love of landscape, when we insist on legislating the care that we have for such places. I am impatient with those who cannot see that landscape—the landscape around us, the landscape we have all shaped, the landscape we all inhabit—is every bit as important as the architecture, archaeology, artifacts, and associations that we also cherish.[6] In fact, these fields are inextricably bound if we are to understand landscape as the hub for collective meaning. Yet we have imposed a landscape understanding that does not coincide with a broader societal view. Have we marginalized ourselves to the point at which our own work is arcane, tedious, and so particular that even we cannot defend it? I like to think that this is not the case.

But in our efforts, we run a great risk of losing the personal equation in the cultural landscape. As we become more entangled in the bureaucratic processes that allow us to think about and act on landscape protection, we have also turned our backs on the individual, intangible memory of, and experience in, that landscape. History is not really what happened, it is the story of what we believe happened. Many of us remember the movement—somewhat seriously, somewhat facetiously—to consider "her-story" instead of "his-story." While that simple, yet powerful, play on words brought to light our gender-focused filters on the past, it also highlighted the degree to which the past as a totality of experience is not known, is not revisited, is not preserved or protected or reproduced. "Living history" truly is an oxymoron.[7]

We seem to be protecting the things of the past, that which has physically survived from an earlier time, rather than been handed down to us. In protecting those things—landscapes, buildings, structures, objects—we attempt as best we can to remember our own place in time and space. It is that memory, as much as the artifact itself, that is so critical to this process, and that—somehow, somewhere—we lose to codification, rationalization, and procedure. Is this necessary? Well, of course it is. In our society we would never be able to achieve the larger goal of enriching lives and meaning were it not for those codes, rules, regulations, and all of the opportunities that they present. I am not suggesting that we abandon that effort.

What we lose, however, is something equally important, equally valuable, yet not at all quantitative or countable; something that cannot fit neatly on a National Register of Historic Places nomination form. It is not more important than those maps and drawings and physical descriptions, but it is no less important. Memory—human memory, human meaning inscribed in a place—is essential, much as the very personal meaning that I ascribe to that landscape that I experienced as a youth in the summer months. How do we find, place, recognize, and protect personal meaning in a landscape? How do we allow for different meanings in the same landscape?[8] There are always different meanings; there are always different histories—or her-stories—always different understandings that are so intensely personal that the very act of societal recognition may negate their vividness, presence, and urgency. I am not sure how we achieve this goal. I *am* sure that if we do not aspire to do so, we risk self-marginalization at a time when meaning, memory, place, and landscape are more important than ever.

There are three broad issues entailed in such an effort: coming to terms with time in the landscape; untangling questions of landscape ownership, practically, politically, and philosophically; and acknowledging and acceding to our intricate relationship with nature. We must engage these issues if we are ever to reach that place of communal acceptance so thoroughly enjoyed by environmental and ecological advocates. These issues are integrally entangled with the meaning of place, the meaning of landscape, and our ability to establish landscape preservation as an equal value on the table with planning, design, and maintenance decisions. The overriding concern is, after all, about real physical places. These issues are not just ideas, and while the record of these places is an essential tool in their protection, the record is not the same as the place, the landscape. Drawings, models, and narratives are imaginative representations of the real thing. Design ideas—three-dimensional ideas—are but fantasies of what may be built, and drawings or depictions of past landscapes are not those places either, but remembrances or historical reconstructions of them.

At its bright core, historic preservation is about the meaning of that past in our contemporary lives; it is about taking explicit human actions to ensure that we do not forget what we did yesterday. Our collective belief and fascination with the past and the future are tightened by the understanding that landscapes change regardless of what we do. It is a wonder and a frustration. We think so much about history sometimes, about the ways in which landscapes were built and managed and enjoyed and enhanced and even destroyed, that we run the risk of only looking backward. As Eugene O'Neill observed in *Moon for the Misbegotten:* "There is no present or future—only the past happening again and again—now. You can't get away from it. . . ."[9]

We continue to revel in the power of the past—or at least our belief in a single understanding of it—but there are, in fact, multiple pasts, pasts that exist in a temporal reality different from our own.[10] How do we reconcile my past with your past, even in the same landscape? How do we ascribe meaning to a landscape—with its broad associations and development history—when that meaning is at once so societal and so personal? We can never fully reconcile these pasts, for they are grounded in visions and memories and emotions so intimate as to defy their explicit elaboration and explanation.

How, then, do we come to terms with *time* in the landscape?[11] We often speak of landscape time, of time passing quickly or slowly, and of the sequence of time. This notion that time is an entity of reality is very much a human construct. Even more confusing is the notion of coordination or regularization of time. The change in calendars through the ages has resulted in a dramatic misreading of past time, one to which we cannot help but succumb while simultaneously supposing that *our* understanding is correct.

Albert Einstein's early work illuminated the essential idea that time is relative, not absolute; yet we are pressed to explain the time of landscape, or landscape time, in references other than our own.[12] For example, at least five major calendars and probably a number of minor ones as well are in use in the world today. Each of these calendars—Chinese, Christian, Indian, Islamic, and Jewish—while measuring the same absolute time, understands time from a relative framework grounded in that culture's history, traditions, beliefs, and myths. Some are based on solar habits, some on lunar, and others on a combination of the two.

Time synchronization, a problem to which Einstein and others devoted substantial effort, only came about in the late nineteenth century. The effort was driven by the expansion of global commerce and the need for precise, consistent geodesy.[13] It was in this period that the zero longitude was established in Greenwich, England. Today, we have extended that societal need for exactitude to the personal moment, with digital watches and clocks wirelessly linked to the atomic clock in Colorado. I can now know, to the second, the exact time, no matter where I am on the globe. We have captured an exact moment, or so it seems, and that belief leads to the notion of a heightened, more authentic reality, a reality that is not any more or less real than those that have preceded it. But this perception makes little sense in the landscape and helps us imagine, wrongly, that time is absolute. Landscape time, like landscape history, is thankfully an inexact science. We are periodically unearthing evidence that alters our previous views, for time and history are inextricably linked.

Our challenge is to recognize that landscape time, as measured by events and people, is more akin to mental mapping than to the watch on our wrists. The process of mental mapping—seeking perceptual understandings of geographies—can assist us to recognize the relative nature of time in the cultural landscape and avoid the trap of seeking exact answers in an inexact world. Landscape time is based, to a great extent, on our perception of landscape and ultimately on our sense of landscape ownership. *Landscape ownership,* in the sense that it is understood in this country, is not universally practiced or accepted.

A colleague in graduate school used to say that someone could own the land, but no one ever owns the landscape. I thought that was merely a turn of phrase so adept that it appeared to be of greater significance than it actually was. But who does own the landscape, and how do we untangle issues of landscape ownership—practically, politically, and philosophically? To address the issue, we must recognize that we view the world through a cultural lens, one shaped, formed, screened, and colored by our own traditions and worldviews, our own constricted cosmology and cosmological interpretations.

In July 1971, Henry A. Kissinger, then Richard Nixon's secretary of state, went to "Red" China to prepare for the president's now famous trip the following year as part of the effort to reestablish political and cultural relationships between the two countries. While in China, an accompanying journalist, James Reston of the *New York Times,* had an acute appendicitis attack. Chinese physicians made an emergency operation to remove Reston's appendix, after which it was reported that they did not use conventional Western anesthetics. Rather, they employed an ancient practice of inserting needles into special areas of the skin safely to deaden the pain, what we in the West learned was acupuncture. Following the trip, Reston wrote about his experience in the *Times,* and Kissinger mentioned the occurrence in a press briefing. The fascination with acupuncture spread, partially because this event had occurred in relationship to Nixon's forthcoming visit, but also due, in part, to a worldview unknown to Western medicine and one that dramatically contradicted known "truths." The lens that said anesthesia was the only way to deaden the sensation of pain had been shattered, or at least fogged over, and in the process our understanding of human systems had been called into question.

Our view of landscapes and the processes by which we take their "vital signs"—as an architect colleague of mine has taught me with regard to buildings—is no less shaped by our cultural hubris. While we still believe in anesthesia as we practice it today, will we one day view it as arcane as the "bleeding" with leeches beginning in medieval times? Our ways of understanding landscape are framed, colored, and informed by our own societal, political, and personal lenses. Thus, we neatly organize our landscape inventories and necessarily, yet artificially, devolve the landscape into its component parts to more fully identify and appreciate that which makes any given landscape important. But where is the next appendectomy? Where is the acupuncture that enables—or forces—us to get beyond the orthodoxy of our own work?

Part of our societal myth is the idea of cultural assimilation, and in that regard landscapes provide us with important lessons. How do we understand, for example, not only how distinct cultural groups have impacted this country, but also how their lives, communities, and cultures have been altered by that experience? While writers such as Oscar Handlin can point us in the right direction, recent scholarship can also inform our understanding, especially with regard to intangible values that often matter most in our increasingly nomadic society.[14] As people move from job to job and from city to city, they carry with them memories, stories, and familiar traditions, as well as tangible aspects of personal histories.

The landscape and our means of understanding it are culturally autobiographical. At times it seems that we inadvertently deny some of that past, if only through the ways in which we ask our questions. The ownership of landscape meaning is a difficult question, for it confronts us with a bifurcated view of landscapes past, present, and future, especially as they collide with racist or romanticized visions of minority cultures and their relationship to landscape.[15] William Cronon's work has been especially instructive in this matter, but there are others who have written eloquently on questions of cultural ownership and forced assimilation. While we may think of this as based in race issues, it is also based in language, religion, and seemingly obscure cultural practices.[16]

The Cajuns in Louisiana are a good example, as that culture has been so "Americanized" as to render it, in its present form, almost indistinguishable from the rest of our society. These people were forced from their homes in Nova Scotia in the nineteenth century, only to face a new discrimination in the American South, and finally to be regarded as hot, chic, and trendy. The trendiness, however, is based in part on an exploited and commercialized vision of that culture as well as its association with the land. While Cajuns have found a way to flourish in the modern world, it has come at the loss of many of their folk traditions, including historic land practices. Who owns that landscape now that it has been transformed into chemical manufacturing plants, hunting grounds for the outdoorsman, or a popularized vision of what it means to be Cajun?[17]

And what do we mean by ownership when we speak of natural values in the landscape? Can we ever come to terms with the most difficult issues of acknowledging and acceding to our intricate *relationship with nature*? We are still mired in a nature-culture dichotomy, and while our acceptance of this relationship has improved, we have far to go. Certainly, the idea of nature is a human construct, as is our present-day notion of wilderness. There really is no wilderness, in the strict sense of that term, left in our continent, and that which we call wilderness is by the very act of being set aside decidedly *not* wilderness. The mere act of setting it aside is a human decision, thereby making it a cultural landscape. More importantly, from the earliest of times, we have sought to conquer nature, overcome wilderness, and tame the landscape for human use, while proclaiming and extolling the beauty, majesty, and wonder of the very lands we were domesticating. One need not look only to recent history, of course, as nature and wilderness were seen throughout Western history as the hiding place for evil and danger, perhaps with good cause.

As Michael Pollan reminds us, the line between the garden and nature is now blurred.[18] Where is the garden, the controlled nature? And where is nature, the wild garden? If we only think of the built or designed or explicitly modified landscape, we are failing in our work. We need to recognize, accept, and respond to our intensely complex relationship with what we view as nature and our desire to honor and control nature at the same instant. How we engage this issue, in particular, will set the future course of our work. How then do we engage and tackle these three big issues—landscape time, landscape ownership, landscape and nature—as we move forward? What, in other words, do we need to do now?

In a recent meeting in the western United States, a number of people working daily in cultural landscape preservation addressed a broad-ranging discussion of the needs in that region. For many of us in the West, and I suppose elsewhere, this is to a great extent a regional question. Cultural landscapes really do vary in different parts of the country. In the Pacific West our landscapes are marked by the vastness of the geography and even the time it takes to travel from one place to another. Lane County, Oregon, where I live, is as large as the state of Connecticut. There are thirty-six counties in Oregon, not all as large as Lane, but this fact does suggest that settlement demographics and landscape scale have a great deal to do with how we think about places and how we work to protect them for the future.[19] Oregon, an essentially rural state with one major metropolitan area and a few small cities, has more places where there are no people than places where there are some people. This complexion affects how we think about the landscape in relationship to human settlement.

The issues that we face in the next generation of work can inform what we must do nationally, region by region, locale by locale, landscape by landscape.[20] These tasks and challenges are not magical, but they are majestic in their scope while particular in their details. My examples are taken, for the most part, from this western landscape but there are equally vivid examples elsewhere.

First, we need to continue to expand our historical understanding of the cultural landscape. How did any specific landscape evolve? What are its detailed dynamics? This point may seem obvious, but it is an unrelenting need. Because histories are merely lenses on the past, how can we learn about multiple histories for the same landscape? And when do we engage, indulge, or deny revisionist history? There are many excellent examples of cultural landscape histories. I am struck as I read Ethan Carr's work, for example, that so much of history is in the asking.[21] When we ask the same question about people and place, we run the risk of arriving at the same conclusions, and in so doing, we fail to understand the complex relationship of people and landscape. There are no right questions, but by asking more questions we add to our multifaceted understanding of any place.

In the West we are asking questions about historic context as well as environmental histories. It was not so long ago that we would *not* ask about the Japanese American internment camps, but now we are beginning to understand the impact of that national political policy not only on a group of Americans but on our landscape as well.[22] We are also learning about the impact of the labor movement, especially the farm workers' movement, on the agricultural landscape. While these are regionally specific matters, the ideas that underlie them are valid throughout the country.

Additionally, we are learning about environmental history, especially the role of fire in the landscape. In the West this is a major issue, fraught with long- and short-term implications. But what do we really know about the role that fire, both naturally occurring and human-ignited, has played in the evolution of our landscape? And what about the environmental implications of ranching, farming, and other agricultural practices? These are not as benign as we sometimes think, but neither may they be as damaging as sometimes claimed.

Second, we need to broaden our horizons and engage colleagues from other disciplines in this work, including archaeologists, anthropologists, horticulturalists, and natural resource specialists, and also some less obvious ones, such as fire managers, ethnobotanists, arborists, foresters, materials conservators, and historic vegetation experts. We need to assemble project teams that can address the particular issues of the landscape without concern about traditional professional rivalries or territoriality. The cultural landscape as an idea can serve as a unifying concept, a place where we can recognize that there is not one way to understand where we are, there are many ways.

Third, there is a gaping lack of knowledge about landscape preservation management and maintenance. In the West, we have become increasingly concerned with range management issues, for example. How can we manage rangeland to protect its historic and associative values while still enabling it to be an economically viable and thriving operation? This is not a modest question, as more and more small-scale ranching operations are being consumed by industrialized ranches that bear little resemblance in size or operation to their forebears. As a working landscape is dynamic and must continue to operate, in the deepest meaning of that term, how do we provide for both past and future? And how do we negotiate the sometimes conflicting values of rangeland operations and environmental health? There are no simple answers.

In another telling example, the National Park Service, under the leadership of Susan Dolan in Seattle, is in the midst of a national orchard study. In the parks and elsewhere, the management of historic fruit and nut orchards is a growing concern, as trees reach the end of their natural life cycle and historic planting and management traditions are no longer practiced. We begin to ask, for example, about tree replacement both in species and location as well as survivability. These are, at one level or another, questions of preservation maintenance, although perhaps not in the traditional vein.

Furthermore, we should not forget about the historic designed landscape. The costs, in a variety of ways, of maintaining those landscapes can seem prohibitive, and we run the risk of protecting a landscape whose future we cannot sustain. I think of this as the "supply lines" problem: once protected, a designed landscape may require constant and ongoing maintenance. Is the will—and are the resources—present to accomplish this goal?

Fourth, and perhaps with the greatest difficulty, we should embrace practices of sustainability, while leading the effort to provide definition to that concept. We should, as well, make sure that our solutions advance environmental and ecological strength, not merely stabilize it. Ideas of sustainability are rampant in our fields, and we would be making a huge mistake to believe that those concerns—environmental, ecological, and energy-related—are not part of what we do. How can we help address, for example, the growing national debate on land use and urban sprawl? What can we learn and say about the relationship between human and natural resources? These are among the big questions we face as a society in how we use our land.

On a more specific level, we face significant challenges in exotic plant control, especially when those plants were part of a historic design. In many areas of the West, as elsewhere, English ivy is considered to be a noxious weed, and there are community work days to remove these invasive plants from the landscape. But what if English ivy is a critical component of a designed landscape? How do we think about "old" ways of design, and what we might do today? And always in the West there lurks the consuming problem of water conservation. The tourist landscape of Las Vegas, magical as it may seem to some people, cannot be sustained, if only because of the water that it takes to create and manage an oasis of this magnitude in the midst of the desert. We can, as a species, exist without many pleasures; water is not one of them.

Fifth, and finally, we must do a better job of engaging the broader community. Many preservationists are already hard at work at this task. The challenge is to continue to expand those efforts so that one day our children and their children think of the value of history in the landscape with the same intensity that they now recognize the need to recycle and reuse. Already, creative and exciting partnerships have emerged, such as the successful efforts at Ebey's Landing National Historic Reserve in Puget Sound, but partnering requires the understanding that community associations, nonprofit organizations, environmental groups, and individuals all have a legitimate stake in the future of the landscape.[23] It means listening to others in order to learn about a landscape, why it is important, what is meaningful, and how it can continue to play a vital role in a community's future.

When I revisit that landscape of my earliest years, that landscape where I, in the most personal of ways, found naive joy, wonder, and trepidation, I am reminded why I care so much about landscape and about its protection. We should ask, once again, what we mean by the essence of preservation. We can all recite the litany of reasons why we believe that preservation is important—the pace of change in our society, the loss of local identity, the decline of human craft and skill, the homogenization of American towns and communities, the McBurbing of our countryside, the need to remember where we have been, and so on. And we can all look to those places—perhaps many, perhaps few—that help us as individuals and as a people to remember, or even find, steady ground in that shifting world of change.

What we have yet to do is fully engage the complexity of our landscape world, the great variety of meanings, and the multiple landscape constituencies—especially in ways that get beyond the visual and historical narrative. We live in a broad, pluralistic society, one that treasures differences. We must remember to value those differences and embrace them as strengths. There are many truths in any landscape. The codified expectation of finding only one truth threatens to divert us from our own feelings, our own understandings, and our own knowledge. We need to think about time, ownership, and nature, and we need to continue to expand our professional and personal landscape horizons. Are we there yet? No, we are not, but I am encouraged that we are well on our way.

Notes

1. Peter Gould and Rodney White, *Mental Maps* (Boston: Allen & Unwin, 1986).
2. Peter Charles Hoeffer, *Sensory Worlds of Early America* (Baltimore: Johns Hopkins University Press, 2003).
3. Neil Evernden, *The Social Creation of Nature* (Baltimore: Johns Hopkins University Press, 1992).
4. David Lowenthal, *Possessed by the Past: The Heritage Crusade and the Spoils of History* (New York: Free Press, 1996).
5. James Marston Fitch, *Historic Preservation: Curatorial Management of the Built World* (New York: McGraw Hill, 1992); Arnold R. Alanen and Robert Z. Melnick, eds., *Preserving Cultural Landscapes in America* (Baltimore: Johns Hopkins University Press, 2000).
6. Howard Mansfield, *The Same Ax, Twice: Restoration and Renewal in a Throwaway Age* (Hanover, N.H.: University Press of New England, 2000).
7. Jesse Kornbluth, "When Furnishings Say Family," *New York Times*, 29 January 2004, D8.
8. Emily Eakin, "History You Can See, Hear, Smell, Touch, and Taste," *New York Times*, 20 December 2003, A21.
9. Eugene O'Neill, *A Moon for the Misbegotten* (New York: Random House, 1952), 18–26.
10. Brian Greene, "The Time We Thought We Knew," *New York Times*, 1 January 2004, A23.
11. Kevin Lynch, *What Times Is This Place?* (Cambridge, Mass.: MIT Press, 1972).
12. Peter Galison, *Einstein's Clocks, Poincard's Maps: Empire of Time* (New York: W. W. Norton, 2003), 18–26.

13. P. Kenneth Seidelman, ed., *Explanatory Supplement to the Astronomical Almanac* (Mill Valley, Calif.: University Science Books, 1992).

14. Oscar Handlin, *The Uprooted,* 2nd ed. (1973; Boston: Little, Brown, 1990), 3–6, 94–116.

15. Michael F. Brown, *Who Owns Native Culture?* (Cambridge, Mass.: Harvard University Press, 2003).

16. William Cronon, *Changes in the Land: Indians, Colonists, and the Ecology of New England* (New York: Hill and Wang, 1983).

17. Shane K. Bernard, *The Cajuns: Americanization of a People* (Jackson: University Press of Mississippi, 2003).

18. Michael Pollan, *The Botany of Desire: A Plant's Eye View of the World* (New York: Random House, 2002).

19. William G. Loy, ed., *Atlas of Oregon,* 2nd ed. (Eugene: University of Oregon Press, 2001).

20. Thanks go to Kimball Koch of the National Park Service for previous articulation of the five issues discussed here.

21. Ethan Carr, *Wilderness by Design: Landscape Architecture and the National Park Service* (Lincoln: University of Nebraska Press, 1998). See also Linda Flint McClelland, *Building the National Parks: Historic Landscape Design and Construction* (Baltimore: Johns Hopkins University Press, 1998).

22. See, for example, Sharon Yamato, *Moving Walls: Preserving the Barracks of America's Concentration Camps* ([Los Angeles]: by the author, 1998); Jeffrey F. Burton et al., *Confinement and Ethnicity: An Overview of World War II Japanese American Relocation Sites,* rev. ed. (Seattle: University of Washington Press, 2002); and Janice L. Dubel, "Remembering a Japanese-American Concentration Camp at Manzanar National Historic Site," in *Myth, Memory, and the Making of the American Landscape,* ed. Paul A. Schackel (Gainesville: University Press of Florida, 2001), 85–102.

23. For discussion, see Nancy D. Rottle, "A Continuum and Process Framework for Rural Historic Landscape Preservation: Revisiting Ebey's Landing on Whidby Island, Washington," chapter 7, this volume.

Contributors

SUSAN CALAFATE BOYLE works for the National Park Service, specializing in interpretation, planning, and historic highways and trails. Her publications include *Los Capitalistas: Hispano Merchants and the Santa Fe Trail, Social Mobility in the United States,* and numerous articles in professional journals.

SUSAN BUGGEY is adjunct professor in the School of Landscape Architecture at the Université de Montréal. As director of historical services for Parks Canada, she was responsible for the service's national multidisciplinary research program on history and the built environment, including cultural landscapes.

MICHAEL CARATZAS is a historian on the staff of the New York City Landmarks Preservation Commission.

COURTNEY P. FINT is an architectural historian with the West Virginia Division of Highways.

HEIDI HOHMANN is a registered landscape architect and associate professor of landscape architecture at Iowa State University. She has worked as a preservation planner and landscape architect for the National Park Service and for private-sector firms on the East Coast and in the Midwest.

HILLARY JENKS is a doctoral candidate in American studies and ethnicity at the University of Southern California. She was managing editor of *American Quarterly,* the journal of the American Studies Association.

RICHARD LONGSTRETH is professor of American studies and director of the graduate program in historic preservation at George Washington University. A past president of the Society of Architectural Historians and vice president of the Vernacular Architecture Forum, he has written extensively on architectural and urban history as well as on historic preservation subjects. Currently he is completing a detailed study, *The Department Store Transformed, 1920–1960.*

Randall Mason is associate professor in the graduate program in historic preservation at the University of Pennsylvania's School of Design. With Max Page he edited *Giving Preservation a History: Historic Preservation in the United States,* and he has written several research reports published by the Getty Conservation Institute.

Robert Z. Melnick is professor of landscape architecture at the University of Oregon, where he served for ten years as dean of the School of Architecture and Allied Arts. He subsequently spent two years as a Visiting Senior Program Officer at the Getty Foundation in Los Angeles. He is coeditor of *Preserving Cultural Landscapes in America,* coauthor of the *National Register Bulletin* on rural landscapes, and author of numerous articles on landscape preservation.

Nora Mitchell is founding director of the National Park Service's Conservation Study Institute, which provides a forum to discuss contemporary issues and practice, conservation history, and future directions for the field. She is coeditor of *The Protected Landscape Approach: Linking Nature, Culture and Community.*

Julie Riesenweber teaches historic preservation at the University of Kentucky, where she is pursuing a Ph.D. in geography.

Nancy D. Rottle is a registered landscape architect and associate professor in the Department of Landscape Architecture at the University of Washington, where she teaches landscape planning, design, construction, and preservation courses.

Bonnie Stepenoff is professor of history at Southeast Missouri State University. She is author of *Thad Snow: A Life of Social Reform in the Missouri Bootheel* and *From French Community to Missouri Town: Ste. Genevieve in the Nineteenth Century.* Her articles have been published in *Labor History, Labor's Heritage, Missouri Conservationist, Missouri Historical Review,* and *Pennsylvania History.*

Index

Page numbers in italic type refer to pages with illustrations.

Lightning Source UK Ltd.
Milton Keynes UK
UKHW031835071021
391776UK00005B/251